This book expertly removes the ambiguity of facilitation and highlights the value an influential facilitator adds to a ~~~~~~~~~~~~~~ through relatable stories, practical advice, and technique ~~~~~~~~~~~~~~ nd this book to anyone, including managemer ~~~~~~~~~~~~~~ ent, regardless of their use of Scrum.

—Nic Easton, Product Deve~~~~~~~~~~~~~~ onsultant

Brilliantly blends practice and theory. Real-life Scrum scenarios throughout the book paint a clear picture of how to put facilitation principles, skills, and techniques into action to overcome common Scrum challenges. Visualize what it looks like to guide people from not-so-effective collaboration toward greater creativity, responsibility, alignment, and improved outcomes.

—Stephanie Ockerman, Founder of Agile Socks LLC and co-author of the book Mastering Professional Scrum

Working with Scrum teams? Then buy this book! It's packed with advice and real-life examples to support your desired goals. The stories shared by the experienced authors resonated with me, and I loved the practical facilitation ideas. I will be returning to this book again and again.

—Caroline Stacey, Scrum Master and Agile Coach

The authors' insights into Scrum facilitation are transformative. Drawing from my own Agile expertise and teaching at Harvard, I can attest to the book's profound value. It's a must-read for anyone striving for high-performance teams. Kudos for this enlightening guide!

—Richard Kasperowski, CTO, Agile Expert, and Harvard University Instructor

This book is a must-have for anyone working with Scrum teams. Packed with practical tips, relatable scenarios, and a sprinkle of humor, it offers invaluable guidance to not only boost your Scrum team's success but also turn up the dial on effective facilitation on every-day scenarios. Kudos to the authors for sharing their expertise and compelling insights.

—Saniya Khalil, Product Owner

I started out as a Scrum Master ten years ago. Reading this book back then would have speeded up my journey helping Scrum teams to work more effectively. It covers everything that Scrum Masters need to get started facilitating Scrum events in a practical yet entertaining way.

—*Simon Flossmann, Professional Scrum Trainer*

Read this book if you want potent techniques to take your team facilitation to another level. You're likely facing some of these scenarios already. Use these approaches to get effective results.

—*David Boyd, Agile Coach, Scrum, and Kanban Professional*

Facilitating Professional Scrum Teams

The Professional Scrum Series by  Scrum.org

Visit **informit.com/scrumorg** for a complete list of available publications.

The **Professional Scrum Series** from Pearson Addison-Wesley and Scrum.org consists of a series of books that focus on helping individuals and organizations apply Scrum and agile leadership to improve the outcomes of customers and organizations. Approaching the challenge from different perspectives, each book provides deep insights into overcoming the obstacles that both teams and organizations face as they seek to reap the benefits of agility.

All Scrum.org proceeds from the series go to Year Up, an organization whose mission is to close the Opportunity Divide by providing urban young adults with the skills, experience, and support to empower them to reach their potential through professional careers and education.

Pearson

twitter.com/informIT

Facilitating Professional Scrum Teams

IMPROVE TEAM ALIGNMENT, EFFECTIVENESS, AND OUTCOMES

Patricia Kong
Glaudia Califano
David Spinks

◆◆ Addison-Wesley

For information about buying this title in bulk quantities, or for special sales opportunities (which may include electronic versions; custom cover designs; and content particular to your business, training goals, marketing focus, or branding interests), please contact our corporate sales department at corpsales@pearsoned.com or (800) 382-3419.

For government sales inquiries, please contact governmentsales@pearsoned.com.

For questions about sales outside the U.S., please contact intlcs@pearson.com.

Visit us on the Web: informit.com/aw

Library of Congress Control Number: 2023947398

Copyright © 2024 Pearson Education, Inc.

Hoboken, NJ

Cover image: Ibaneza_stock/Shutterstock, Bonny Munandar/Shutterstock

Chapter 1-9, Illustration of Gerjon Zomer: Gerjon Zomer

FIG01-05, FIG02-01: Roman Pichler

FIG04-03: Dave Gray

FIG05-01: Jeff Gothelf

ISBN-13: 978-0-13-819614-1
ISBN-10: 0-13-819614-1

1 2023

Pearson's Commitment to Diversity, Equity, and Inclusion

Pearson is dedicated to creating bias-free content that reflects the diversity of all learners. We embrace the many dimensions of diversity, including but not limited to race, ethnicity, gender, socioeconomic status, ability, age, sexual orientation, and religious or political beliefs.

Education is a powerful force for equity and change in our world. It has the potential to deliver opportunities that improve lives and enable economic mobility. As we work with authors to create content for every product and service, we acknowledge our responsibility to demonstrate inclusivity and incorporate diverse scholarship so that everyone can achieve their potential through learning. As the world's leading learning company, we have a duty to help drive change and live up to our purpose to help more people create a better life for themselves and to create a better world.

Our ambition is to purposefully contribute to a world where:

- Everyone has an equitable and lifelong opportunity to succeed through learning.
- Our educational products and services are inclusive and represent the rich diversity of learners.
- Our educational content accurately reflects the histories and experiences of the learners we serve.
- Our educational content prompts deeper discussions with learners and motivates them to expand their own learning (and worldview).

While we work hard to present unbiased content, we want to hear from you about any concerns or needs with this Pearson product so that we can investigate and address them.

- Please contact us with concerns about any potential bias at https://www.pearson.com/report-bias.html.

CONTENTS

FOREWORD BY SAM KANER

1.

I've been surprised for many years that our K–12 schools don't teach the skills for effective collaboration from a relatively young age.

If I were the president of the universe, and I could somehow have those skills installed into the mental-model repertoire of every human being early in their structured-learning lives, part of my strategy would be to help youth develop some foundational *mindsets*.

For example, do little kids have any inherent capacity for staying present and connected to conversations where other people are doing all the talking? Can kiddos feel and show empathy? My answer is: watch them sit in front of their favorite Disney videos. Then ask them to describe what they saw. Maybe also, ask them how their favorite characters felt at key moments, when they lost a friend or had to gear up for a fight or met someone they were attracted to. I'll bet we could figure out how to strengthen those skills early on, before they were swept away by performance pressures induced by all the incentives we load on kids to prioritize *achieving results* in every context.

Likewise for learning process management skills. (Ever watch four-year-olds play with their action figures and dolls and plushy-bears?)

How soon can children absorb the principle that *full participation is everyone's responsibility*? Kindergarten? How soon can we teach that diversity is a fact of life—and one to be treasured, not shirked. And what about valuing the process and goal of trial-and-error: supplying some youngster-friendly pictures and stories about the continuous improvement cycle? Maybe use some incentives (gold stars in the workbook?) for accepting feedback and using it for upgrades?

I could go on.

My point: Foundational "group process" principles may seem mysterious or magical to many people—but only because they weren't taught those principles at the same age they learned to do basic math or play sports. I wish those grounding principles for collaboration were valued and taught and practiced as widely as math and writing and geography and history, the sciences, the social sciences, the arts . . .

And why does this matter? Well, umm . . . look around. Here we are, a planetary collection of nations and societies, billions of everyday people interdependent with a tiny percentage of power-holders and other key influencers. As we face into the mega-challenges of the 21st Century, do the everyday people look to you to be empowered, planful, capable? Or do we look more like lemmings, following our so-called leaders into the abyss?

I so wish that those power-holders and key influencers were inspired advocates and sincere implementers of participatory values, such as continuous learning; extensive and ongoing consultation with multiple stakeholders; inclusive, both/and problem-solving; information access and transparency; and the other cornerstone values and guiding principles that could help the planet collaborate its way back from the brink. If only . . .

All of which brings me to the practice of Agile, and then to the importance of the book you have in your hands.

2.

Essentially, I think the practice of Agile project design, Agile planning and Agile management might be an effective way forward to solving tough problems collaboratively—not just for software development but for a wide array of non-technical challenges that require project-oriented design and management. And if so, Agile initiatives might well become learning labs for adults, in replacement for the K–12 classroom, to teach and install participatory values effectively, broadly, and with successful outcomes across an enormous range of innovative solutions to the world's toughest problems. Here's what makes me see it this way:

Take another look at the *12 Agile Principles*.[1]

Combined, these 12 principles are powerful guidance to place everyday people in the driver's seat: to support them, in other words, to think together and act with alignment. I'm not saying that Agile principles are adopted effectively in every company that claims to use "agile methods." I'm saying the potential is real, and most important, the potential (I believe) is real for those 12 principles to *guide the transformation of non-technical organizations too*.

What makes me believe in this claim? Why do I think Agile principles can be transplanted from their native context of software-product development into the context and language of non-technical—but still goal-oriented—project design, planning, and management? In other words, into the context and language of social-change and system-change initiatives? I contend that it's not difficult to read Agile principles as a set of coherent and interwoven parameters and specifications that can be applied to organize pretty much *any* cross-functional team:

- to engage in continuous improvement;
- to collaborate closely and frequently with diverse stakeholders;
- to use functionality as the marker for benchmarking incremental success;

---

1. agilemanifesto.org/principles.html.

- to strive for and create platforms for enlightened access to relevant information;
- to employ iterative and incremental sprinting to do inclusive, real-time problem-solving;
- and to use simultaneous interactivity (whether in-person or online) to greatly reduce the wasted time and effort of reporting up and down the siloed ladders of hierarchical decision-making.

All of those words reflect the intention of Agile. None of those words are the exclusive province of software or high-tech product development.

3.

When Jeff Sutherland and Ken Schwaber created Scrum—a framework in alignment with the Agile manifesto—they successfully focused our attention on a critical *practical* dimension of Agile: the down-into-the-weeds use of *teams*. Yes, the 12 principles are absolutely clear that cross-functional teams are a prerequisite of Agile; but! Those principles are quiet on how to implement the day-by-day, week-by-week getting-things-done part of working in teams. That's what Scrum brings into the foreground: a clear, integrated set of "team capacity-enabling" roles, procedures, and tools. By utilizing a well-designed system that centers on teams, Scrum succeeds in putting Agile principles into practice.

Even so, operating that system—that is, planning and leading and participating in those Scrum Teams—focuses our lived experience on one more attribute, one additional layer of practicality: *the human element*.

Here's a claim I take as self-evident: The characteristics of Scrum-enabled teams are more likely to succeed when those teams can understand and manage the *human dimensions* of working together.

To put it differently: What good is it to say, "Task a cross-functional team to use an iterative process with a cyclical, well-defined timebox, organized into clear frequent short cycles punctuated by opportunities for learning and upgrading." What good is it to say all that, if leadership is unclear, and/or participants can break the agenda to talk about whatever they want, and/or accountability for follow-through is poorly addressed, and/or it's common for deals to be made on the side . . .? What good is a procedure manual about team structure and roles and shared meeting principles, if people don't follow it in practice? What good is a "continuous improvement" framework when some or many of the team members are uncomfortable giving and receiving feedback?

Thus, one remaining link needs to be made.

4.

Scrum provides the opportunity to optimize the "people parts" of Agile. Almost by definition, the team's "group dynamics" have been brought to the foreground where they can be talked through, defined, resolved, and managed just like every other element of the process.

However.

And this however is a significant one. You probably noticed in the preceding paragraph that I referred to "*the opportunity* to optimize the people parts." The opportunity, yes; the actualization of that opportunity: not necessarily. That's because of what it really takes to support a group to actually think together.

I'm talking about what it takes to help people say what they're really thinking; or share feelings under pressure; or detach themselves from their biases; or overcome their long-held personal habits to talk too much or keep silent too often; or transcend their defensiveness when it's time to give and receive feedback; or manage their triggered reactions to people with more authority than they have, or with less authority than they have; or express themselves with a digestible blend of patience and directness when dealing with their teammates' poor follow-through or unrealistic pronouncements. These are just the bread-and-butter varieties of the "people parts" of working together.

In a nutshell, working together can be a slog, it can be messy, it can require patience and courage and tolerance, any or all of which may have to be developed over time.

Scrum does not solve for that part of the puzzle. In order for cross-functional teams using Scrum to be optimized, they also need *group facilitation*.

Which means, in other words, that a Scrum Team with substantial objectives often needs support from someone who understands how to handle communication, group energy, and group dynamics. Someone who:

(a) can see what's going on through a human lens,

(b) can put some language to their observations, so other people can see it too; and

(c) has skills and tools to work with the group to strengthen communication, bolster group energy, and channel group dynamics.

Or to put it in slightly different terms, an optimized cross-functional team needs someone in their midst who knows how to encourage full participation, promote mutual understanding, foster inclusive, both/and thinking, and cultivate shared responsibility.

Authors Patricia Kong, Glaudia Califano, and David Spinks have done a superb job of incorporating insights from their depth of knowledge about group facilitation, and foregrounding that knowledge, aligning it, and weaving it in with the objectives and practices of Scrum while staying true to the values and principles of Agile. They have, essentially, provided Agile professional practitioners with the missing link.

5.

I'm not a high-tech aficionado. (In fact, I barely qualify as an end-user.) So my admiration for the Agile Manifesto and its potentials must be taken with some rocks of salt. But I can't help speculating that when the history of the information revolution is written, there's a reasonable chance that its historians will look back at Agile as an enormous innovation, maybe in the same class of importance as the steam engine, or the discovery of electricity, were for the industrial revolution.

And if it turns out that Agile does become recognized as the innovation that enables innovations, then the milestones in its development are likely to include the Manifesto, the 12 Principles, the popularization of Scrum, and perhaps even this book you're reading now.

No question in my mind, *Facilitating Professional Scrum Teams* is the lens that magnifies the human elements, foregrounding them against the background of the many structure-and-process wisdoms of Scrum and foundational values of Agile. As the authors demonstrate conclusively group facilitation is not esoteric or "special" in some way; it's learnable. And it's necessary. It's the key that opens the door to project success when communication and group dynamics are challenging. Open sesame!

And that goes double for the future of our planet. *Facilitating Professional Scrum Teams* might turn out to be the missing link that lets us turn Agile into a surrogate classroom for project-planners and doers of technical and non-technical contexts alike. Good facilitation opens that doorway to human-optimized Scrum—a space in which practitioners—in technical and non-technical contexts alike—can set up and operate their Agile process tools with greater confidence and with a higher expectation for engagement, motivation, and commitment by all parties.

Imagine the potential impact if you—the readers who use this book to strengthen your facilitation skills—found time to apply your own wisdom and your fresh learning (from this book) to new contexts beyond your regular work. Maybe volunteer some time with your local community initiatives and teach them how to apply Scrum to their projects. Or pull together a reading group with group facilitators and coaches who don't know Agile or Scrum. Or take a shot at practicing fee-for-service Agile-based consulting for non-profits and other initiatives. If you can imagine any context that lets you bridge what you already know about Agile with the enormous number of opportunities to bring that wisdom to the everyday contexts that need transforming, *the knowledge and tools in this book will support you* to put your professional values into practice.

So thank you Kong, Califano, and Spinks for your gift to our planet. Your many efforts across the years have given Agile practitioners that missing key to unlock access to Agile ways of working for countless people who need to learn, as adults, how to collaborate in the project-achievement context of solving the world's toughest problems.

Open sesame!

—Sam Kaner

FOREWORD BY DAVE WEST

Have you ever been to a horrid meeting? A meeting that was frustrating and left you with a feeling that you wasted your time? The reality is that many interactions with groups of people can be challenging. Everyone comes with a different agenda. Some people want to speak more. Others want to avoid talking at all. Emotions and communication styles get in the way. And often, there needs to be clarity as to what the outcome should be. But when you leave a good meeting, the opposite happens. Not only has the group accomplished something, but the positive feeling also carries to other interactions and work. Good meetings are an effective way to create a positive atmosphere throughout the organization while reaching outcomes. They help to shape people's perceptions of each other and, ultimately, the organization.

If facilitating conversations and meetings is so important, why do we never formally learn how to conduct them well? I have attended multiple leadership training programs, and facilitation was never part of the learning. It is assumed that humans are innately good at working with others and that coordinating effective interactions in a meeting or an event is easy and something everyone can do. It does not matter how much experience we have that contradicts that assumption; we continue to follow that belief.

During the 2020 pandemic, my lack of facilitation skills became painfully apparent. I ran many meetings where the outcome could have been better. I also attended many confusing meetings where everyone was distracted. At Scrum.org, Scrum is our foundation for delivering value, and even the Scrum events needed more clarity than usual. But then I realized that there was one set of meetings that got excellent outcomes and were pleasing to attend. And I realized those meetings had the same person driving them. Over time, I asked that person to introduce those skills to our teams and me. We practiced in large meetings, smaller working sessions, and our Scrum events. We even used those skills to help run social events such as virtual happy hours. It solidified for me and our organization that facilitation skills are foundational to success in Scrum.

In the book *Facilitating Professional Scrum Teams,* Patricia, Glaudia, and David have written a guide to how agile practitioners can improve their facilitation skills. This book does not mechanically describe every facilitation technique. Instead, it provides a simple and practical resource for selecting and applying those techniques for Scrum Teams and the people they work with.

The book is organized in a very accessible way. Each chapter includes a story that illustrates a situation or example where a particular element of the Scrum framework is used to explore some aspect of facilitation. These stories not only provide very realistic examples to illustrate the application of the principles, but they also help the reader connect the sometimes abstract ideas of facilitation with their work. Each chapter can be used as a reference guide. For example, if you are working with two or more Scrum Teams, then look at Chapter 8, which will provide some precious ideas for bringing two or more Scrum Teams together to achieve a good outcome.

Lastly, I want to describe the importance of facilitation in dealing with conflict. Scrum is an approach designed to help teams solve complex problems. Scrum encourages transparency, and transparency is not always a comfortable place for Scrum Teams or stakeholders. For example, a stakeholder attending a Sprint Review who expresses firmly held views, but the Increment and empirical evidence show those views are wrong can be uncomfortable for everyone at the event. Addressing those issues and learning those hard lessons are crucial for delivering value. A well-facilitated meeting can reduce much of the pain associated with these situations. Applying the ideas and techniques in this book will not solve the challenges that Scrum uncovers, but it will make the process more effective, more enjoyable, and less stressful.

A well-facilitated Scrum is a much better one!

Scrum On!

—Dave West
June 2023
Burlington, MA

PREFACE

We know there is no shortage of books on Scrum or on facilitation, yet we found a need to write this one because it uniquely blends the two topics. Our goal for this book is to offer you facilitation ideas, tips, and techniques to guide you in specific Scrum settings. It can assist you when you confront common Scrum Team scenarios and questions like the ones we have encountered again and again:

- I find some team members are very quiet. How can I get them to contribute more?
- How do I deal with members on the team who dominate our Sprint events by speaking over everyone?
- How can we run Sprint Planning so that everyone agrees on a single Sprint Goal and the items to be taken into the Sprint?
- What do you do when stakeholders do not give feedback at the Sprint Review?
- How can I energize the team and make them feel more connected?
- What should I do when people are blaming each other?
- How do I encourage people to participate in virtual meetings?
- How do I deal with conflict?

Effective facilitation helps teams take advantage of Scrum and their creative differences in a positive way, guiding team members to frame their discussions with a clear purpose when engaging with one another. This helps them reach agreements where they have created shared responsibility for their results.

There's another reason we found this book necessary. Effective facilitation is a great skill to develop for mindfully guiding Scrum Team interactions. Unfortunately, we have encountered numerous ineffective and misapplied facilitation that is annoying, dreadful, and intrusive, such as when the facilitator impedes effective conversations rather than enables them. We would like to break that cycle by providing the context, principles, skills, and techniques for facilitation.

We have worked with scores of Scrum Teams and organizations to help them become more effective at using Scrum. Sometimes we were successful, and sometimes we were not. In our combined experiences, we found that teams were more effective when we nudged them using deliberate facilitation techniques.

Whether you are new to facilitation or looking to further develop your ability at helping Scrum Teams thrive, we hope this book is helpful to you and your teams.

—Patricia, Glaudia, and David

Register your copy of *Facilitating Professional Scrum Teams: Improve Team Alignment, Effectiveness, and Outcomes* on the InformIT site for convenient access to updates and/or corrections as they become available. To start the registration process, go to informit.com/register and log in or create an account. Enter the product ISBN (**9780138196141**) and click Submit. Look on the Registered Products tab for an Access Bonus Content link next to this product, and follow that link to access any available bonus materials. If you would like to be notified of exclusive offers on new editions and updates, please check the box to receive email from us.

Acknowledgments

This book would not have been possible without the experiences that we gained from working with all the different Scrum and agile teams throughout our careers. There are too many individuals to mention here, but we give thanks for everything we have learned from each and every one of them.

Thanks to Caroline Stacey, David Boyd, and Simon Flossman for their feedback and suggestions during the writing and development of this book. They helped make this a better book!

We give thanks to Todd Miller for his contributions and ideas in facilitation for Scrum Teams.

Thanks to Kenny Sime for sharing his experience, over numerous cups of coffee, in working with Scrum Teams. This helped inspire some of the suggestions we made in this book.

Our thanks go to Kurt Bittner, who helped us immeasurably with his feedback, suggestions, knowledge, and experience.

We want to thank Sam Kaner for writing a Foreword and for his work in the field of facilitation. We owe much of our thinking and success with facilitation to him.

Our thanks also go to Dave West for his Foreword and his leadership in helping people and teams across the world use Professional Scrum to solve complex problems.

We thank Gerjon Zomer for his excellent and entertaining illustrations that have helped bring this book to life.

We want to thank the team at Pearson and those who helped to make this book a reality: Haze Humbert, Mary Roth, Manjula Anaskar, Jayaprakash P, Sandra Schroeder, Karen Davis and Donna M.

Finally, we want to thank Fred, our BFF.

About the Authors

Patricia Kong helps organizations thrive in a complex world by focusing on enterprise innovation, leadership, and teams. She is a people advocate and fascinated by organizational behavior and misbehaviors. She emerged through the financial services industry and has led product development, product management, and marketing for several early-stage companies in the US and Europe. She is co-author of the books *The Nexus Framework for Scaling Scrum* and *Unlocking Business Agility with Evidence-Based Management,* as well as the *Guide to Evidence-Based Management* and *The Nexus Guide*. She is a sought-after speaker at conferences and events. Patricia lived in France and now lives in her hometown of Boston.

Glaudia Califano is an agile and lean practitioner and mentor, working with and within teams. She loves to be hands-on, coming up with new ideas, and learning from those around her. Glaudia divides her time between the UK and Spain with her partner and her two dachshunds.

David Spinks is an experienced software developer, Scrum Master, and accredited trainer of Scrum and the Kanban Method. He believes in creating environments where empowerment, autonomy, and flexibility enable teams to do the best work possible. David is based in the UK. He enjoys traveling, keeping fit, the outdoors, and spending quality time with his guitar.

Together, Glaudia and David founded the company Red Tangerine with the mission to release people's potential and transform work environments. They are co-authors of the books *Adopting Agile Across Borders* and *Mastering Collaboration in a Product Team*.

INTRODUCTION

Understanding and using Scrum effectively requires the individuals within a Scrum Team, and those who work with them, to understand the intention of the framework and each of its accountabilities, events, and artifacts. Doing so helps the Scrum Team learn during each interaction and to inspect and adapt quickly. When Scrum Teams do not understand the elements of Scrum, their Scrum events are less effective—they run over their timeboxes, and they lack focus and balanced participation, eventually leading to frustration, boredom, and disengagement.

To work well, Scrum requires healthy collaboration, not just between the members of the Scrum Team, but also between the Scrum Team and its stakeholders to gather feedback and input. These stakeholders include users and customers of the product developed by the Scrum Team. Healthy collaboration entails embracing and leveraging individual experiences and perspectives, a dynamic that is at the core of solving complex problems and an everyday phenomenon for a Scrum Team. The results of this type of collaboration are usually impressive, but achieving them is not always easy when it uncovers conflicting ideas that lead to disagreements about what to do and how to work.

From our own experiences and those of others, we believe that effective facilitation can guide people to explore their differences positively by framing conversations with clear purpose. This enables people to engage and understand one another better, which in turn helps them solve problems collaboratively.

PURPOSE OF THIS BOOK

Each Scrum Team addresses its issues differently. However, teams typically encounter similar challenges. We have written this book to provide ideas and guidance on facilitation for those who would like to help their Scrum Teams work through these challenges. We do that predominantly by including real-life scenarios with sample facilitation skills and techniques. With new insights, we hope readers can further leverage facilitation as a powerful complementary practice to Scrum.

FACILITATION AS A COMPLEMENTARY PRACTICE TO SCRUM

Effective facilitation rests on principles that guide the actions of facilitators and the techniques they use. In other words, effective facilitation engages everyone fully (participative), has an objective that everyone understands (purposeful), enables collective progress toward the objective (process), creates shared understanding (transparency), and occurs in a secure environment and respectful manner (healthy).

Falling back on these principles can help facilitators work with Scrum Teams to achieve objectives collaboratively in different situations. These principles can also help facilitators decide which facilitation skills and techniques might be appropriate and useful. This holds true not only when creating an energetic environment in which the Scrum Team is engaged and focused on achieving an objective together, but also when interactions do not go as anticipated.

For more details on the facilitation principles, visit Appendix A of this book, "Facilitation Principles."

Scrum has facilitation implicitly built into the framework. Therefore, a Scrum Team generally only needs lightweight facilitation. Sometimes more is needed, and sometimes not; a good facilitator knows the difference and when to apply more or less facilitation, even within the same event.

Many assume that the Scrum Master should facilitate all events and other interactions for the Scrum Team. Although the Scrum Master may take on the role of the facilitator in various scenarios, relying on the Scrum Master for all facilitation creates a potential bottleneck and impediment. It also takes away self-management opportunities from others.

Rather than let facilitation constantly fall on the Scrum Master, others on the Scrum Team should share the responsibility to not only develop their own skills but also shift the dynamic of conversations. As long as the team agrees, facilitation can come from anyone, be it the Product Owner, a Developer, the Scrum Master, someone from outside the Scrum Team, or a combination.

WHO SHOULD READ THIS BOOK

This book can be beneficial to people who have a variety of responsibilities:

- **Scrum Masters and Agile Coaches** who want to develop their facilitation skills and acquire more facilitation techniques to help their Scrum Teams.
- **Scrum Team Developers** who want to work more collaboratively and be more aligned with other Developers and stakeholders on the work that they do.
- **Product Owners** who want to create alignment around their product vision and unlock the potential of the Scrum Team to solve complex problems.
- **Professional facilitators working in a Scrum environment** who want to understand how best to apply facilitation skills and techniques with Scrum Teams and agile organizations.
- **Managers** who support and empower Scrum Teams while maintaining team alignment and progress toward goals.

HOW THIS BOOK IS ORGANIZED

The book is organized around the typical scenarios that Scrum Teams experience, from struggling to decide on a Sprint Goal to engaging with stakeholders, and ways facilitation can help in these cases.

Each scenario includes a story, a breakdown of the dynamics of that story, a debrief, and a section called "Try This!," which focuses on the facilitation techniques you can try to address those scenarios. We describe how to try the techniques, when to use them, how you can combine them with other techniques, and what objective they can help you achieve. The scenarios serve as a basis for introducing various facilitation skills and techniques, giving context and examples as to how and why they might help.

Although these scenarios are fictional, they are based on our own experiences. We also share our own personal experiences. Each chapter ends with a summary called "Keys to Success" and a Conclusion.

The purpose and focus of each chapter follows:

- Chapter 1, "Facilitating Alignment," provides scenarios and ideas for getting started as a Scrum Team, such as creating a Product Goal, the Definition of Done, and a working agreement.
- Chapter 2, "Facilitating Sprint Planning," presents common scenarios and facilitation approaches to try when facilitating the Sprint Planning event.
- Chapter 3, "Facilitating the Daily Scrum," presents common scenarios and facilitation approaches to try when facilitating the Daily Scrum event.
- Chapter 4, "Facilitating Team Dynamics," discusses facilitation that can help with conflict and group dynamics.
- Chapter 5, "Facilitating Product Backlog Refinement," discusses approaches for facilitating refinement of the Product Backlog so that it is well defined, well ordered, and helps the Scrum Team get Product Backlog items ready for a Sprint.
- Chapter 6, "Facilitating the Sprint Review," presents common scenarios and facilitation approaches to try when facilitating the Sprint Review event.

- Chapter 7, "Facilitating the Sprint Retrospective," presents common scenarios and facilitation approaches to try when facilitating the Sprint Retrospective event.
- Chapter 8, "Facilitating Beyond a Single Scrum Team," discusses how facilitation can help with challenges that span beyond a single Scrum Team.
- Conclusion, "Moving Forward," ends the book with some final thoughts and guidance on getting started, watching for common facilitation mistakes, navigating group dynamics, and improving as a facilitator.
- Appendix A, "Facilitation Principles," introduces the five facilitation principles that are core to effective facilitation.
- Appendix B, "Adapting for Virtual," shares some ideas and considerations for facilitating virtual settings.
- Appendix C, "Facilitation Checklist," is a guide for items that a facilitator may need to think about when preparing to facilitate a session and following up afterward.

HOW TO READ THIS BOOK

You can read this book cover to cover. You can also use it as a reference guide.

You may want to come back to various sections that describe situations that your own Scrum Team is facing for techniques that might help, so bookmark information or pages in a way that is helpful for you to find content you find important.

We offer many facilitation techniques and ideas in this book. Keep in mind that we believe an empirical approach should apply to the techniques. Once you understand the purpose of the techniques, feel free to get creative and adapt them where you see fit to help you facilitate in a way that gets the most valuable outcomes for your context. We encourage you to experiment with the techniques themselves and use them in combination. Think of them as tools for your toolbox; if one does not work in a particular context, go back to your toolbox to find another that might be a better fit.

FACILITATING ALIGNMENT

Getting a group of people on the same page.

People do not naturally align on, commit to, or buy into goals and outcomes that they do not feel they have a stake in. This is a big risk for leaders or Product Owners who have a vision and define a goal in isolation and then expect everyone to follow it.

In addition to working toward a vision, Scrum Teams have other things to align on, such as how to work together or how to collaborate with their stakeholders.

Creating alignment can be difficult because people have different opinions and priorities and unique ways of communicating. A facilitator can bring value by helping Scrum Teams with these challenges. In this chapter, we share some facilitation tips and techniques that a facilitator can bring to a Scrum Team for creating alignment.

THE SCRUM TEAM FIGURING OUT HOW THEY WANT TO WORK TOGETHER

Vicky gets things started. "Okay, everyone, what are the worst possible things we can do as a team when working together? In other words, how can we be as ineffective as possible? You have five minutes to individually write down your thoughts in silence on sticky notes and add them to the board."

After five minutes of team members writing, Vicky breaks the silence, "Okay, your time is up!" She briefly looks at the sea of sticky notes on the board. "Wow, I can see some truly terrible ideas. Well done! We need to organize this a bit, so please start grouping stickies together. We're looking for items that are duplicates or similar. Anyone can move any sticky note. Feel free to ask each other questions if you need clarification."

The team gets to work, moving sticky notes around the board. "What does *planking at the Daily Scrum* mean?" asks Sajid.

Beatrice's hand shoots up. "That's my terrible idea. At the Daily Scrum, instead of a standing up, we should all do a daily plank! That will help us to easily keep the meeting under 15 minutes. But as a bonus it will help us all to get fitter, which will make us more productive."

Carter chimes in, "That's truly a horrible idea, Beatrice!" He continues, "I'm interested in this one: *To help ensure we meet the Definition of Done, if we have any failing tests, we should remove them so that the test suite always passes.* Wow, that is a terrible idea!"

After a couple of minutes, some of the team members have started to arrange the sticky notes into groups on the wall. Vicky gives some more instructions. "Now that we have some grouped items, if you can think of a name for a group, go ahead and call it out and write it next to the cluster of stickies." A few moments later, there are groups of sticky notes, and each group has a name. One group is labeled "Scrum events," one is "Definition of Done," and a third is called "Liaising with Stakeholders." The team members reflect on the items they grouped together and agree that most of the things they identified would be detrimental to the effectiveness and collaboration of the team.

Vicky continues, "Now that we know how *not* to work together and what would make us ineffective as a team, let's flip this around. Instead of bad ideas, now I want you to think of good ideas that will help us work together effectively. Also, keep the Scrum values[1] in mind. Again, let's timebox this to five minutes."

Everyone goes back to working individually to capture their own ideas on sticky notes. After the timebox has expired, the team members share their good ideas on how they should work together. They capture these on a different part of the board, and they repeat the process of grouping and naming the groups. Next, they refine the wording and carry out a fist of five vote on each proposed idea. Any item in which all team members give a score of three or more automatically goes into their working agreement. The team discusses those items that do not meet this criteria in more

---

1. For a detailed explanation of the Scrum values, see https://guntherverheyen.com/the-scrum-values/.

detail, and members either rewrite them and vote again or reject them outright.

They end up with a working agreement that includes *All team members attend Scrum events and arrive on time, Team members who attend Product Backlog refinement sessions brief those who did not attend on what happened as soon as possible, Cameras are on in virtual meetings; however, we will not make a big deal of any team member who does not turn their camera on, trusting that they have a good reason not to do so.*

The team members step back and read through their working agreement that they have written on the whiteboard. "So, that's our working agreement. Well done, everyone!" says Vicky. "There's just one more thing we haven't decided on. What is our team name going to be?"

There is a short pause while everyone gives it some thought. "How about From Worst to Best?" suggests Carter.

FORMING A TEAM WORKING AGREEMENT

Although the Scrum framework provides a set of rules and guidance for the Scrum Team to follow, relying only on Scrum is highly unlikely to be enough. Scrum is a container for context-specific practices and processes, and Scrum Teams can benefit from facilitators running workshops to agree and make transparent their ways of working and capture them into a team working agreement.

A Scrum Team can collaboratively create a team working agreement so that members have a set of guidelines they collectively agree to follow in addition to the rules of the Scrum framework. Team working agreements help all team members understand what is expected of them as they collaborate. It helps to give people clear boundaries and policies to guide their decision-making.

In the preceding story, Vicky facilitated a session for the Scrum Team to agree to its working agreement, but she was doing so in a way that enabled the team to do this collaboratively. A Scrum Master, manager, or someone else deciding what is in the working agreement takes away an opportunity for self-management from the Scrum Team, which has a greater risk of team members either not buying into it or ignoring it completely. However, self-management happens within boundaries, so to set the boundaries for which decisions and ways of working a Scrum Team can decide for itself, management and the Scrum Team can use delegation poker, which we discuss in Chapter 7, "Facilitating the Sprint Retrospective." Vicky used a technique called worst possible ideas, in which everyone was encouraged to first think of the worst ways to answer the question, and affinity mapping to organize the ideas. She then asked the team to turn the question on its head and come up with good ideas. Vicky also used the fist of five technique as a decision-making tool, which we will discuss in Chapter 4, "Facilitating Team Dynamics." We also saw that there was a decision rule of *Any item in which all team members give a score of three or more automatically goes into their working agreement*. We will discuss decision-making rules, and some facilitation tools for making decisions, in Chapter 4.

Vicky also reminded everyone to keep the Scrum values in mind. The Scrum values are a valuable tool for a facilitator to refer to when helping a Scrum Team create its working agreement. The values of *commitment, courage, focus, openness*, and *respect* provide guidance for a Scrum Team to think about what behavior and actions are appropriate when working together.

A Scrum Team can include anything in its working agreement that will guide members on how to work together. Examples can include:

- Agreed collaboration hours
- Do not disturb times
- What qualifies as an emergency issue that is expedited immediately into the Sprint
- How the team communicates
- What tools members use
- What days people work from home
- When everyone should be in the office together

Working agreements are context specific, and a Scrum Team should regularly inspect and adapt its working agreement, for example, in its Sprint Retrospective or in another facilitated session.

When team members follow the working agreement but things do not work out, the Scrum Team can see if the working agreement could be improved. By implication, this means that people are less likely to blame individuals and resort to personal attacks when the problem is with the policies in the working agreement and not the individual, assuming that the person was not behaving in a way that ignored the team working agreement.

Definition of Done and the Team Working Agreement

A Scrum Team might decide to make the Definition of Done part of its team working agreement and also include agreements on how to ensure that the Definition of Done is met. For example, a team might have this clause in its Definition of Done: *All work must be peer reviewed and conform to standards.* The working agreement might then include something like this: *If, during a peer review, the two people cannot agree if something meets our standards, they invite a third team member who will arbitrate.*

TRY THIS! IDEATE AND ORGANIZE

Vicky demonstrated a few facilitation techniques in the story to guide a Scrum Team to create its working agreement. We will describe these techniques in more detail.

Besides creating working agreements, Scrum Teams can use these techniques together or let them stand alone in many different scenarios, such as for creating a Definition of Done, generating ideas to solve a user's particular problem, or ideating on what to do about a particularly difficult impediment.

Worst Possible Ideas

What are the worst possible ways to solve a problem?

People's creativity is not a switch that they can simply turn on. Many people need to warm their creative juices before they can generate ideas. Other people can be fearful of sharing their ideas in case they are criticized or ridiculed by others. Some are just daunted by a blank piece of paper or whiteboard staring back at them.

This is where the worst possible ideas technique can help. As the name suggests, the aim is for people to generate the most terrible ideas possible. It helps people get their creative minds into gear and get them comfortable with sharing their thoughts because they are encouraged to generate bad ideas—the worse the better! As we saw in the story, participants often have fun with it.

With a collection of worst possible ideas, a facilitator can then get the group to reflect on them. The group can think about opposites or explore what is actually so bad about the ideas. Ironically, this can lead to some great ideas.

A facilitator can run a worst possible ideas activity as follows:

1. The facilitator sets the context for the group of participants, in the form of the problem to be solved.

2. The facilitator should make it clear to the participants that they should aim to come up with the worst possible ideas that they can. They set a time limit, such as five minutes, for everyone to individually write down as many bad ideas as they can. Alternatively, with a larger group, a facilitator can divide people into pairs or smaller groups for them to discuss and come up with their worst possible ideas together.

3. Each individual, pair, or subgroup then shares its worst possible ideas with the whole group. Alternatively, participants can capture their ideas on sticky notes and collaboratively group them together in an affinity map.

4. As an optional follow-up, a facilitator can ask participants to dot vote to determine the top three worst ideas. We discuss dot voting in Chapter 4. A facilitator can also ask the team to discuss what is so bad about the ideas.

5. Follow up the worst possible ideas activity by asking participants to repeat the process, but this time with good ideas.

A Scrum Team can use this technique in any situation that requires creative collaboration, from what it needs to do to be able to release an Increment, to how to meet a particular user's needs, to dealing with impediments, to creating a team working agreement.

Some people might recognize this technique as the Liberating Structure called triz. Liberating Structures[2] are evolving practices for facilitating when people work together. *Worst possible idea* is the name given to the technique in the design thinking space.[3]

With this technique, participants can generate a lot of data. One way for a group to organize a large amount of data following an activity like worst possible idea is through the creation of an affinity map.

Affinity Mapping

Ideation sessions result in the output of a lot of data and ideas. People may feel overwhelmed by a physical wall or virtual space covered in sticky notes. Affinity mapping is a simple technique to help a group converge by getting its data quickly organized.

Participants should add the output from an ideation session, such as a worst possible idea activity, on sticky notes or index cards with one thought per note. They then stick these up or spread them over a shared space. Participants can move the notes around into groups where the items appear to be related. They can do this in silence or discuss as they go.

As groups of stickies emerge, the participants start to give each group a name that reflects the collection of notes in the group. They can split or break down the groups until they are satisfied with the resulting affinity map. An example is shown in Figure 1.1. Together, the group of participants can then study the results for insights and discuss what action to take next.

---

2. Liberating Structures, https://www.liberatingstructures.com.
3. www.interaction-design.org/literature/topics/worst-possible-idea. The origin of the technique can be traced back to Bryan Mattimore, author, cofounder, and "chief idea guy" of the Growth Engine Company. See Mattimore, Bryan (2012). *Idea Stormers: How to Lead and Inspire Creative Breakthroughs*. Jossey-Bass; 1st edition.

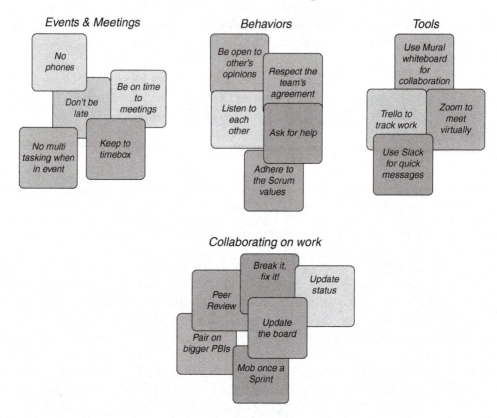

Ideas on how to work together

Events & Meetings

No phones

Be on time to meetings

Don't be late

No multi tasking when in event

Keep to timebox

Behaviors

Be open to other's opinions

Respect the team's agreement

Listen to each other

Ask for help

Adhere to the Scrum values

Tools

Use Mural whiteboard for collaboration

Trello to track work

Zoom to meet virtually

Use Slack for quick messages

Collaborating on work

Break it, fix it!

Update status

Peer Review

Update the board

Pair on bigger PBIs

Mob once a Sprint

Figure 1.1 An example of grouping insights and ideas in an affinity map.

THE SCRUM TEAM THAT ALIGNS WITH ITS STAKEHOLDERS TO DELIVER VALUE

Xiao, Li, Juri, Heiko, Isabella, Danny, and Yolanda pull their chairs into a semicircle in front of their team whiteboard. They are midway through their Sprint, and although the development work for the Sprint is going well enough, a few things came up in the Daily Scrum that they felt they needed to talk through as a whole team.

Yolanda, one of the Developers and the team's Scrum Master, kicks things off. "So we have some outstanding questions about this Product Backlog item," she says, pointing at one of the index cards stuck on the board. "Xiao, that's why we called you here. We thought that as the Product Owner, you might have an answer for us. Basically, the question is whether the users need to have a cleaner screen, or whether it is more important to see all the information in one place." Li spins his chair around to show the mockups of the two options on his computer screen.

"Hmm," says Xiao thoughtfully. "I'm really not sure. We should probably check with the people who are going to be using it."

"That makes sense. Who would that be?"

"Well... I suppose we could talk to the call center managers."

"The managers?" asks Juri. "Why not the actual call center agents? They are the ones who use the system day in and day out."

"Good point," answers Xiao. "But aren't these screens used for monitoring and reporting? They are not just for the call center agents."

"You're asking us?" says Juri.

Yolanda cuts in. "Well, it seems we need to talk to someone who knows all the uses and users for what we're building. Xiao?"

"This company has more than 3,000 employees. This system will be open to a good number of them, and many people will be interested in the information, not just here, but for the other pages we will be building."

"Do we know who to talk to and whose needs are most important if we are to design this thing?"

Xiao doesn't know how to answer. Heiko jumps in. "Why don't we just build what we think is best? People can then come to the Sprint Review and tell us what they think. That's the whole point of Scrum, right? Build something, put it in front of your users, and then we can make changes if there's anything they don't like."

"That seems really wasteful," says Isabella.

"Well," says Danny, "we already invited the whole company to our last Sprint Review. We even held it virtually so anybody could come. No one did."

"Everyone knows this project is going on. You would have thought people would have enough interest to come to the Sprint Review," Isabella adds. "As well as our work is going, something is not right here. It feels like we are working in isolation from the rest of the company."

"So what can we do to make things better?" Yolanda asks.

KNOW YOUR STAKEHOLDERS AND WHEN YOU NEED THEM

People's different perspectives make aligning difficult!

Scrum identifies the Scrum Team as the "fundamental unit of Scrum." As a small group of highly skilled and cross-functional professionals, a Scrum Team can be an effective force in solving problems and producing value. However, the danger is this unit becoming an island that is isolated from other entities, especially when Scrum Teams are formed within large organizations. A Scrum Team can become highly efficient and productive, but if it is not aligned with the rest of the organization, it may not be effective and add as much value to the organization as it could.

In the story, Yolanda and her team seemed to have a good process in place in terms of developing things. However, from the conversation the team was having, it appears that the Scrum Team was disconnected from its stakeholders. The team knew it had different users of its product, but how each one used the product and why was unknown. The team had knowledge at a high level of what was needed, but when it came to a particular detail, there was a risk that the team would produce a product that was not a good fit for some of its stakeholders. The Scrum Team has not interacted with its stakeholders as part of Product Backlog refinement or the Sprint Review. Although the team may have the mechanics of Scrum and the opportunities for inspection and adaptation in place, it is meaningless without stakeholder engagement and collaboration. Transparency is reduced, and risk grows.

Many Scrum Teams operate under these conditions, where there is a poor connection between Scrum Teams and stakeholders. Although facilitation of the Scrum events and the delivery of value is of course important to a Scrum Team's success, facilitation of the Scrum Team's interactions with its stakeholders, and not just at the Sprint Review is also important.

TRY THIS! STRATEGIES FOR INTERACTING WITH VARIOUS STAKEHOLDERS

Collaboration is a key ingredient in Scrum, but this means much more than just collaboration within a Scrum Team. It should extend beyond the Scrum Team to its stakeholders. Here we share some strategies that you can use to facilitate engagement from the stakeholders with your Scrum Team.

Stakeholder Mapping

A facilitator can use a stakeholder mapping session to help the Scrum Team identify anyone involved with, or impacted by, the product that the team is working on and identify who can give valuable insights. This includes customers and end users. An example is shown in Figure 1.2. A stakeholder map can be created with a Scrum Team through the following steps:

1. Team members write down on sticky notes all the people that they can think of who are stakeholders for their product.
2. Participants add their stickies to a (virtual) wall and then group them in whatever way feels right. These groups do not have to follow

organizational functions or departments. Example groups that emerge could include end users, influencers, financial interest, pricing strategy, market and sell the product. Some stakeholders might appear in more than one group.

3. Team members then name each group and draw lines between them to describe how the groups interrelate and communicate with each other.

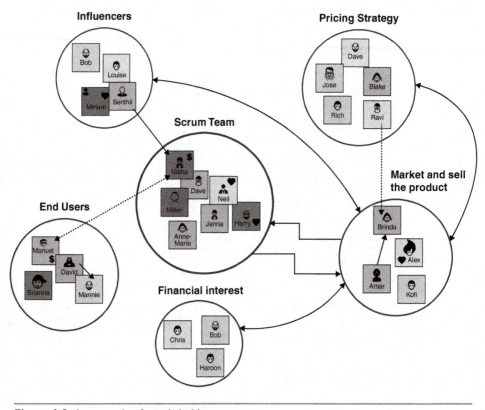

Figure 1.2 An example of a stakeholder map.

Armed with a stakeholder map, a Scrum Team can create a decision matrix to come up with strategies for the different stakeholder groups.

Decision Matrices

The decision matrix method is also known as the Pugh method,[4] after its creator, Stuart Pugh. A decision matrix can become complicated with several criteria and multiple rows and columns, but for the purposes of stakeholder engagement, we believe that there are two main dimensions that Scrum Teams need to consider: influence and interest. To create a decision matrix, the Scrum Team can follow these steps:

1. Draw a 2×2 grid, creating four quadrants.
2. Label one axis so that it represents stakeholder influence, ranging from low influence to high influence.
3. Label the other axis so that it represents stakeholder interest, ranging from low interest to high interest.
4. Team members add the different groups from the stakeholder map in each one of the quadrants according to their judgment on the stakeholders' interest and influence on the Scrum Team's work.

An example is shown in Figure 1.3. A facilitator can then use this as a starting point for team members to strategize for engagement with the different groups.

- Scrum Teams should frequently engage with stakeholders they placed into the "high influence, high interest" quadrant. At the very least, they need to invite these stakeholders to the Sprint Review, and the Scrum Team may consider facilitating other touch points as well. This may include collaborating with stakeholders as part of Product Backlog refinement.
- For stakeholders that the team placed in the category of "high influence, low interest," the Scrum Team needs to understand why they are in this category. Encourage team members to discuss and decide if the stakeholders here really need to be at the Sprint Review. If so, the facilitator can assist the team with finding a strategy that will help these stakeholders feel more engaged. Or if there is genuinely no need to have them at the Sprint

---

4. Pugh, Stuart (1981). *Concept Selection: A Method That Works.* Proceedings of International Conference on Engineering Design, Heurista, Zürich, 1981, pp. 497–506.

Review, find some other mechanism to give them what they do need, such as a regular update.

• The Scrum Team needs to be aware of those stakeholders in the "low influence, high interest" quadrant, include them in updates, and ensure that they do not influence things when really they should not.

• Lastly, it is useful to be aware of those in the "low influence, low interest" quadrant. The Scrum Team should monitor the situation and be aware if this changes and inform the people in this quadrant only when needed.

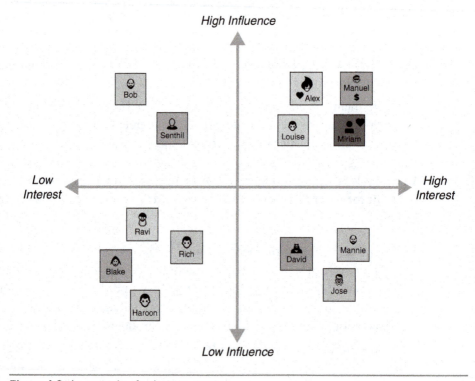

Figure 1.3 An example of a decision matrix.

Scrum Teams do not need to create a perfect stakeholder map and decision matrix. What is important for the Scrum Team is the conversations that creating them invoke, helping them be more aware and aligned with their stakeholders. Transparency is the key here. We would advise Scrum Teams to make the Sprint Review an open invite event, but they should be clear whose attendance they really need and whose attendance they consider as optional. One way a facilitator can help stakeholders decide if they should attend the next Sprint Review is by engaging them beforehand with an email invite that includes prompts to ask themselves what they expect to get out of the Sprint Review and what value they might contribute. We discuss this in Chapter 6, "Facilitating the Sprint Review."

The Scrum Team should regularly revisit their stakeholder map and decision matrix. The influence and interest that different stakeholders have in the product can change over time, particularly if the Scrum Team accomplishes or abandons a Product Goal and moves on to a new one. Where a product is in its lifecycle, from inception to initial development, introduction to the market, growth, maturity, and through to decline is another factor that can mean that different stakeholders will have different levels of influence and interest at different times.

How Long Has It Been...?

A stakeholder map and decision matrix are great tools for a Scrum Team to collaborate with its stakeholders, but an additional tool that asks the Scrum Team, "How long has it been since we engaged with each stakeholder?" adds the dimension of helping the Scrum Team manage the regularity of the relationships. One way for a Scrum Team to visualize this is as follows:

1. Draw a series of ever-larger concentric circles.
2. Draw a line from the center to the outermost circle's edge.
3. Create a scale along this line where each circle represents an increment of days, weeks, or months. Depending on your context, for example, it could go from "today" in the center to "more than 2 months ago" at the outer circle.
4. In the circles, add cards or sticky notes for each of the stakeholders identified from the stakeholder map and decision matrix that the Scrum Team needs to regularly engage with. Arrange the cards or sticky notes in the circle's timeline according to how long it has been since the Scrum Team has interacted with each stakeholder, with the more recent contacts in the center.

5. The team updates this visual regularly and use it in conjunction with the stakeholder decision matrix to keep stakeholders engaged appropriately.

An example of this visualization is shown in Figure 1.4.

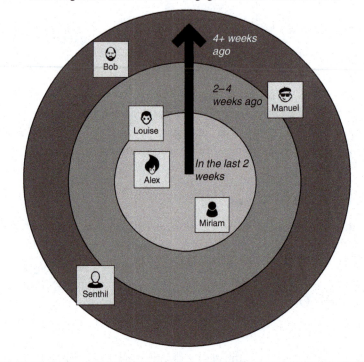

How long has it been since we engaged with our stakeholders?

Figure 1.4 An example of a how long has it been visualization.

Facilitate Early and Continuous Feedback

At the Sprint Review, stakeholders have the opportunity to see the work Done by the Scrum Team and provide feedback. However, a Scrum Team and its stakeholders can also do this earlier on in the Sprint. Scrum Teams can practice ways to improve the flow of work and contribute to completing it earlier, for example, by limiting work in progress, or pairing, mobbing, or swarming.

This enables the Scrum Team and stakeholders to review Done Increments throughout the Sprint.

The Sprint Review is a collaborative working session, so any reviews during the Sprint should be collaborative as well. They might involve just one or two key stakeholders, with the rest being informed during the Sprint Review. The Scrum Team needs to work out which stakeholders to involve in these in-Sprint interactions and which just need to be at the Sprint Review. A stakeholder map and a decision matrix are useful tools for this decision-making.

When a Scrum Team facilitates reviews as soon as possible once work is completed according to the Definition of Done, it enhances its agility. By getting early feedback, the team can validate if what it is doing is meeting stakeholder expectations, reducing its risk of doing the wrong things. This can also enhance the value of the Sprint Review because the Scrum Team can center the conversation on feedback—including early feedback on completed work from the Sprint that customers might already be using. The Sprint Review can become more strategic with focus on validation of value, the direction of travel for the product, and any changes in wider business conditions.

Although carrying out reviews with the stakeholders during the Sprint and at the Sprint Review helps a Scrum Team with its pursuit of continuously delivering value, remember that the relationship with stakeholders should not start and end there. A Scrum Team can benefit greatly from involving stakeholders in activities such as story mapping or buy a feature. We discuss these techniques in Chapter 5, "Facilitating Product Backlog Refinement."

THE SCRUM TEAM ALIGNING ON A VISION

"Who would like to go first?" asks Jared.

"We'll go first!" says Alma on behalf of herself and her partner Rob. "Our headline is this: 'Genysis Product revolutionizes the agricultural industry.'"

"Nice," says Jared. "What does everyone else think?"

"I like it," says Nick, "but I think something is missing. It's great that the headline causes a stir and is ambitious with the use of the word *revolutionizes*, but what is missing is how it will make a difference to our industry. Having said that, our headline certainly doesn't do that either."

"Would you like to share it with the group?" Jared asks.

Nick answers, "Genysis product makes $1 billion profit!"

"Ha ha! We should have expected that from the finance guy!" says Rob.

"Okay," says Jared, "whose headline is next?"

Fernando and Dana look at each other and nod. "We'll go," says Dana. "We had this: 'Germinator Genysis, the fully automated mass seed-planting machine that guarantees healthy crops with less waste!'"

"Oh that's good!" says Rob. "Germinator Genysis—maybe we should rename the product to that!"

The Scrum Team and its stakeholders, which include Nick, the company's CFO, and Nuno, the company's head of marketing, continue to review their imagined trade magazine headlines that they have written about the product they are planning to develop. Once all the pairs share their headlines, the group continues to discuss the elements of what they like about each one so they can craft them together into one headline.

"I think we have something that I am happy with now," Jared says. "Nuno, as the head of marketing, why don't you have the honor of reading it aloud for us?"

"You are the Product Owner. I think it should be you!"

"Well, if you insist. 'Germinator Genysis: state-of-the-art technology efficiently and sustainably producing fresh, delicious crops, as nature intended.' That's our future headline and our product vision!"

ALIGNING THE SCRUM TEAM ON THE PRODUCT VISION

Scrum Teams take steps toward fulfilling a vision.

The Product Owner officially sets the product vision, but the Product Owner does not have to create it in isolation or without the help of someone else facilitating discussions to encapsulate it.

We saw in the story that Jared, the Product Owner of a new product in the agricultural industry, facilitated a workshop that involved the Scrum Team and some of its key stakeholders, including Nick, the chief financial officer, and Nuno, the head of marketing. Yet Jared used a technique that broke down any sense of hierarchy by pairing stakeholders with Scrum Team members. All the pairs presented their ideas, and they gave each other feedback. The group then worked together to craft the final articulation of the product vision.

Note, too, that Jared made it clear that the product vision was his account-ability as Product Owner. He stated, "I think we have something that I am happy with now." Yet he facilitated in a way that has enabled the rest of the Scrum Team and the stakeholders to give input. Jared also created greater transparency around the process and the thinking that has gone into the vision by including others.

The product vision drives future Product Goals, which are intermediate steps taken one at a time to fulfill the product vision. A Product Goal in turn gives a direction for each Sprint Goal. Transparency of these layers and the fact that they are created collaboratively, from the Sprint Goal at the Sprint level to the overarching product vision, creates alignment and understanding. Scrum Teams that have a shared understanding of the product vision and Product Goal find it easier to craft their Sprint Goals because everyone understands what they are trying to achieve with the product.

TRY THIS! DESCRIBE DESIRED FUTURE OUTCOMES

The Product Owner is accountable for the creation and communication of the product vision and the Product Goal. Doing this in collaboration with the rest of the Scrum Team and the stakeholders can create more of a sense of shared purpose and communicate inclusiveness for shared responsibility for all aspects of the product development. By including others in the process of creating visions and goals, the Product Owner is more likely to achieve strong buy-in.

Here we describe some techniques to support the Product Owner in defining the product vision and a Product Goal collaboratively.

Divergence and Convergence

Divergence is the process of two or more things moving away from each other. *Convergence* is the state of things coming together. A divergence and convergence approach can be used to leverage the diverse perspectives within a group. When using divergence and convergence as a collaborative approach, participants first generate a number of ideas or insights independently (divergence stage), and then participants explore the results as a group to consolidate the ideas and insights to a collective output (convergence stage).

Each individual's perspective is usually one part of the bigger picture. The parable of *The Blind Men and the Matter of the Elephant* provides a useful metaphor.

The metaphor goes like this. All inhabitants of a city were blind. A king and his army arrived and camped nearby. Among them was an elephant. Word of the animal's arrival spread. The city inhabitants were curious about the elephant because they had never encountered such an animal before so they went out to find it. When they found it, they inspected it by touch. Each person gathered information from a different perspective. One person found the elephant's trunk. "It is like a long, thick snake," they declared. Another discovered the elephant's legs and feet. "It is like a pillar," this person said. One found an ear. "It is like a rug." A fourth person found the tail. "It is like a rope." A fifth found the elephant's side and declared, "It is like a large wall." Another person found its tusk, observing, "It is like a spear." Each person had one perspective out of many, but their individual perspectives were incomplete. It is only when all the people touching the elephant came together and collaborated, taking time to understand each other's perspectives, that the whole picture of the elephant emerged.

And so it is with divergent and convergent thinking: everyone's perspective is taken into consideration, a shared understanding is built, and then the group comes to an agreement.

Divergence can happen before or during a meeting. For example, a facilitator can ask the Scrum Team to reflect on the Sprint before the start of the Sprint Retrospective by using a simple team survey. The Scrum Team then discusses the results during the Sprint Retrospective. To give team members more time to reflect at their own pace first, a facilitator should ensure that quiet time is allowed for individual thinking. Many techniques take a divergence and convergence approach, including 1-2-4-all, affinity mapping, and silent writing. We discuss 1-2-4-all in Chapter 2, affinity mapping in this chapter, and silent writing in Chapter 4.

Tomorrow's Headlines

Tomorrow's headlines is a facilitation technique that focuses the team on the outcome as the starting point. It helps people to think about future success and challenges them to succinctly capture what that success means. Therefore, it could be a suitable technique to help a Product Owner collaborate with others to form a product vision, as Jared did in the story. It could also help a team create Product Goals and even Sprint Goals. The technique is based on the cover story activity featured on the gamestorming.com website[5] and the

---

5. See https://gamestorming.com/cover-story/.

book *Gamestorming: A Playbook for Innovators, Rulebreakers, and Changemakers*.[6]

As we saw in the story, Jared was facilitating a session in which the participants were imagining the future state of their product and thinking about what might be written as a headline about it in their industry trade magazines. Thinking in headlines helps participants imagine the outcomes and benefits of the product so they do not worry about particular features too early.

One way to facilitate the activity with a divergence and convergence approach follows:

1. Split a group of participants into pairs to create a future headline together.
2. Have the pairs share their headline with the rest of the group. Each pair could simply read out their headline as we saw in the story, or each group could place their headline in a shared area on a sticky note, such as on a physical wall or a virtual whiteboard.
3. Encourage the group as a whole to discuss and agree on a single headline, which could be a combination of several suggestions.

Alternatively, people could first work individually before the group converges.

Some groups might go further and also write a press release to accompany the headline. This might include details on the market for the product, the benefit that users of the product experience, and some imaginary testimonials.

Elevator Pitch

The elevator pitch is a template that expresses a product vision. The template looks like this:

For <target customer or user>

who <statement of need or opportunity>

---

6. Gray, Dave, Sunni Brown, and James Macanufo (2010). *Gamestorming: A Playbook for Innovators, Rulebreakers, and Changemakers*. O'Reilly Media; 1st edition.

the <product name>

is a <product category>

that <key benefit, compelling reason to buy>

unlike <primary competitive alternative>

our product <statement of primary differentiation>

The elevator pitch is a tool for capturing elements of a product vision in a succinct way: the target customers or users, their needs, the product itself and its category, what distinguishes the product from its competitors, and the product's main competitive advantage.

Product Vision Box

The product vision box is another way of having people think about the future state of the product that the Scrum Team is going to work on. The challenge is to design the "box" that the product comes in, even though the product might not yet exist. The technique originates from the series of *Innovation Games* created by Luke Hohmann.[7]

When designing a product vision box, participants should try to include the product's name, an image, a tagline or slogan, and two or three points that promote the benefits of the product to the users. Most important of all to include is the value proposition—in other words what value the customer or user gets from the product. The trick is to focus on benefits and not simply list features. Apple, with its message of "1,000 songs in your pocket" when it launched the iPod,[8] is a great example of a company providing a value proposition. Its competitors fell in the trap of listing features, such as "mp3 support" or "reprogrammable firmware." A vision that describes benefits is much more motivating than a list of product features.

---

7. Hohmann, L. (2006). *Innovation Games: Creating Breakthrough Products Through Collaborative Play*. Addison-Wesley Professional.

8. See www.youtube.com/watch?v=6SUJNspeux8.

Facilitating a Virtual Product Vision Box Workshop

In my experience, when we don't know what to create, it is best to just start creating something. This approach is often referred to as "thinking with your hands." It unleashes creativity and increases the level of engagement. I used to facilitate the creation of a product vision box with teams in a physical setting by giving participants materials such as cardboard, sharpies, markers, and glue and asking them to collaboratively create a physical box. I have since experimented on how to replicate this same experience in a virtual setting.

Facilitating a virtual product vision box workshop for the first time took some extra preparation, but it was still possible. I sent a set of materials to everyone beforehand. I also asked for volunteers to be "build hands." I sent these people extra materials and checked whether they had a camera and lighting that was good enough for them to show the box they would be building.

I reiterated to participants that they should not worry about how their creation would look and that the workshop was not an art class. My reassurance that the objective of the session was to convey a message and not create a perfect-looking box made them feel more comfortable in letting their hands do the work.

Each participant built a box and then took a picture of it, which they uploaded to an online whiteboard. The group discussed the concepts and asked each other questions about their thought processes behind each box. The participants then worked in breakout rooms to converge, using insights from their individual boxes, and built a single box together in small groups. The people who had volunteered to be build hands did the building of the box for their group, pointing the camera on their hands while creating it, while the others in the group gave instructions. Once the box was ready, the build hands uploaded an image of their group's box onto the whiteboard. The whole group came back together again in the main room to show and discuss the boxes from their smaller groups. From there, the participants discussed concepts, built upon ideas, and then collectively as a group created one box, with one of the build hands volunteering to create it and the rest of the group giving instructions.

—*Glaudia Califano*

Creating a product vision using a divergent and convergent approach using either the elevator pitch template or the product vision box can also be facilitated in a similar way to what we described for tomorrow's headlines.

Roman Pichler's Product Canvas

With a product vision, the Product Owner can collaborate with others to define the first next step to fulfill the vision, which is the Product Goal. The Product Goal is part of the Product Backlog along with the Product Backlog items.

Scrum Teams looking for an alternative to the top to bottom linear Product Backlog can instead use the product canvas from Roman Pichler,[9] as shown in Figure 1.5.

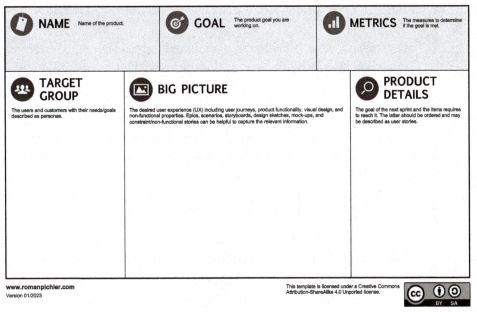

Figure 1.5 Roman Pichler's product canvas.

Author: Roman Pichler. Source: www.romanpichler.com.

License: Creative Commons Attribution-ShareAlike 4.0 Unported (CC BY-SA 4.0), https://creativecommons.org/licenses/by-sa/4.0/.

---

9. The product canvas is available for download at www.romanpichler.com/tools/the-product-canvas/.

A facilitator can help the Scrum Team with creating and maintaining the product canvas. The product canvas has sections for each of the following:

- The product name
- The Product Goal
- Metrics used to measure progress toward the goal
- The target group of the product, which could take the form of personas
- The big picture, which could be expressed with workflows, story maps, or high-level Product Backlog items
- Product details, which a Scrum Team might use for the Product Backlog items in Sprint and those that are candidates for the next Sprint

The product canvas is deliberately designed to be a lean representation of the Product Backlog, avoiding having dozens or even hundreds of detailed Product Backlog items.

A Scrum Team and its stakeholders can create and evolve a product canvas collaboratively to create alignment and increase shared understanding of the content and intent of the Product Backlog.

KEYS TO FACILITATING ALIGNMENT

A facilitator can bring a lot of value to a Scrum Team by creating alignment. The facilitator's skills and techniques can help the team gain alignment with its goals, with each other, and with its stakeholders. We look now at a summary of the main things to consider when facilitating alignment for a Scrum Team.

SCRUM TEAM COLLABORATION OVER COOPERATION

Many people and teams mistake collaboration for cooperation. "We worked well as a team" is an often-used phrase to describe what went well during a Sprint. Oftentimes, the sentiment is because team members were cordial to one another and efficiently passed information to each other. What is described is cooperation in which a group of people work toward the same goal but essentially do their own jobs.

Collaboration is what turns a group of people into a team. Collaborative team members assist each other outside their own function when they can, and when they cannot, they seek to grow their skills and knowledge. Their focus is on producing value, not utilization and keeping people busy. Team members empathize with each other and care about achieving a shared goal.

BUILD EMPATHY BETWEEN THE SCRUM TEAM AND ITS STAKEHOLDERS

Although the Sprint Review is the formal event for interactions between the Scrum Team and its stakeholders, ongoing collaboration between the two increases transparency, reduces risk, and aids decision-making.

It is important for a Scrum Team not to isolate itself from its stakeholders, with the only interaction possible at the Sprint Review. This isolation would be counterintuitive to the transparency that is so important to the successful use of Scrum. These interactions could encompass informal reviews and feedback of work as it progresses during Sprints and involving stakeholders in Product Backlog refinement activities.

Good facilitation is one of the keys to keeping the stakeholders engaged, to bringing transparency to the Scrum Team of the stakeholders' needs and expectations, and to keeping the stakeholders informed about progress being made. Effective and efficient facilitation makes these interactions positive, productive, and timely.

MAKE IT INCLUSIVE

To really get people to buy into a vision, they need to feel like they are part of its development. Facilitating a session where the vision can be contributed to and crafted with everybody who is going to be involved with an initiative, including stakeholders and the Scrum Team, can create alignment from the start.

CONCLUSION

An organization consists of employees, systems, rules, goals, and countless other factors that affect its business. When an organization achieves alignment, with its vision, goals, and strategy transparent and customer-driven, it has a clearer sense of what to pursue at any given time. The same can be said for a single Scrum Team in an organization.

A Scrum Team that invests time and effort in creating alignment within itself and with those external to it sets itself up for success. This includes collaborating on the vision for its product, how it will work as a Scrum Team, and how it will collaborate with its stakeholders.

Conversations around alignment and goals can be difficult. Although it is good for a Scrum Team and its stakeholders to think about what they want to achieve, as a facilitator, you can help the group think about what is most important—the outcomes their customers want. Not only will this deliver better results for customers and the organization in the long run, but it gives Scrum Teams a greater sense of purpose and more space to be creative.

FACILITATING SPRINT PLANNING

Targeting the Sprint Goal.

Sprint Planning is the first event of a Sprint. In it, the Scrum Team defines a Sprint Goal that supports the Product Goal, and the Developers create their initial plan of action by selecting Product Backlog items from the Product Backlog to work on in the Sprint. In doing this, they discuss three questions about the Sprint:

1. Why will the work of the Sprint be valuable? (the Sprint Goal)
2. What work will the Developers focus on? (the Product Backlog items forecasted for the Sprint)
3. How will the Developers get started? (the initial plan)

The result from these discussions forms the Sprint Backlog.

An effective Sprint Planning event contributes to the success of the Sprint. However, Scrum Teams often struggle with meeting the purpose of the Sprint Planning event. For example, they end Sprint Planning with a low-value Sprint Goal or even no Sprint Goal, the team members do not have a shared under-standing of the selected Product Backlog items for the Sprint, or the Developers do not know how to get started with the work. Outcomes from Sprint Planning like these set up the Scrum Team for failure from the outset. Effective facilitation can reduce these risks.

THE SCRUM TEAM STRUGGLING TO AGREE TO A SINGLE SPRINT GOAL

Team Hustle is in its Sprint Planning event. Four hours have passed without a Sprint Goal being created. After a coffee break, the team reconvenes in its meeting room. Ben, Team Hustle's Scrum Master, summarizes what the team has discussed so far.

"Okay team, as discussed, we know we should kick off the usability testing to get some feedback on the first prototype of the personal recommen-dations feature, so we have an item for that on the Sprint Backlog. Scott really wants us to get the last of the user stories completed to enable our customers to pay by credit card, so that work is on the Sprint Backlog too."

"Excellent. It will be great to see that one finished," says Scott, Team Hustle's Product Owner.

"Yes," Ben continues, "there is also an item for the work we need to do to support the marketing campaign that goes out next week."

"Don't forget the complaints about the application instability that we heard about at the Sprint Review!" Francisco interjects.

"Right! Before the break, we agreed we would put an item on the Sprint Backlog to investigate that. Francisco, would you mind adding it now?"

"Sure. This one worries me. It could be affecting thousands of customers or just a few. We won't really know how bad it is until we investigate further and put in some analytics. And as for fixing it…"

"Things were so much easier before we launched the product!" observes Pawel. "Remember when we could focus on the next most important feature? Now we have to deal with all these support and maintenance issues alongside the next set of feature work."

Everyone agrees.

"So what should the Sprint Goal be?" Ben asks, trying to bring the conversation back to the topic that they had gotten stuck on before the break.

Ben purposefully lets the silence hang. Kayla eventually breaks it. "Well," she says, "we already have the items on our Sprint Backlog that we think we can do. And we know what we're doing with them. Why don't we just make it the Sprint Goal to finish all these items and be done with it? Why do we even need a Sprint Goal anyway?"

CRAFTING A SPRINT GOAL WHEN THE SCRUM TEAM HAS COMPETING PRIORITIES

Team Hustle had competing priorities for the Sprint, a situation that many Scrum Teams face at Sprint Planning. And even though the team had capacity to work on some of them, the Product Backlog items were not related, making it difficult for Team Hustle to craft a single Sprint Goal.

Scrum Teams need to work on competing priorities for a variety of reasons. It can happen as a product evolves in its life cycle, such as when the Scrum Team continues to develop new features while supporting and maintaining the previously released versions of the product. This can be reflected in a Scrum

Team's Sprint Goal that is littered with the word "and" separating different objectives. Or the team's Sprint Goal may read as a list of Product Backlog items it needs to complete. In both cases, the Scrum Teams have no unifying purpose for their Sprint. When a Scrum Team lacks a unifying purpose, it starts behaving as a group of individuals rather than collaborating as a team.

Lacking a unifying purpose also makes it harder for the Scrum Team to make decisions. During the course of a Sprint, the team learns more about its work. This can lead to the Scrum Team having to make trade-offs in both its way of working as well as the product itself. When lacking a unifying Sprint Goal, a Scrum Team can make flawed or haphazard decisions. A skilled facilitator guides the team to create this single objective. As Patrick Lencioni, CEO, executive coach, and author of *The Advantage*[1] says, "When everything is important, then nothing is."

TRY THIS! CONVERGING ON A SINGLE COHESIVE SPRINT GOAL

Scrum Teams eventually, inevitably, have to deal with multiple separate initiatives in a Sprint. That's what makes it even more important to have a Sprint Goal to focus the team's attention. Here are some ways for you to consider that may help your Scrum Team form its Sprint Goal.

Stakeholder Invite

The stakeholder invite is a useful technique in which a Scrum Team starts with the end in mind. In Sprint Planning, the Scrum Team thinks about what its stakeholders would like to see at the Sprint Review. What would excite them? What would be so valuable to them that they can't wait to join the Sprint Review? Ultimately, what could the Scrum Team include in an invitation to stakeholders to get their attention and create enthusiasm?

The stakeholder invite is an activity in which the team crafts an invitation to the stakeholders during Sprint Planning. A facilitator can use this as a technique to help a Scrum Team think about what the goal of the Sprint should be. The Scrum Team can craft the invite as a group, or it can split up into

---

1. Lencioni, Patrick M. (2012). *The Advantage*. Jossey-Bass.

subgroups, with each coming up with its own suggestions. Each subgroup then presents its suggestion or does a gallery walk so the groups can learn about each other's ideas before having a whole team discussion to converge on a final version. We discuss the gallery walk technique in Chapter 8, "Facilitating Beyond a Single Scrum Team."

The Scrum Team does not need to send the invitation, although the technique may be more impactful if it does. The goal of the stakeholder invite is to help the Scrum Team focus on its stakeholders' desired outcomes for the Sprint, which will lead it back to what its Sprint Goal could be. The team can then start to plan the Product Backlog items for the Sprint that will help it achieve this goal.

Powerful Questions to Uncover the Next Most Important Outcome

The right question at the right time can have a big impact. If a Scrum Team is struggling with its Sprint Goal, as a facilitator, ask powerful questions to focus minds on what the next most important thing is that the Scrum Team should do.

Here are some examples:

- If this was the last Sprint, what would we do to provide the best value?
- If we would invest our own money in this Sprint, what work would maximize our return on investment?
- What Sprint Goal would most excite our customers and stakeholders?
- What could we do next that would reduce the most risk of losing time or money in the future?

Facilitating this as an open discussion and answering these questions as a group may be enough of a prompt for a Scrum Team to define its Sprint Goal. However, here are some things to keep an eye out for:

- The Scrum Team might generate several competing options.
- Another risk is that certain personalities may dominate the conversation, or everyone goes along with whatever the Product Owner suggests. If either of

these is a danger, a facilitator can instead experiment with techniques that enable full participation with divergence and convergence of thought. Combining 1-2-4-all with other techniques to explore options and make a decision is a good option.

1-2-4-All

1-2-4-all is a facilitation technique from the group of practices known as Liberating Structures[2] that can help a Scrum Team form its Sprint Goal in a way that is participative for the whole team. It usually requires a minimum of eight participants. For the purpose of using it to form the Sprint Goal, the Scrum Master and Product Owner can take part alongside the Developers.

Because the Sprint Goal is a step toward the Product Goal, everyone needs a shared understanding of the Product Goal. Allow time for the Product Owner to remind everyone of the Product Goal and to answer any clarifying questions. When everyone is aligned on the Product Goal, the Scrum Team can start to explore what first step can be taken to move the Scrum Team closer to it.

The 1-2-4-all technique consists of the following. First, present the topic for discussion. In this case, it can be posed as the question, "What is the best outcome we can achieve by the end of this Sprint to move us closer to the Product Goal?" Then a first individual reflection round takes place, followed by two more rounds of discussion in growing group sizes. Each round is strictly timeboxed, so a facilitator must monitor and signal the start and end of each round:

1. Participants reflect individually on the question and consider what they believe is the best outcome they can achieve for the Sprint. Timebox of one minute.

2. Participants form pairs, share their thoughts, and develop ideas further together. Timebox of two minutes.

3. Each pair then joins another pair to share and develop ideas further as a group of four. Timebox of four minutes.

4. The whole group comes back together, and each group shares one idea for a Sprint Goal. Timebox of five minutes.

Although the format suggests a group size that is a multiple of four, a facilitator should adjust accordingly. For example, it can be run as a 1-3-6-all.

A facilitator can use 1-2-4-all in many scenarios that call for divergence and convergence of thought. We discuss divergence and convergence in Chapter 1, "Facilitating Alignment." In addition to helping the Scrum Team craft its Sprint Goal, a facilitator can use 1-2-4-all to address other challenges that a Scrum Team is facing. For example, a facilitator can use it in a Sprint Retrospective to help the Scrum Team explore ideas to help them improve and become more effective. And even during the Sprint, when the Developers are stuck on how to implement a particular Product Backlog item, 1-2-4-all can help them quickly explore different options.

This technique is helpful, especially when there are quieter people or authoritative characters in a discussion, because all have the opportunity to put their views forward without the influence of the person behind the idea being a major factor. In theory, 1-2-4-all enables the participants to evolve the best ideas together and helps to naturally build consensus and shared understanding.

However, facilitating a 1-2-4-all has some pitfalls to watch out for.

The short timeboxes mean that participants do not have the opportunity to analyze and critique ideas thoroughly. If this is the case and people feel conversations have not gone deep enough, a facilitator can always run a second round of 1-2-4-all or adjust the standard timeboxes slightly by adding a few minutes more per round.

In addition, although 1-2-4-all gives the opportunity for people who are quieter and more reserved a chance to share an idea, it does the same for those who are more vocal and dominant.

Strong Personalities Can Still Beat Strong Ideas in 1-2-4-All

I think 1-2-4-all is a great interactive way to share and converge on ideas, and I use it regularly when facilitating. There is something to watch for. One time I had a challenge when I was working with a large group and thought that 1-2-4-all would be a good technique to give everyone in the group a voice, but what I observed was a particularly outgoing person who held strong opinions pushing their ideas through every round of discussion. The short timeboxes allowed this person to dominate the conversations, and other people did not have a chance to contribute.

—Patricia Kong

As a facilitator, share guidelines upfront, such as maintaining one conversation at a time in group discussions and living the Scrum values of openness and respect.

1-2-4-all results in a number of options being generated and developed by the different groups. It usually requires some follow-up to further explore the generated output and decide on actions.

Follow Up 1-2-4-All with a Gallery Walk and the Selection of a Sprint Goal

Ensure that each group's response is visibly recorded for everyone to see, perhaps by placing it on a (virtual) wall.

Once each group has shared its results as part of the final part of 1-2-4-all, the Scrum Team can conduct a short gallery walk to explore the different Sprint Goals further and note any thoughts, concerns, or questions. This can be timeboxed to 12 minutes, for example. For more on the gallery walk, see Chapter 8.

After team members have shared and discussed any major concerns, questions, or thoughts on the suggested Sprint Goals, the Scrum Team selects the outcome it wants to achieve for the Sprint, which brings it closer to the Product Goal. This could be done by a dot vote for example. We discuss dot voting in Chapter 4, "Facilitating Team Dynamics."

The Sprint Goal Template

One facilitation aid that is useful for Sprint Planning is Roman Pichler's Sprint Goal template,[2] which is shown in Figure 2.1.

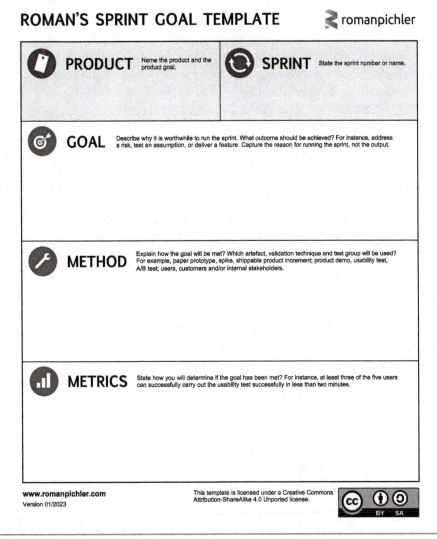

Figure 2.1 Roman Pichler's Sprint Goal template.

Author: Roman Pichler. Source: www.romanpichler.com.

License: Creative Commons Attribution-ShareAlike 4.0 Unported (CC BY-SA 4.0), https://creativecommons.org/licenses/by-sa/4.0/.

2. To download Roman's Sprint Goal template, see www.romanpichler.com/tools/the-sprint-goal-template/.

Scrum Teams can fill in this Sprint Goal template as a way to facilitate conversations about the Sprint Goal in Sprint Planning. In the header section, the Scrum Team describes what the product is, and it highlights its Product Goal. The Sprint Goal template includes a section to capture the Sprint Goal and a section for the method that the Scrum Team can use to capture how it intends to meet the goal. This can include a description of the future state of the Done Increment as a tangible new version of the product. Alternatively, it can include descriptions of prototypes for the Scrum Team to get feedback on or other experiments when the goal is learning. The last section prompts the Scrum Team to think about what metrics to measure to determine if the goal has been met.

From a facilitation perspective, Roman Pichler's Sprint Goal template provides guidance and helps the team think about not just the Sprint Goal, but also how the planned work for the Sprint fits in with the Sprint Goal in a way that is simple and visible to the whole Scrum Team. The Scrum Team can make the resulting canvas accessible to its stakeholders after Sprint Planning, providing transparency for the Sprint, encouraging collaboration, and minimizing surprises at the Sprint Review.

THE TEAM MEMBER WHO PUSHES THE TEAM TO OVERCOMMIT

Why are so many items being pulled into the Sprint?

"Look, I'm not 100 percent sure it is even feasible," says Andie. "I'm happy to create a spike and pull that in, but I don't think we can commit to this Product Backlog item until we really know what's involved."

Donnie sighs. "You want a spike for everything! We'll never get anything done if we are always doing spikes. The best way to learn how to do it is to start it. Scrum tells us to have courage, so let's just bring it in."

"Any objections to Donnie's proposal?" asks Arjen, the team's Scrum Master. "No? Great! Let's put it on the Sprint Backlog then. So, what's next, Steven?"

"The next item from the Product Backlog is item 312," replies Steven, the team's Product Owner. "We looked at it in refinement a few days ago. It's the one we said we needed input on from Ian, but he's still on vacation."

"It's fine," replies Donnie. "There's nothing to it."

"I'm not so sure," says Andie.

"Does anyone else have a concern? If not, let's try and do it without Ian," says Arjen. Ulrika, Kristina, and Dave are all silent. "Okay, then. Glad we agree. I'll move it onto the Sprint Backlog."

Andie lets out an audible huff that she makes no attempt to hide. "We're going to take too much on again," she mutters.

"What about 313? I'd love to get that one in as well," says Steven.

"Sure! That should only take half a day. You can add it to the Sprint Backlog," says Donnie. Ulrika and Kristina look on quietly. Andie rolls her eyes and sighs again.

"Great!" says Arjen. "I'm adding it now."

Donnie catches the look that Andie gives him. "Don't worry, Andie," he says. "I know the last Sprint was stressful, but I just feel like we will be fine this time. We learned from what happened the last time."

"What exactly did we learn, Donnie?" she asks.

CREATING A SPRINT FORECAST COLLABORATIVELY

When forecasting the work for the Sprint, Developers may be overly optimistic. This could be the Developers as a collective, or one or more dominant voices are pressuring the rest of the group to add more work to the Sprint Backlog, similar to how Donnie acted in the story. We also saw Steven, the Product Owner, pushing the Developers to do more. In other cases, the opposite can happen: people can be risk averse and afraid to add too much work to their Sprint Backlog in case they do not deliver what was "committed" to; they see this as failure.

A facilitator should avoid asking questions that imply a promise during the selection of Product Backlog items for the Sprint, such as "Is everyone okay to commit to getting this Done by the end of the Sprint?" Everyone should know that when forecasting Product Backlog items for the Sprint, the Developers make assumptions based on available information and evidence. Everyone should be aware that Developers can't get their plan for the Sprint 100 percent right in Sprint Planning, and the initial Product Backlog items that they selected in Sprint Planning may change as more becomes known throughout the Sprint. When their forecast is not met, the Scrum Team should take it as a learning opportunity. The Developers should explore ways to improve future forecasts using empirical evidence.

Bringing in too much work during Sprint Planning can cause Developers to feel overwhelmed and result in them working on many Product Backlog items at the same time during the Sprint. Good facilitation in Sprint Planning encourages collaborative conversations based on data and evidence instead of relying on pure guesswork.

TRY THIS! MAKING BETTER-INFORMED DECISIONS AS A TEAM

In the prior story, Andie was the only Developer in the Scrum Team who raised concerns about the team taking on too much work, while Donnie was pushing the others to accept everything that was suggested into the Sprint. The other Developers, Ulrika, Kristina, and Dave, sat passively. Steven, the

Product Owner, continued to push for more work to go into the Sprint. Arjen, the Scrum Master, noted the acceptance of the work without question.

This Scrum Team was not collaborating effectively. Their behaviors during Sprint Planning were likely setting them up for another Sprint of incomplete work and rising tensions. In cases like this, a facilitator should have participants step back and reflect on the behavior of the group and their interactions.

Uncovering Everyone's Point of View

Some facilitators mistake silence in response to a closed question as consent, as we saw when Arjen assumed Ulrika, Kristina, and Dave were in agreement. Asking a question like "Does anyone else have a concern?" can be effective when team members have healthy working relationships with each other and feel they are able to voice their concerns; otherwise, team members are highly unlikely to express their true thoughts. Scrum Teams can use decision rules and decision-making facilitation techniques, which we discuss in Chapter 4, to clarify the level of agreement they should have as a collective for potential decisions.

When a few individuals are dominating a conversation, a facilitator can try a few different tactics to create space for the other participants to share their thoughts. For example:

- Stepping in with the invitation, "Let's hear from the people who did not have a chance to share their thoughts yet"
- Suggesting that the participants form smaller groups to create more intimacy and more space for individuals to contribute
- Allocating time for individual reflection
- Giving each individual an opportunity to speak by using a round robin approach

Whatever technique is used, a facilitator should avoid controlling or berating people who are more vocal. This potentially brings even more attention to them and more weight to their opinions.

At the very least, a facilitator can use open questions that require more than a yes or a no answer. A simple change in how a facilitator asks questions can make a big difference in how people respond. For example, compare the question, "Does anyone have concerns about getting this item Done this Sprint?" to "What are some risks that we might not be able to get this item Done this Sprint?"

What Does the Data Say?

One of the inputs to the Sprint Planning event is whatever the Developers know about their past performance. Many teams base their forecast on gut-feel, which is okay, but when it comes to forecasting, human beings tend to be overly optimistic. Developers should use data that shows what they have *actually* achieved in the past to help them forecast the work they think they can complete according to the Definition of Done during the Sprint. Forecasting using past information and data also helps team members respond to pressure about taking on too much work in an evidence-based way. Part of empirical theory is to use what is known from the past to help with decision-making.

Metrics for past performance come in different forms and nomenclature. An example is throughput, which is the amount of work Developers get Done in a unit of time. It could be the number of Product Backlog items Done per Sprint. Although people argue about the usefulness of some of these metrics, their primary purpose is as a planning tool for the Scrum Team. To spark valuable conversations and help the team make better informed decisions, a good facilitator should point the team to reliable and relevant data and ensure that it is accessible for everyone during Sprint Planning.

Facilitate the Discussion Toward the Next Most Important Thing to Start Next

Developers can and should update their Sprint Backlog during the Sprint because, as we've mentioned, it is unreasonable to expect them to be able to forecast exactly what Product Backlog items they will complete according to the Definition of Done in Sprint Planning, Sprint after Sprint. A simple way for a Scrum Team to avoid taking on too much work is to not attempt to plan all Product Backlog items for the Sprint. Instead of Developers asking themselves, "What Product Backlog items can we get Done this Sprint?," an easier question is, "What are the most important Product Backlog items to start next?," aligning what is important with the crafting of the Sprint Goal. When they are ready to, Developers can then bring items onto the Sprint Backlog *during* the Sprint. This is still within the rules of Scrum—the Developers just need enough to get started.

The Importance of Collaboration Toward the Sprint Goal

One of the most successful Scrum Teams that I worked with had really effective and lean Scrum events. We had 2-week Sprints, and our Sprint Planning event was typically done in about 30 minutes. Our Product Backlog refinement activities involved the whole team. Everyone was fully participative and had a really good understanding of the Product Backlog items by the time they were considered in Sprint Planning. But what made our Sprint Planning really smooth was that we would focus on creating a Sprint Goal, select the first Product Backlog item that would contribute to the goal, and then create an initial plan for it. Once we had that, we would end the Sprint Planning event with the understanding that the Developers would pull items from the Product Backlog onto the Sprint Backlog during the Sprint. Our working agreement included clauses such as Developers first seeing if they could help with the item in progress; if they could not, they would then look to the Product Backlog for the next item that could contribute to the Sprint Goal. If nothing was available, Developers might select something else valuable to work on.

This did require a shared understanding of the product, the Product Goal, our Sprint Goal, excellent ongoing collaboration between the Developers and the Product Owner, a well-refined and up-to-date ordered Product Backlog, everyone living the Scrum value of courage, and an environment of high trust. With these things in place, this approach worked really well for us.

—Glaudia Califano

With this approach, facilitation of the Sprint Planning event then becomes much more lightweight and simpler, while still adhering to the purpose of the Scrum event. It does require all parties being comfortable with ambiguity of what Product Backlog items might be delivered by the end of the Sprint. Developers need to collaborate closely so they can hit the ground running each time they pull in a new Product Backlog item. This approach also needs trust in the environment that the Developers will continually pull the next piece of work once they have capacity.

THE TEAM MEMBERS WHO DON'T KNOW WHERE TO START

Getting off the start line in a Sprint.

Marty looks from his screen to the index card lying next to his keyboard. Written on the index card is the Product Backlog item he is supposed to be working on, in the form of a user story and its acceptance criteria.

Three hours have passed since the conclusion of this morning's Sprint Planning event, but Marty has still not made a start. And now it is almost the end of the working day and time for Marty to go home.

He is confused about how to approach this work. Marty is not a bad Developer. On the contrary, he has many years of experience. Looking at the Product Backlog item by his keyboard, he knows some of the elements that need to exist. He just has no idea where to start.

CREATE AN INITIAL PLAN FOR HOW THE WORK WILL GET DONE

At Sprint Planning, the Developers create an initial plan for completing the chosen Product Backlog items for the Sprint. They need to consider what work for the Sprint would be valuable to do, and how they will meet the Definition of Done to produce at least one Increment. They may also need to think about ongoing Product Backlog refinement and implementing any agreed-upon improvement actions.

Ideally, as soon as Sprint Planning ends, the Developers have what they need to hit the ground running and start making progress with the development work. But that is not always the case. We have certainly seen Scrum Teams struggle with getting started in the Sprint. The first couple of days of the Sprint slip by, and no real progress is made as Developers grapple with what they should do first. This is often a consequence of the Scrum Team rushing Sprint Planning and the Developers not giving adequate attention to planning the work of the Sprint during the event. In many cases, Scrum Teams identify their Sprint Goal and select Product Backlog items for the Sprint, but that is only half the battle. The Developers need to plan how they will actually get started.

A facilitator should support the Developers during Sprint Planning so that they finish the event with an immediately actionable plan.

TRY THIS! DECOMPOSE PRODUCT BACKLOG ITEMS AND CREATE AN INITIAL PLAN

Facilitation can be used to support the Developers in creating their initial plan. However, facilitators need to be careful not to infringe upon the self-management of the Developers. Here are some tips for how to facilitate and support the Developers as they create their initial plan for carrying out the work of the Sprint.

Breakdown into Tasks

Many Scrum Teams have no problem selecting their Product Backlog items for the Sprint and are able to get started with them without much further effort needed. In that case, no further facilitation is really needed. However, if Developers struggle with how to get started, they need to spend some time in Sprint Planning working out their initial plan of action, and this often takes the form of decomposing the Product Backlog items into subtasks.

It can often be hard to get started with this discussion. Some Developers may say they do not know what subtasks will be involved until they start looking at the Product Backlog items in detail for themselves. The danger of leaving the conversation there is that people end up working in isolation, which leads to the scenario that we saw in the story with Marty. When that happens, transparency is lost, resulting in time being wasted and the Developers not knowing how to get started.

Instead of accepting "We don't know until we start" as an answer, a facilitator could ask a prompting question like this one: "Let's imagine that you do know. Where would you start?" Remember that the Sprint Backlog evolves over the Sprint, and Developers can add new subtasks as they learn more. The objective is not to try to identify every subtask or decompose every Product Backlog item selected for the Sprint, but to do enough to create a plan to get started.

Visualize Tasks

Visualization is another handy facilitation tool. Displaying the Product Backlog items with their related subtasks as the Developers identify them, either on a physical board or in an electronic tool, helps to create a shared understanding of what needs to be done. It may also help the Developers identify any gaps. At this point, Developers can go into detail, discussing designs and implementation detail as they identify subtasks of one day or less. It might involve Developers sketching ideas on a physical or virtual whiteboard, drawing flow diagrams or workflows. This is a perfectly appropriate exercise for Developers to do in Sprint Planning. During the rest of the Sprint, the Developers can continually refine their plan.

KEYS TO FACILITATING AN EFFECTIVE SPRINT PLANNING

We have looked at some common challenges that Scrum Teams have with Sprint Planning and scenarios that can result from mediocre facilitation of the event. We described some facilitation techniques that may help with some of these challenges. Here is a summary of the primary keys to success in facilitating an effective Sprint Planning event.

PREPARE INPUTS

The effectiveness of Sprint Planning is coupled to the quality of the inputs. Knowledge of the Scrum Team's past performance, the team's capacity for the upcoming Sprint, a well-defined and understood Definition of Done, a shared understanding of the Product Goal, the objective for the Sprint, and an ordered Product Backlog all have huge parts to play.

Facilitation does not begin and end at the door of the event or meeting. Facilitation includes preparation and follow-up actions. Interactions need to be facilitated to ensure the Scrum Team treats Product Backlog refinement as an ongoing concern with collaboration between the Product Owner, Developers, and the Scrum Team's stakeholders. A good, shared understanding of the Product Backlog and its content, including having Product Backlog items that are deemed to be ready for selection, makes a big difference in the smooth running of the Sprint Planning event itself.

Other useful items to prepare for Sprint Planning include detailed data about Scrum Team's past performance and the team members' availability. Many teams may only have a qualitative feel for what they can deliver. Or they may take an average velocity or throughput. Averages do not take into account variation, so additional information on the Scrum Team's ranges of velocity or throughput is more useful. Facilitation may be needed to help everyone analyze and understand the data.

The Definition of Done is another important input to the Sprint Planning event. Without a shared understanding of what it means for items to be Done, Developers have a difficult time understanding what they will need to do in the Sprint, therefore making it harder for them to plan what items they can get Done with confidence.

Each Sprint Goal should act as a step toward achieving the Product Goal. Without a Product Goal, a Scrum Team will have no overarching view for the desired future state of the product and what it is supposed to achieve.

Without a Product Goal, the Sprint Planning event is more challenging to facilitate because the direction that a Scrum Team should be going in is unclear.

We discuss facilitating creation of the Product Goal in more detail in Chapter 1.

TAKE A GOAL-ORIENTED APPROACH

Many Scrum Teams have trouble crafting a Sprint Goal when they attempt to retrofit it around a set of Product Backlog items they selected for the Sprint. When crafting goals in this way, success is tied to completing the forecasted Product Backlog items and the Sprint Goal is almost meaningless.

The alternative is to facilitate the conversation by taking a goal-oriented approach and starting with the "why." The Product Owner shares their objective for the Sprint, explaining why it would be valuable. The Scrum Team collaboratively crafts a Sprint Goal while discussing the work for the Sprint. During Sprint Planning, the Scrum Team can continually revise the Sprint Goal and the selected Product Backlog items as it creates its plan for the Sprint, but centering on the Sprint Goal and how it will take a step toward the Product Goal helps the Scrum Team focus on doing the next most valuable thing.

This is not to say that every item on the Sprint Backlog must contribute to the Sprint Goal. It is likely that the Scrum Team has other valuable work it can do that does not directly relate to this Sprint Goal. Examples include improvement actions from the Sprint Retrospective, small fixes, and learning something new in the product's technology space. Or the Scrum Team might just have capacity to work on other valuable Product Backlog items during the Sprint in addition to those that help the team meet the Sprint Goal.

ENCOURAGE PULL, DON'T PUSH

Developers select the work for the Sprint. Good facilitation of the Sprint Planning event supports the Developers in deciding what they think they can do. A facilitator should challenge any kind of pushy behavior in Sprint

Planning. This might come from the Product Owner pushing a pre-decided list of Product Backlog items that they have planned for the Developers to do in the Sprint. This often happens when a bigger plan involving a Sprint-by-Sprint roadmap exists over the long term. Such an approach is counterintuitive to the empirical approach of Scrum and requires education. Push might also come from within the group of Developers, such as when there is an optimistic and dominant personality, or an anxious developer is worried that not enough work is getting delivered, and feels pressure to accept more Product Backlog items into the Sprint.

In both cases, the job of facilitation is to protect the team from these push actions. It involves empowering the Developers to self-manage and select the work for the Sprint by themselves in a way that involves everybody so they can arrive at a decision that everyone is comfortable with.

LEAVE SPACE FOR THE DEVELOPERS TO PLAN

A facilitator of Sprint Planning should allow space for the Developers to plan how to conduct the work. Sprint Planning is more than crafting the Sprint Goal and identifying the Product Backlog items to work on in the Sprint. It should also include time for the Developers to create an actionable plan that they can act upon as soon as Sprint Planning is over.

This may include the Developers decomposing Product Backlog items into subtasks and discussing in more detail what they will do. It could even involve discussion among the Developers in which they are sketching ideas, drawing diagrams, and doing whatever else they need to do to think through their plan. The Developers can do this during the Sprint, but it should be perfectly fine for them to do this in Sprint Planning as long as it supports them in creating their plan of action.

The Developers are solving complex problems, which often necessitates the creativity, innovation, and diversity of perspectives of the whole Scrum Team. Combining facilitation techniques that allow divergence of thought and convergence to decisions for the way ahead helps to maximize the chances of success.

DO JUST ENOUGH PLANNING

Sprint Planning is timeboxed to eight hours or less. It may be tempting for Scrum Teams to fill this timebox and investigate every nuance of the Product Backlog items that have been selected for the Sprint to come up with the perfect plan. A facilitator can steer the Scrum Team to do just enough planning to make a start. The team must still craft and articulate a Sprint Goal that everyone understands to be able to create an initial plan.

The sooner the Developers start the development work of the Sprint, the better. They will discover false assumptions about what is feasible, and uncover complexity by starting the work instead of trying to plan for every eventuality in the Sprint Planning event.

CONCLUSION

Sprint Planning kicks off the Sprint with the team members coming together to consider the latest product Increment, their capacity, and what they have learned from their stakeholders from the Sprint Review and refinement to select a Sprint Goal. They also consider what work they think they can achieve at a minimum to pursue that goal. As long as that Sprint Goal is relevant, it serves as the North Star, a focus that guides the Developers when making decisions about that Sprint.

Developers deciding what can be Done in a Sprint is a control mechanism that enables a Scrum Team to learn more quickly and more frequently about value. But it is hard. A Scrum Team can get lost during and after Sprint Planning for multiple reasons:

- Unable to create a single valuable Sprint Goal
- Unequal representation of ideas and voices during planning
- Overcommitting to work
- Lack of clarity on the plan

How the Scrum Team manages its Sprint Planning event largely affects the tone of the Sprint and the team's ability to collaborate in it. As a facilitator, your objective is to make sure the Scrum Team collaboratively develops and shares an understanding of its initial plan of action for the Sprint. That includes ensuring that the relevant feedback and input from the previous Sprint Review and Retrospective is brought forward into Sprint Planning. To get to that point, you will likely need to rely on the facilitation principles of participative and process for effective facilitation.

3 FACILITATING THE DAILY SCRUM

Synchronizing in a timebox of 15 minutes.

The Daily Scrum should, as the name suggests, take place every day. It is the formal opportunity for the Developers of the Scrum Team to get together and synchronize. They do this by reviewing the progress they have made toward the Sprint Goal and updating their plan of action that is represented in the Sprint Backlog.

Developers align and produce an actionable plan for the upcoming day of work at the Daily Scrum. It is the event for Developers to self-manage, raise impediments, and make decisions collaboratively, all within a 15-minute time-box.

Although the Daily Scrum is a short time period during the day for the Developers to communicate and focus on the day's work toward the Sprint Goal, in our experience and likely yours, it is often misinterpreted and not focused on the Sprint Goal at all. You have likely seen this event interpreted in different ways, perhaps as a status update meeting or a problem-solving session. This chapter explores that.

THE DAILY SCRUM WHERE EVERYONE PROVIDES A STATUS UPDATE

Team Swift is relatively new to Scrum. The whole team is initially excited about the new way of working, but some team members feel like they are not getting the value out of the Scrum events that they thought they would. This includes Naveen, a new Scrum Master who has recently taken a two-day Scrum training class. As a result of the training, Naveen feels like he has a good understanding of the basic rules of the framework. It seems to him that Team Swift is doing the right things. All the events are in place, and Naveen thinks that the rules of Scrum are being followed, so he is particularly puzzled as to why it feels as if the Daily Scrum has been lacking energy lately.

Four days into their current Sprint, the team gathers for its Daily Scrum, which is held by Naveen's desk in the open plan office.

"Hi, everybody!" says Naveen. "Let's make a start. Blake, let's begin with you. What did you do yesterday, what are you going to do today, and do you have any impediments?"

"Yesterday I continued working on Product Backlog item 1653," Blake replies. "As I said yesterday, it will be a few days of work, so I will be on that again today."

"How far through do you think you are? Give me a rough percentage."

"Oh, about 60 percent, I guess. So it will be another couple of days, I would think."

"Okay. Amr, what about you?"

"I'm working on the UI. I thought I would get it done yesterday, but I had a problem when I ran the regression test suite, and some of the tests failed. I don't know why."

"Okay. Keep me posted on that. Rodrigo?"

"Well, yesterday I…"

APPROACHING THE DAILY SCRUM AS A TEAM PLAN FOR THE DAY

In the story of Team Swift, the Daily Scrum appeared to be more like a status update meeting in which team members seemed unconcerned with progressing toward the Sprint Goal. The Developers only talked about what they had been doing over the previous day in various degrees of detail. Amr even raised a difficulty he was having—a prime example of the need for team collaboration. However, the conversation quickly moved on to get the next Developer's status update, and the impediment was left unmanaged.

The Developers addressed Naveen with their updates as if he was some kind of authority figure who had to be kept informed of progress. The Developers did not interact, and they may not even have been listening to each other.

If this situation is similar to your Daily Scrum, many facilitation techniques can improve it. When experimenting with these techniques, the Developers should choose what works for them. Whatever approach they use should enable inclusion, participation, focus on the Sprint Goal, and the creation of a plan for the day.

TRY THIS! USE QUESTIONS AND VISUALS TO DRIVE FOCUSED DISCUSSION

Here are a few popular Daily Scrum facilitation formats that many Scrum Teams use to keep the Daily Scrum focused, and things to look out for when using these formats. Although you may be facilitating this event, you do not have to ask the questions or lead the conversation. A facilitator guides the team to the purpose of the discussion.

The Three Questions

The three questions is a common format many Scrum Teams use to facilitate the Daily Scrum. The first version of the *Scrum Guide* back in 2010 described this approach, although the format has its origins from even earlier in the Daily Stand Up meeting in Extreme Programming.[1] One at a time, each Developer considers the three questions that are centered on what they accomplished the day before, what they aim to work on that day, and what problems they may have that might cause delays or risk completion. It became an optional technique in Scrum in subsequent versions of the *Scrum Guide*, and any reference to it was removed entirely in the 2020 version to emphasize that Scrum does not prescribe a particular format. However, the use of the three questions remains common.

If a team uses the three questions, we recommend exploring the questions in a way that focuses all minds on the Sprint Goal:

- What did I do yesterday that helped the Developers meet the Sprint Goal?
- What will I do today to help the Developers meet the Sprint Goal?
- Do I see any impediment that prevents me or other Developers from meeting the Sprint Goal?

The three questions facilitation format gives space for each Developer to speak. Everyone knows that they will have an opportunity to speak, reducing the risk of interruptions and increasing the chances that the Developers will listen to each other. This does not mean that everybody *has* to speak. With

---

1. Wells, Don (1999). "Daily Stand Up Meeting." www.extremeprogramming.org/rules/standupmeeting.html.

the purpose of the meeting understood and everyone knowing that it is not about people justifying their time or existence in the team, it is perfectly acceptable for someone not to make use of their turn. For example, if a team does a lot of pairing or mobbing, where more than one person works at the same work station on the same problem at the same time, they can share their progress as one.

Team-Based Questions

If a team likes questions to trigger the Daily Scrum conversation, but the three questions lead to individual updates, a lack of collaboration toward the Sprint Goal, or a challenge to complete the Daily Scrum in 15 minutes or fewer, an alternative facilitation approach is to encourage team-based open-ended questions. With this approach, the questions can be explored openly for a group discussion instead of everyone responding individually. Example questions include these:

• How is the team progressing toward the Sprint Goal?
• What is the next step for us to move toward the Sprint Goal?
• What impediments do we face, and how can we approach them?
• What or who do we need to help us make this decision?

Walking the Board

Most Scrum Teams use some kind of board, whether physically or virtually, to visualize their Sprint Backlog. At a minimum, such a board typically helps the Developers understand the work in progress, work that is blocked or impeded, and work to be started. A board is a useful artifact to help teams focus and create alignment. Walking the board focuses on the work to be done and its flow, rather than what individuals contribute toward achieving the Sprint Goal.

Walking the board involves the team looking at the items on the board and discussing them in turn. It should not be used to push for more work to be started; therefore, the focus should be on the items that are in progress. The Developers may talk about the current progress of active work items, discuss what happened to them since the last Daily Scrum, and then make a plan of action for each. Walking the board usually starts with items on the right side of the board because the items here are closest to being Done, and discussions proceed "right to left." Avoiding the starting of more work before finishing valuable work in progress reduces the risk of lots of incomplete work at the end of the Sprint.

Visualization of work is not only helpful for the day-to-day work but also is a great facilitation tool for the Daily Scrum because it helps to trigger the right questions at the right time. When facilitating the Daily Scrum using this format, focus is on the flow of Product Backlog items instead of what individuals are doing. Ensure questions are being raised, such as these:

- What work is blocked?
- Is there anything we are working on that is not visualized on the board?
- How can we collaborate today to improve the flow of work?
- Can we still achieve the Sprint Goal?

It is key that the Developers have good discipline in keeping the board up to date. There needs to be trust that the visualization of the Sprint Backlog provides the right transparency of what is going on to the whole team.

Making the Sprint Goal visible on the board also acts as a reminder for the team. However, to really ensure that focus toward the Sprint Goal is not lost, Developers can end the walking the board Daily Scrum with the open question, "How are we doing toward achieving our Sprint Goal?"

Work in Progress and Work Item Age

Some teams focus their Daily Scrum on how many items are in progress and how long individual items have been in progress. The amount of work in progress, how far it has progressed, and the work item age for each item help teams decide what they should focus on that day. Scrum Teams can provide focus for the Developers' conversations in the Daily Scrum by visualizing how long each Product Backlog item has been in progress. Most electronic work tracking tools will show how many days it has been since work started, or if using a physical board, the Developers can add a check mark on the physical card each day. We like to encourage the Developers to finish the items that have been in progress the longest or those that are most at risk of violating stakeholder expectations.

Like some of the other formats, an important question to ask while using this technique is this: "Is this work still valuable?" That way you do not lose sight of the Sprint Goal or the value of the work.

THE DAILY SCRUM WHERE DEVELOPERS DIVE INTO PROBLEM-SOLVING MODE

Emily listens intently. Jason's voice projects from her speakers as his image fills her screen while he speaks.

"... and I thought I had the wording worked out, but then I found that it doesn't really fit with the images we're using, and now I'm back to square one." Even though they were working remotely, Emily felt like Jason was looking directly to her for help.

"Hmm…" began Emily. "Did you go back over the original brief for some inspiration?"

"I did. The thing is, I'm not sure if it still makes sense for this marketing campaign given what we learned earlier in the week about our customers. I think we need to be thinking about targeting a different demographic, or we should be going back to the drawing board with the campaign itself."

"I see," replied Emily. "Have you spoken to Trudi?"

"I had a quick chat with her yesterday. All she said was to do my best and we'll have a look during the Sprint Review. I'm not sure how much she gets what I am saying because she hasn't seen the outputs from the focus groups."

"Well, as the Product Owner, she's the one who needs to make a decision."

Raymond, one of the other Developers, jumps in. "Could we go and talk directly to the customer? I could see if Derek is available."

"Or how about if we develop two prototypes?" asks Annaliese. "One based on the original brief, and one that we can say we came up with because of the findings of the focus group. We'd still meet the Sprint Goal, and then we'd have some options for Derek and Trudi to think about."

"Do you think we have time? I was going to work on the graphics today," says Emily.

"I think it could be doable," says Jason. "I just need to bounce some ideas off the team. Then I can go away and flesh them out."

"Wait, everyone," says Raymond. "We've been on this call for 18 minutes already, and there is some stuff that I need to talk about as well…"

"Oh, yeah," says Emily. "But let's focus on helping Jason first. Then we can continue with the rest of the Daily Scrum."

KEEPING THE DAILY SCRUM FOCUSED AND CONCISE

At first glance, Emily and her team's Daily Scrum appeared to be quite healthy. They were having good conversations, collaborating, and supporting one another. However, what was really happening was that they were losing focus and getting bogged down in talking about one particular issue. They ended up trying to solve it during the Daily Scrum itself and risked not uncovering issues that Raymond wanted to discuss.

We saw the team get into details and start to problem-solve, which is a common way for teams to go off track at Daily Scrums. Some team members offer their suggestions, whereas others have to wait for their opportunity to make transparent other things that are going on elsewhere in the team. The timebox passing by without the outcome of a plan for the day is a clear sign that this team's Daily Scrum could be facilitated in a more productive way.

TRY THIS! FOCUS THE CONVERSATION

Daily Scrums can become a problem-solving discussion. Here are some ways for you as a facilitator to refocus the Daily Scrum.

Take It Offline

The plan for the day, which should be the result of a Daily Scrum, can include making plans for follow-up discussions, which may include all or a subset of Developers to go into particular issues more deeply. If a facilitator starts to see the Daily Scrum turning into a problem-solving discussion, they should step in with a suggestion to pause the conversation and plan for a follow-up discussion. This would include identifying those who need to be part of the follow-up, anybody else who wants to be there, and anyone beyond the Developers who may need to be invited.

The After-Party

A Scrum Master told me about a technique that his Scrum Team used to deal with discussions that come up in the Daily Scrum that are too involved to be completed within the timebox.

They had something that they called the "after-party." After-parties were scheduled for 10 minutes to be held straight after the Daily Scrum. Issues that required deeper discussion would be parked until the after-party. The Developers would not need to have an after-party every day, but having the time reserved meant it was there if they needed it, and any conversations could happen straight away. Those Developers who needed to be part of the after-party conversation would stay, and everyone else could leave.

—Patricia Kong

ELMO

One way to pause a conversation is with our friend Elmo, the red furry Muppet that lives on *Sesame Street*. He's quite popular. But ELMO is also used worldwide when facilitating timeboxed events.

ELMO stands for "enough, let's move on!" When facilitating an event such as the Daily Scrum, you can use ELMO if there is a danger of the conversation going into a rabbit hole.

If you notice that a lot of your Daily Scrums or any other meetings are unfocused, create an agreement that involves ELMO. The agreement is that if any participant in the meeting feels as if the conversation is going off-track or becomes too detailed for the purpose of the meeting, they can call out "ELMO!" The participant could simply shout out "ELMO!" or raise an ELMO toy, picture, or card into the air. If other participants hear or see an ELMO, and if they agree that it is time to move on, they too call ELMO. It is a clear signal to the entire group that they need to stop the current conversation and refocus.

It is entirely optional whether you use actual Elmo toys. People can just raise a hand. We should point out that we have no affiliation with Elmo toy manufacturers!

THE SCRUM TEAM ACTING AS A GROUP OF INDIVIDUALS

It is the last day of the Sprint for team Tigers, and it appears as if, once again, the team is not going to have achieved anything. Sam, the Product Owner of the Tigers, stares anxiously at her screen, willing for some indication, any indication, that something can be salvaged from the Sprint.

Twenty-four hours earlier, everything felt very different, with much less anxiety. After yesterday's Daily Scrum, when the Developers welcomed Sam as an observer, it seemed as if the team had just a few hours of work left to finish the remaining tasks on the Sprint Backlog and complete the planned work of the Sprint. The Developers had even joked about taking a long lunch break and going out to celebrate a successful Sprint; they were that confident about finishing everything. The burndown chart backed up this level of confidence, showing only fifteen hours of work remaining, and Sam knew that this was well within the capacity that the team of six developers had before the Sprint Review.

It was later in the afternoon when Sam started to realize that everything was not as it appeared. She had asked the Developers if she could look at the product Increment to start preparing for the Sprint Review. The Developers just mumbled, "It's not ready yet." It was only after she called Justin, the Tigers Scrum Master who also served as one of the Developers on the team, that she saw a clearer picture.

Sam now looks at the electronic tool displaying the Sprint Backlog. Lesley, Uri, and Fern each have their name on different tasks, but as was discovered yesterday, not one of them was the one remaining critical task that was needed to complete the functionality for the must-have Product

Backlog item. Each of them had assumed that someone else was taking care of the task, but it turned out that no one was! Sam thinks back to the last retrospective when the Tigers had agreed to an improvement action to coordinate and communicate better at the Daily Scrum because they had failed to deliver an Increment and meet a Sprint Goal in that Sprint as well. The Developers did seem to talk more this time around.

So why does this keep happening? Sam wonders.

ALIGNING AROUND THE SPRINT GOAL AT THE DAILY SCRUM FOR COHESION

Sam reflects on an interesting question as we leave the story. The chaotic end to the Sprint could have been due to several reasons. We saw that there was little alignment and cohesion. It seemed as if Developers were working in silos, and the team had a lack of transparency about the true progress it was making as it approached the end of the Sprint. A common root cause of teams with similar problems to the Tigers is having too much work in progress and a lack of alignment around a Sprint Goal.

Daily Scrum formats such as the three questions "force" all Developers to speak. However, having all attendees at a meeting speak should not be the aim. Instead, it is about enabling all people to make meaningful contributions when necessary. Just because all Developers have spoken does not mean progress toward the Sprint Goal is as transparent as it could be. "Participation with purpose" is our guiding mantra here.

TRY THIS! BRING EVERYONE BACK TO THE PURPOSE

Ideally, the Developers leave each Daily Scrum with a plan for the day and transparency about the progress they are making toward the Sprint Goal, but that is not always the case. We love Mitch Lacey's The Fourth Question in Scrum from his book *The Scrum Field Guide: Practical Advice for Your First Year*[2] for this problem. It tests the Developers' confidence in meeting the Sprint Goal. This technique could have helped the Tigers.

---

2. Lacey, Mitch (2012). *The Scrum Field Guide: Practical Advice for Your First Year*. Addison-Wesley Professional.

The Fourth Question in the Daily Scrum

In a nutshell, Lacey's fourth question involves asking the Developers at the Daily Scrum to rate their confidence that the Sprint Goal will be met. A facilitator invites everyone to score their confidence level on a scale from 1 to 10, with 1 being the lowest confidence and 10 being the highest. If there are even one or two outliers with a low score, it is worth discussing as a team any concerns that have not been raised already. Sometimes the impediment may not be obvious, but some individuals may have a gut feeling that something is not quite right. Adding the fourth question to the Daily Scrum helps people put a number on something intangible (their confidence) and can surface issues that might not have come up otherwise. It also gets people thinking about progress toward the Sprint Goal rather than individual Product Backlog items or tasks.

The use of the fourth question can be facilitated as follows. After everyone has answered the usual three questions, or the Developers have walked the board, have everyone write their confidence level anonymously on a sticky note. When everybody is ready, gather up and reveal the scores on the sticky notes. The added anonymity may help because some people on the team may be introverted or reluctant to speak up.

A facilitator can implement the fourth question just as effectively virtually as in-person. People can use the chat function (most virtual conferencing tools have these), with the facilitator giving a countdown to signal to everyone that it is time to reveal their score. Or a facilitator can use a virtual whiteboard with virtual sticky notes for people to put their score on anonymously.

When a team is using the fourth question, the event can risk running over the 15-minute timebox. More importantly, a team might find out too late—at the end of the event—that confidence is low, and then that has to be addressed in an additional meeting. We would recommend opening the Daily Scrum with the fourth question rather than asking it at the end, regardless of the rest of the Daily Scrum format. This enables the team to explore any concerns with meeting the Sprint Goal during the rest of the Daily Scrum.

ABSENTEES OR LATE COMERS TO THE DAILY SCRUM

A Daily Scrum with a missing team member.

The Purple Wizards have been using Scrum for several months. Their company has a flexible work-from-home policy, and the team members had previously agreed that they would usually work away from the main office. This was okay as long as they felt communication among the group was not a problem.

On the second to last day of the team's fifteenth Sprint, the Developers start to arrive at the Daily Scrum one by one via their virtual conferencing tool.

Sally, Preeti, and Rafael are already on the call as Marcus joins. "Good morning," says Marcus.

"Morning!" comes the chorus of replies. Two voices are missing: Morayo's and Peter's. The clock ticks around to 9:32 a.m. as the group waits. The Purple Wizards' Daily Scrum is supposed to have started at 9:30. Preeti sends an instant message to Morayo and Peter to see where they are. Sally and Marcus have opened their email applications to check for any new messages, and Rafael is looking at the code that he had been working on the previous day. 9.32 becomes 9.33. And then 9.34.

"Shall we just get started?" Sally suggests. The others mumble their acquiescence just as Morayo appears on their screens. His arrival is greeted by sarcastic cheers, and Marcus states sharply, "You're late again, Morayo! This must be the third time this Sprint!"

"At least he is here now," says Sally. "Anything from Pete?"

"Nothing," answers Preeti.

"I guess he's not coming then... *again!*" Marcus says with more than a hint of frustration in his voice. "Oh well, we might as well get started..."

RESPECTING THE DAILY SCRUM

Some teams do not even acknowledge there is an issue when Developers are often late or miss the Daily Scrum. They do not discuss the behavior, and it becomes normalized. This may be because everyone just accepts it as the way things are, or it could be because people are uncomfortable calling out their peers. Either way, the situation may never be improved if an open and respectful discussion is lacking.

Teams that invest in learning about the motives people being late or missing the Daily Scrum could in turn start to learn about how they could make their Daily Scrum accessible and effective for everybody.

Developers might arrive late to the Daily Scrum or be absent from it for entirely innocent reasons. The reasons could be personal. Perhaps a Daily Scrum at the start of the working day is difficult for some Developers because they need to drop their children off at school before the workday starts. Or perhaps they are in a different time zone, and the Daily Scrum is planned at a time that is inconvenient for them.

Others might not even understand the purpose of the event and know that the Daily Scrum is mandatory for Developers. Or perhaps a Developer is unclear about when the event takes place or where. Before making assumptions or judgments, an important part of facilitation comes back to our facilitation principle of healthy facilitation, which involves building empathy and respect for others on a human level. We recommend that any discussions to address the issue of late or absent Developers start from a place of building understanding into the rationale behind the behavior.

On the other hand, Developers might not find the event valuable and choose to ignore it or come late. Reasons could include the event being used as a status update for individuals to report to a central figure, Developers feeling like they are not listened to, impediments are not acknowledged or acted upon, team members giving long, invaluable commentary in the event, or the team is not aligned on a shared objective, so Developers have no interest or need to know what others are doing.

Whatever the root cause of people coming late to or skipping the Daily Scrum, it is much more effective if one of the Developers raises the discussion about issues around the attendance at the Daily Scrum rather than the Scrum Master or a manager. Such a figure raising the issue could be seen to be using authority or coercion. Although this could result in a change of behavior, any change may be made begrudgingly and likely would be unsustainable. However, recognizing that a behavior is affecting or considered unacceptable by other Developers is more influential toward changing that behavior.

The Developers should hold each other accountable for attending the Daily Scrum. The Daily Scrum is the Developers' meeting; it is their formal opportunity to self-manage.

TRY THIS! LEVERAGE THE SCRUM VALUES AND TEAM AGREEMENTS

Facilitating a conversation within the team that allows issues to be discussed openly and respectfully can be the most effective path to improving uncomfortable situations. What follows are some concepts for you to consider.

Use the Scrum Value of Respect as a North Star

Using prompting questions around respect is one way to start the conversation. The Scrum value of respect can be used as a North Star to guide a Sprint Retrospective conversation about late or absent Developers to the Daily

Scrum. The facilitator can remind the group that the successful use of Scrum depends on the Scrum Team members becoming proficient in the Scrum values, which include respect. A facilitator can pose these open-ended questions for the team to reflect upon and discuss:

- How are we respecting the Scrum framework?
- How are all team members showing respect to each other?
- What behaviors display a lack of respect or misunderstanding?
- What can we do as a team to be more respectful to one another?

In our experience, at least one of these questions will be enough to trigger a conversation about an undesirable behavior.

Note that, in this example, we are not encouraging the facilitator to jump straight in to highlight the problem. Instead, the facilitator sets the scene and guides the Scrum Team in finding a way to start talking openly about the problem by themselves without feeling judged, rejected, or humiliated. The facilitator can always fall back on the Scrum values of courage and openness. With this approach, it is possible that the subject might not be raised at all. That might actually be okay. The team might not be ready to have the conversation yet if trust and psychological safety have not been built up within the group. The challenge to the team is to work together constructively to solve their problems rationally when they are ready to do so.

Enable Consistency and Accessibility

Setting clear expectations about attendance and punctuality is a basic but necessary first step for facilitating the Daily Scrum event. A basic rule of the Daily Scrum is that it should be held at the same time and place every day. We would also add having it at the same time and place every day that is suitable to all Developers. Varying the location or timing might be a cause of confusion that leads to people missing it or being late. Or the time and place that has been set might just not be suitable for certain people. Maintaining consistency of time and place that works for all Developers instills a routine.

> ### Agree on a Daily Scrum Time Suitable to Everyone
>
> One team that I worked with included distributed team members with people join-ing remotely spread as far apart as the UK, the US, and India. For whatever reason, the team held a false belief that the Daily Scrum had to be held first thing in the morning (defaulting to UK time since that was where the majority of the team were based). That was a very unsocial time for those in the US, who were having to get up in the middle of the night. The unsuitable time was a main reason for the poor punctuality and attendance of this team. Simply agreeing on a mutually suitable time for all Developers solved the issue.
>
> —David Spinks

KEYS TO FACILITATING AN EFFECTIVE DAILY SCRUM

We have explored some scenarios in which the Daily Scrum might be subopti-mal. We have also explored some facilitation skills and techniques to improve the Daily Scrum. Here, we look at some of the primary keys to success in facilitating an effective Daily Scrum.

FOCUS ON THE SPRINT GOAL

Many teams do not recognize the importance that the Sprint Goal has in Scrum, particularly when it comes to the Daily Scrum. When they do not take the Sprint Goal into consideration, they devalue and miss the intent of this crucial event. In many Scrum Team's Daily Scrums, Developers report prog-ress on completion of tasks, but whether the team is actually achieving the Sprint Goal is often never discussed.

The Sprint Goal is the guiding light and purpose for the Sprint. Facilitation of the Daily Scrum should be with the intent of Developers inspecting progress toward the Sprint Goal and achieving the outcome of an updated plan that reflects the Scrum Team's alignment toward meeting the Sprint Goal.

This focus on the Sprint Goal should become second nature to the Developers once they get into a routine of well-facilitated Daily Scrums, regardless of the format they use.

KEEP IT FOR THE DEVELOPERS

The Daily Scrum is for the Developers, and only the Developers are required to participate in it. However, if the Product Owner or Scrum Master is actively working on items in the Sprint Backlog, they should also participate in the Daily Scrum as Developers.

The Developers should be confident about facilitating and reaching the expected outcomes for the event by themselves. Many teams rely on the Scrum Master to facilitate the Daily Scrum and make sure it happens, and that includes Scrum Teams that have been using Scrum for quite some time. Although the Scrum Master is accountable for making sure the event happens and may provide support if needed or requested, it is really the Developers themselves who should be facilitating the Daily Scrum.

Given the short timebox and the event being for the Developers, a facilitator can focus minds on the purpose of the Daily Scrum, ensuring the event starts on time and is not hijacked or interfered with by others having different agendas. We see non-Developers interfering in the Daily Scrum. They run the meeting on the Developers' behalf, elicit status updates, admonish or give kudos based on task completion, influence or even overrule Developers' decisions on how to act, assign tasks, and focus on keeping people busy, all while neglecting the Sprint Goal. These behaviors in the Daily Scrum may be well intended, but they can be detrimental for several reasons. Besides putting focus on individuals and tasks instead of on the Sprint Goal and value delivery, it stifles self-management. The Daily Scrum is one of the elements of the Scrum framework that gives the Developers the opportunity to self-manage.

MANAGE TIME EFFECTIVELY

The Daily Scrum should achieve a lot in a short amount of time to minimize waste. A delicate balance needs to be struck in which the Developers keep the event to 15 minutes or fewer yet still have discussions that run granularly enough for them to end it with their plan for the day. Well-facilitated events need good time management, but it is important to understand that this does not just mean sticking strictly to timeboxes. It is about ensuring that valuable conversations and collaboration happen within the time, with agreement made on any follow-up discussions or needed actions.

Numerous factors can cause overly long Daily Scrums. Some Developers make tedious and irrelevant contributions. Sometimes a complexity has become apparent that the Developers need extra time to plan for. Some Daily Scrums deteriorate into lengthy problem-solving discussions. Or a Daily Scrum format is used that is unsuitable for a Scrum Team that has a large number of Developers, which makes it difficult to be inclusive and give everyone the opportunity to contribute while still keeping the meeting to 15 minutes or fewer.

From a facilitation point of view, encourage any discussion that does not directly contribute to the purpose of the Daily Scrum to be taken offline with a plan for a follow-up discussion. Developers should be continuously collaborating throughout the day anyway, which includes supporting each other and solving problems that they encounter while doing the development work of the Sprint.

Enable Transparency and Visualization

Daily Scrums involve planning—in a short amount of time—of the work of the Developers for the upcoming day. The discussions inevitably create a high cognitive load on participants who are engaged, actively listening, and participating. People have a lot to keep track of, so regardless of the facilitation technique or Daily Scrum format employed, we recommend that a visualization of the Sprint Backlog is available to the Developers during the Daily Scrum.

The facilitation principle of transparency supports this idea. The Sprint Goal should be part of the Sprint Backlog. Although Scrum does not prescribe how the Developers design their Sprint Backlog, most teams have some kind of visual board. Making the Sprint Goal visible as a constant reminder can be as simple as writing it on such a board.

For true transparency, all of the Developers need to have a shared understanding of what the Sprint Goal actually means. A well-facilitated Sprint Planning event is key for this, as we discuss in Chapter 2, "Facilitating Sprint Planning."

USE A PARTICIPATIVE FACILITATION FORMAT

A Daily Scrum can take many formats. Whichever format is used, the facilitation principles of participative, purposeful, and healthy facilitation in particular act as a guide for what a successfully facilitated Daily Scrum means. A great Daily Scrum has the following characteristics:

- All Developers are actively engaged.
- All Developers are respectful of each other.
- Every Developer has had opportunities to contribute.
- It promotes learning, alignment, shared understanding, and transparency.
- It re-energizes the team for the day ahead.

Given the fact that the Daily Scrum occurs every day, Developers can quickly fall into a repetitive routine with the way the event is facilitated. It becomes a mundane process to take time out of the day to attend the Daily Scrum before getting back to work. The danger is teams viewing the event as losing value and going through the motions of their Daily Scrum just because it is part of the wider Scrum framework. Developers' behavior in the Daily Scrum is at risk of changing and may even become an impediment. They might become less transparent, stop actively listening to other Developers, lose focus on the Sprint Goal, concentrate only on what they are doing individually, or not attend the Daily Scrum at all if they feel particularly strongly that the event does not have value for them. These behaviors themselves are then seen to be the problem when, in reality, they are often symptoms of underlying issues with the event itself and the actual value it brings.

Teams need facilitation techniques that enable the Developers to meet the objectives of the Daily Scrum, that are inclusive, and that enhance collaboration. Using a participative facilitation format, focusing on a shared goal, encouraging active listening, and managing time effectively are just a few ways of steering the Developers into running a valuable Daily Scrum.

CONCLUSION

The Daily Scrum acts as the heartbeat of the Sprint, focusing attention to a 24-hour period. It is when Developers come together to discuss their plan for the day and ask for help from others on the team. Everyone should be curious about how they can be helpful to other Developers. But this short 15-minute meeting is not as easy as it sounds on paper.

As we've described in this chapter, teams can easily fall into anti-patterns, such as using the Daily Scrum as a time to report on statuses or dig into solving problems. Multiple facilitation techniques are available for you and your teams to conduct the Daily Scrum to correct these approaches. All are aimed at one objective: facilitating the team's progress toward the Sprint Goal.

Above all, if you are facilitating the Daily Scrum, whether you are a Developer on the team or someone else the Developers have invited to facilitate, keep an eye on how you can help the team sense, as soon as possible, whether the Sprint Goal is in jeopardy. You can do this by discussing the work on the Sprint Backlog and asking open-ended, team-based questions.

If, by chance, the team thinks the Sprint Goal is in jeopardy, it can cause angst. As a facilitator, your role is to let the team know that it is okay and help them consider next steps forward, such as how the team might approach its impediments and how it can reset expectations with the Product Owner and the Scrum Team stakeholders. Your primary concern as a facilitator is to guide the team of Developers in discussion and toward action.

FACILITATING TEAM DYNAMICS

Team dynamics can involve fireworks!

Many people view facilitation as preparing for a session, creating an agenda, running the meeting itself, and then following up. And they consider the facilitation successful when they manage to keep participants on track according to their plan and timebox.

Something important is missing with this approach: the human element. When people work in groups, complex interpersonal dynamics are at play that a facilitator needs to be aware of. Because of these dynamics, things often do not go according to plan. Good facilitators know how to guide the interactions of a group, so they get the most out of their work together. Let's get into it.

Leveraging the Diverse Perspectives of a Team

The greater the diversity in a team, the greater the range of skills, knowledge, experience, and perspectives. Team diversity includes all the aspects that make each individual unique, such as their experiences, backgrounds, professions, skill sets, and culture. However smart one person is, their ideas will always be from a narrower perspective than that of a group of people. Broader diversity opens up a more expansive spectrum of perspectives and thinking, which leads to a greater potential for innovation.

To leverage the diverse perspectives of a group, individuals need time and space to explore their own and others' ideas before aligning. However, the dynamics at play in group interactions can lead to misunderstandings and clashes.

Understanding group dynamics is a core competency for anyone involved in facilitation. With this knowledge, a facilitator can help a group work through its differences in a way that fosters collaboration and results in shared understanding.

THE SCRUM TEAM MEMBERS STUCK ON THEIR OWN IDEAS

Team Sparkling Chandeliers is discussing how to get started with a Product Backlog item titled "Market Our New Product in Time for Its Launch." The acceptance criteria include clauses for running one experiment to see if the team can reach its target demographic and a target for the number of people who sign up to receive a brochure.

"As I said in refinement," Amelia says, "we will do an email campaign."

"Amelia, you're not listening," says Johnny. "That won't be as effective as my idea of running social media ads."

"Both of those ideas are shooting in the dark. If we want signups, we want people who already have an interest in the industry. We need to go to trade shows and talk to people face to face and sell our idea directly," Bill says.

"We can hit thousands of people with an email at the same time," says Amelia.

"Social media ads target particular demographics. We'll have confidence that the people we want to know about our product will see it," says Johnny.

"And we can easily get hold of a list of email addresses," continues Amelia.

Bill interjects, "Well, with trade shows, you can really explain your product to people. It's way more effective for conversions than any other approach."

"Can't you all just listen to my idea first?!" yells Johnny.

There is a slight pause before Omar interjects with, "I want to put my idea out there as well. We should get an influencer on board and leverage their connections."

They continue to go back and forth. The official timebox of the Sparkling Chandeliers Sprint Planning expires before they agree on a plan, yet the discussions continue.

UNDERSTANDING GROUP DYNAMICS

The Sparkling Chandeliers were not really having a discussion. No one was listening to anyone else, and team members were stuck on their own ideas. As we saw in the story, Johnny started to express his frustration at not being listened to, and the others in the group were likely feeling the same. This is a common scenario when a group of people get set on their own ideas to solve a problem and do not consider and explore the options given by others.

A facilitator should have a good understanding of group dynamics and the complexities of divergence and convergence to be able to help a group navigate through its difficulties to reach its desired outcomes.

The Diamond of Participatory Decision-Making

People often believe that a healthy problem-solving process should look like a smooth, linear sequence of steps, as shown in Figure 4.1. Participants discuss the topic, everyone works at the same pace, they generate and keep track of each other's ideas, and agree to a solution.

Figure 4.1 What people think a healthy problem-solving process looks like.

Although such a smooth process would make a facilitator's job much easier, it does not reflect reality. In real life, people go off track from the main topic, lose focus, and have different perspectives and ideas they get attached to. Some people may already be three ideas ahead, whereas others are still thinking about the original question. Confusion and frustration kick in.

Many group conversations start off by covering safe and familiar territory. When a group is discussing a simple problem with a simple solution, participants can decide quickly. However, most groups try to bring *every* discussion to closure quickly. When groups are working their way through a complex problem, they need to go beyond the obvious solutions and explore a wider range of options. Facilitators actually want to encourage a range of ideas, but people often struggle to integrate different ways of thinking that are not their own. This experience is usually unpleasant, with people repeating themselves if they do not feel like they are being heard or acting defensively or aggressively about their ideas. This leads to misunderstanding, frustration, clashes, and sometimes even complete disengagement.

Sam Kaner describes this dynamic as the "Groan Zone," which is part of the Diamond of Participatory Decision-Making model in his book *Facilitator's Guide to Participatory Decision-Making.*[1] Figure 4.2 illustrates the Groan Zone and shows that the transition between divergence and convergence is not smooth and takes a group some effort to work through. Each of the small light bulbs represent examples of different ideas. The vertical arrow shows the diversity of thoughts and ideas, and horizontally from left to right represents a timeline.

---

1. Kaner, Sam (2014). *Facilitator's Guide to Participatory Decision-Making*, Third Edition. Jossey-Bass.

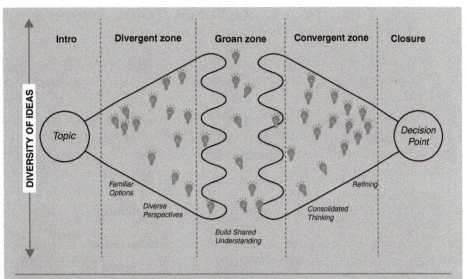

Figure 4.2 The Diamond of Participatory Decision-Making model.

One of the most damaging things a facilitator can do is push participants to come to a premature agreement when they are going through the Groan Zone. This can lead to the most vocal people dominating the group's decision. When this occurs, it may appear that the group has made a decision, but more than likely, not all participants are really committed to it.

Sometimes facilitators mistakenly feel that the best way to get things moving is to make the call on behalf of the group, in which case they have just shown bias, and participants may wonder what the point of having a group discussion was if the facilitator was going to decide anyway.

In both circumstances, the facilitator loses credibility and trust. Additionally, decisions are likely to result in low acceptance by the team, creating a weak outcome.

Facilitators should help groups and Scrum Teams work their way through the Groan Zone. Participants need to know that the frustration they feel in the Groan Zone is natural. Facilitators can help them create a shared understanding to integrate their ideas and achieve better shared outcomes.

Some Scrum Teams assume that they are dysfunctional because they experience discomfort during group interactions. They should not. Misunderstanding is a normal and natural aspect of group dynamics and an inevitable consequence of a healthy diversity of opinions.

TRY THIS! NAVIGATING SCRUM TEAMS THROUGH PARTICIPATORY DECISION-MAKING

The Diamond of Participatory Decision-Making model helps facilitators understand the group dynamics when teams work on complex problems. Using this model can help the facilitator plan and facilitate interactive sessions. It can also help them guide people to understand and legitimize the emotions they experience when working in a group. Once people understand that having different opinions is natural and beneficial for creativity, that they can expect to feel some level of confusion, apprehension, and frustration, and that building a shared understanding and reaching a strong outcome take effort, then they can navigate the Groan Zone more easily.

Throughout this book, we discuss many techniques for a facilitator to help a group navigate through the process of participatory problem-solving and decision-making. Additional examples follow.

Sample Techniques to Use in the Divergent Zone

In the divergent zone, the facilitator should focus on helping the group create new ideas.

Silent Writing

Silent writing is a simple facilitation technique for generating numerous ideas with a group.

Participants spend a short set amount of time, such as five minutes, independently writing down as many ideas as they can think of in response to a question or problem. As the name suggests, they do this in silence so that they can think without distraction or influence from others in the group. It is best to have participants write one idea per sticky note so that they can be treated independently in follow-up activities.

Silent writing is a technique that supports divergent thinking. It should be followed up with other facilitation techniques that help the participants organize their collective thoughts and create a shared understanding of all the options, before deciding on the best ones and taking them forward.

Participants can use affinity mapping, which we discuss in Chapter 1, "Facilitating Alignment," to help them converge their thoughts and ideas.

Silent writing helps to ensure that everyone has the opportunity to contribute. It gives everyone an equal voice, neutralizing any loud voices that might be in a group of participants.

Crazy 8s

We know the crazy 8s technique from the book *Sprint*.[2] It is a powerful technique that a group of people can use for divergent thinking to come up with a lot of ideas quickly.

Crazy 8s works like this:

1. All participants have paper to capture their eight ideas on. A piece split into eight panels should be enough, or if facilitating virtually, you could use a tool to give each participant a virtual space with eight panels.

2. The facilitator should remind everyone of the question they are trying to answer or the problem they are trying to solve with the ideation session. A How Might We question, as we discuss in Chapter 7, "Facilitating the Sprint Retrospective," is a great format to use to express this.

3. The facilitator signals the start of the ideation session, perhaps by ringing a bell. From there, everyone has eight minutes to sketch out eight ideas (one for each panel), with participants spending one minute on each idea.

4. The facilitator signals every minute to prompt participants to move on to their next idea. The content that participants create in their sketches can be pictures, text, flow diagrams—anything goes!

The tight timebox that comes with Crazy 8s helps to unlock people's creative ideas that might not have surfaced otherwise. Most people can come up with two or three ideas, but using Crazy 8s pushes people to go beyond obvious and familiar options. People discover and capture ideas without worrying about if they are actually any good, and the facilitator should emphasize that

---

2. Knapp, Jake (2016). *Sprint: How to Solve Big Problems and Test New Ideas in Just Five Days*. Bantam Press; 1st edition.

no one else ever has to see the initial results of an individual's efforts. The best ideas can be crafted into something presentable later.

Participants have different options with what to do with the results. One option is to give more time for individuals to pick their favorite two ideas and spend some time refining them into a presentable version.

To move to convergence, people can work in small groups to share, compare, and refine their ideas together. Then participants can post the results on a wall or virtual whiteboard. Because people often need time to reflect, the group can decide to leave the ideas on the board for a few days. That gives them the opportunity to visit the ideas, add questions, give feedback, and come up with new ideas that build upon the existing ones. This also works well if there is a big group and too much cognitive load for everyone to take in all the ideas at once. If there is a lot of content, the group can create an affinity map with the ideas. Finally, once everyone has had the opportunity to visit and contribute to the ideas, a facilitator can organize a dot vote for the group to decide on the best ideas. This could be done together at an agreed-upon time, or people can vote during this review period. We discuss dot voting later in this chapter.

Sample Techniques to Use in the Groan Zone

For the Groan Zone, the facilitator should focus on helping the group create shared understanding by building empathy and comprehension of each other's ideas and perspectives.

Active Listening

Listening is an underrated but essential skill. People's minds tend to be active and focused on their own response rather than listening intently to others. Active listening is a purposeful act that gives full attention to others without judging or thinking how to respond. A facilitator can lead by example by applying active listening and encouraging and teaching others to do the same.

Scrum Teams that apply active listening build empathy and understanding between team members, but it takes practice. Here are a few general tips on active listening, whether you are a facilitator or a participant:

- Leave space for other people to talk, and avoid interrupting them. Silence is okay; you do not have to fill the space when there are a few seconds of quiet. Sometimes others are just collecting their thoughts to finish something they are saying. The quiet time gives you and others time for reflection.

- Slow down so that other people have space to express themselves.

- Listen without judgment and without making assumptions.

- Do not listen to respond. When people listen and are already planning what to say back, they are not focused on really listening to others.

- Do not impose opinions, propose solutions, or push advice when no one is asking for it. Often people just want to get things off their chest and feel listened to. If you really feel a need to give advice, ask for permission. For example, you might ask, "Would you like me to share some advice?" If the answer is no, respect that and keep your ideas and your opinions to yourself.

- Be curious and ask relevant clarifying questions to further your understanding.

- Paraphrase what has been said to validate your understanding and so that the speaker feels heard.

Paraphrase

Paraphrasing is expressing what someone has said in different words to make sure your understanding is correct. It is an essential part of active listening. When a facilitator paraphrases what a participant said, the participant feels that their opinion is valued. It also allows the participant to clarify or confirm what they said to clear up any misunderstanding. Paraphrasing is especially powerful in the following situations:

- The participants need a shared understanding.

- The topic the participants are discussing is complex.

- There is a higher risk for miscommunication when people are using different terminology or have different first languages.

- The speaker is not concise; their message is convoluted or confusing.

- Distractions are abundant.

Here are a few tips for paraphrasing:

- In your own words, share what you think a speaker means.
- Frame the paraphrase as a question so that the speaker can clarify, confirm, or correct. For example, "What I hear you are saying is…. Is that correct?"
- Try to keep the paraphrase short. If the speaker's message is lengthy, summarize when paraphrasing by using key points.
- A facilitator should encourage participants to practice paraphrasing during discussions.

Sample Techniques to Use in the Convergent Zone

In the convergent zone, the facilitator should help the group consolidate and refine ideas.

Pros and Cons

Pros and cons is a simple technique to encourage people to think critically about their own ideas and give the ideas of others due consideration with positivity. Pros and cons can be facilitated like this:

1. Each participant presents one idea to the rest of the group and addresses any questions the group has.
2. In this first round, for a short timeboxed period of time such as four minutes, each person analyzes their own idea and lists all the potential negatives for the idea.
3. In the following rounds, for each timebox, each participant takes one of the ideas from another participant in the group and only lists the positives for it.
4. The rounds continue until everyone has had a chance to give positives to all ideas.
5. The participants stick the ideas to a wall or put them on a shared virtual space, and they add their pros and cons to each, consolidating any duplicates.

6. The facilitator provides some reflection time for people to look at the content they generated.

7. Finish with a group discussion on the insights the participants generated.

Six Thinking Hats®

Six Thinking Hats®[3] is a technique in which a group of participants purposefully explores a topic, problem, or idea from different perspectives together. It helps to promote critical and parallel thinking for discussions that are constructive and to avoid unhelpful arguments.

Six differently colored hats are available, each metaphorically representing a direction of thinking.

- White represents facts. Participants focus only on the available information.
- Yellow represents optimism. Participants explore the positives only, looking for value and benefits.
- Black represents critical judgment. Participants look for risks and where things might go wrong.
- Red represents feelings. Participants talk about emotions they feel, such as fears, likes, and dislikes.
- Green represents creativity. Participants ideate to generate alternatives and new ideas.
- Blue is the process control hat. Participants use it for organization.

Here is a brief description of how to facilitate the Six Thinking Hats® technique.

- All team members "wear" the same hat at the same time for a short, timeboxed discussion, such as 10 minutes.
- Everyone contributes under the direction of the hat in play.
- A facilitator indicates the end of the timebox and instructs the participants to have another conversation under the direction of a differently colored hat. This is repeated for all the hats.

---

3. de Bono, Edward (2016). *Six Thinking Hats: The Multi-Million Bestselling Guide to Running Better Meetings and Making Faster Decisions.* Penguin Life.

- With the exception of the blue hat, participants can wear hats more than once and use them in any order.

- Participants use the blue hat at the start of a session for the group to gain alignment around the topic they will be exploring and to decide the sequence of the hats. They again use blue at the end of the session for the group to summarize insights, draw conclusions, align on outcomes, and decide next steps.

THE SCRUM TEAM WITH GROWING CONFLICT BETWEEN TWO TEAM MEMBERS

The Red Arrows are just finishing their Daily Scrum using their virtual conferencing tool.

Bertram says, "So I am just starting to code the algorithm for the pricing rules. It is complex, and I could use some help. Linda, you're really knowledgeable about how the pricing rules work. Why don't we pair on it?"

"Oh, erm... I already had plans to start looking at collating the data from our user surveys," Linda says.

"I can do that!" says Reshma. "I'm ready to start on something else. Bertram is right. You're the best person to look at the pricing with him!"

"Well, okay. I suppose so," says Linda.

"Great!" says Bertram. "I'll send you an invite with new conference call details straight after the Daily Scrum."

"No, Bertram. Let me familiarize myself with the rules again. I'll invite you."

With that the Red Arrows complete their Daily Scrum and get on with their day.

An hour goes by. Then another. Bertram, still waiting for Linda's invite, sends her an instant message.

Hi Linda! Are you ready to pair yet?

He waits a couple of minutes, but there is no response. Bertram picks up his phone and calls her. Bertram listens to the rings until finally an automated voice invites him to leave a message.

"Hi, Linda!" he says. "It's Bertram. I just sent you an instant message. Are you ready to collaborate with me on the pricing rules yet? Let me know."

Just to make sure, he sends Linda an email.

A few minutes later, Bertram receives an instant message from Linda.

Hi, Bertram. Sorry. I got caught up on something else. Can you carry on by yourself for today?

Bertram immediately starts typing.

Sure! Let's get together straight after the Daily Scrum tomorrow then. I'll send you a meeting invite so your calendar is blocked out for the whole morning.

With that Bertram sets up the meeting invite and does his best to progress with the pricing rules.

It is the next day, and in the Daily Scrum Bertram updates the rest of the Red Arrows on the pricing rules Product Backlog item as they walk the board. He tells the team that he struggled without help, but he expects to make progress when he works on it together with Linda today. The Daily Scrum call finishes, and Bertram immediately starts the new call for Linda to join. He waits for a couple of minutes and then receives an email notification. Linda has declined his meeting request.

The rest of the Red Arrows would be shocked to hear the next words that come out of Bertram's mouth.

A few months pass. The Red Arrows are in a Sprint Retrospective and Clayton, one of the Red Arrow's team members, is facilitating the event. He is using the format mad-sad-glad. The team members are writing their responses to these prompts and putting their stickies on the virtual wall under these headings.

"Okay, everyone. Let's see what we have on the board," Clayton says. "I'll start with what made us mad. I'm immediately drawn to this one that says, *CERTAIN TEAM MEMBERS ARE UNCOLLABORATIVE AND DISRESPECTFUL!!!* Wow. it's written in all capitals, and there are three exclamation marks! I can sense some tension from whoever wrote this. I guess we need to talk about it. Who wants to tell us what this is about?"

There are a few seconds of awkward silence.

"Is this about when I said Emmanual's cat looks like Ed Sheeran?" asks Pippa. "It was just a joke."

"I wrote it," says Bertram, "and it has nothing to do with Emmanual's cat! I have been feeling really disrespected by Linda over the past few Sprints. I'm always willing to collaborate with others in pairs or small groups. Pippa and I work together all the time. Reshma and I did some great stuff together this past Sprint. But for some reason Linda refuses to collaborate with me. She says she will pair with me, only to suddenly not be available. I send meeting invites, and then she cancels at the last minute. What is your problem, Linda?"

"Bertram," Linda starts, "to be honest, you are overwhelming me. You don't give me any space. You are constantly messaging me to pair. You instant message me and send me emails and meeting requests all the time. If anything, you disrespect me. You try to fill up my day without permission. I feel like you're micromanaging me!"

"Well, you never do what you say you are going to do. Maybe you do need micromanaging!" Bertram retorts, his voice raised and his cheeks flushing red.

"MAYBE YOU NEED TO LEAVE ME ALONE!" Linda shouts. Everyone is stunned into silence. "I'm sorry, everyone. I didn't mean to shout like that. Please give me a moment," she says, her voice quivering. Linda turns off her camera and microphone.

Bertram's face is even redder. "HOW DARE YOU SHOUT AT ME LIKE THAT, LINDA!" he yells. "Linda? LINDA?!"

"Give her a moment, Bertram," Clayton says. Nobody says anything for a few seconds.

"So, should we go back and talk about Emmanual's cat?" asks Pippa. "I still feel bad about that."

UNDERSTANDING CONFLICT AND PEOPLE'S NEEDS

Team solidarity or team conflict?

Conflict often occurs in a team when people have misunderstandings. There are different levels of conflict, from someone disagreeing with another's ideas to people making personal attacks. At higher levels, the goal is no longer about critiquing an idea; sides are forming, and people want to win and see their opponents lose.

The Five Levels of Team Conflict Model

The five levels of team conflict is a model by author Speed Leas that facilitators can use to understand how conflict can escalate and how to mitigate it. The levels, with mitigating options, are as follows:

Level 1: Problem to Solve. People have differences of opinion or experience uncomfortable misunderstandings. However, those involved are focused on getting to a resolution and do so positively, openly, and factually.

At this level, build consensus where people can collaborate to understand one another and arrive at a decision that everyone can back.

Level 2: Disagreement. Here, self-preservation has become as important as solving the problem. Offline discussions may occur and subgroups form. Initially, friendly jokes become nastier, although open hostility is absent. Communication is less clear, not all information is shared, and there may be some confusion about what is actually happening.

Step out of the immediate issue and use a facilitation approach that restores a sense of safety and encourages collaboration or helps the participants build empathy with each other. The aim is to help participants regroup around their shared values and mission.

Level 3: Contest. Unresolved issues become larger issues and different "causes." Factions emerge within the wider group around each cause, from which politicking arises. Conversations are emotional, and exaggerations or sweeping generalizations are made. Views become distorted, and a culture of blame emerges.

Facilitate for negotiation and compromises to be made, if possible. Use data and have facts established to help avoid more emotional or speculative responses.

Level 4: Crusade. Resolving the situation is no longer enough. Factions have become entrenched, making them more identifiable to people than the whole group or team. People and positions are seen interchangeably, leading to personal attacks. Language is focused on principles and ideology ahead of talking about specific issues and facts.

At this level, diplomacy may be called for rather than facilitation. A "go-between" or mediator may be necessary for communication between the parties until the level of conflict has de-escalated.

Level 5: World War. Besides winning the argument, those on the other side must be seen to lose. A resolution to the group's misunderstandings is virtually impossible at this level. The only viable option is to break up the group.

Focus on stopping participants from causing harm to one another.

Fundamentally, the needs that people have are universal. All of us should be able to relate to the needs for belonging, support, acceptance, appreciation, respect, and privacy, to name just a few, and experience most, if not all of them at some point in our lives. However, we have different needs at different times in our lives. We also have needs in different contexts, and we may have different needs from other people in the same situation or scenario.

Team conflict arises because of the approach people on the team take to fulfill their individual needs. For example, a person who has a strong need for harmony may just ignore another person if what they are saying is controversial or uncomfortable. Their response might be to deflect and try to change the conversation and move on. This is their strategy on how to fulfill their need for harmony. The other person, however, may have a need for self-expression, and their strategy is to say what they really think, but as a consequence of the first person's strategy, they feel shut down. Here, two people do not understand each other's needs and do not have empathy for one another's point of view. Their strategies to fulfill their needs are clashing, leading to frustration. This can easily escalate into a destructive conflict between the two.

In the story of the Red Arrows, tensions were growing between two of the team members, Linda and Bertram, until the tensions finally erupted into an unhealthy conflict. Some might point to Linda's behavior as being uncooperative. Some could accuse Bertram of being self-imposing. It is not a case of one party being right and one party wrong, but about their clashing strategies for fulfilling their respective needs. Bertram may have the need for connection and learning, and his strategy to fulfill these needs is to pair and bounce ideas off of others. As part of this strategy, he organized conference calls and calendar invitations, and he messaged people to make it happen. Linda saw his approach as forceful. She may have a need for space. Her strategies were to work on her own first. She was noncommittal, she found excuses, she canceled meetings at the last minute, and she generally tried to avoid Bertram just to get some space.

Both Bertram and Linda made assumptions about why the other person behaved like they did. Bertram interpreted Linda's behavior as not wanting to work with him and that she was that she was being selfish. As time has gone by, Bertram felt this as a personal attack, and he was offended and hurt. Linda, on the other hand, felt annoyed, disrespected, cornered, and micromanaged by him. While Bertram and Linda have not understood each other's needs and continued to employ their respective strategies, their conflict escalated to the point where it finally boiled over.

TRY THIS! FACILITATE THE BUILDING OF EMPATHY AND UNDERSTANDING NEEDS

Conflict is a natural occurrence, and it happens all the time within groups. Once conflict reaches a certain level, it is difficult for individuals or teams to recover.

Humans tend to act with emotions first, and there is usually a delay before the logical part of the brain kicks into gear. Creating space is an effective method to deal with conflict in the moment.

A longer-term strategy is to help people build empathy with one another so they understand each other's needs. This reduces the chances of tensions reaching a high level of conflict.

As a facilitator, you can employ techniques to help people create space and foster empathy with each other. Following next are some tools and techniques to build empathy and create alignment. However, be aware that there may be some pitfalls a facilitator should avoid. For example, some people find sharing personal information to be invasive. A facilitator should create an environment in which people do not feel pressured to share anything they feel uncomfortable with. When sharing sample templates and canvases, a facilitator should emphasize that participants can use their own versions and decide for themselves what information they feel comfortable sharing. Some participants may be comfortable sharing certain things with their immediate team members but do not want that same information to be known outside the team. As a facilitator, you can introduce the Vegas rule: *What happens in Vegas stays in Vegas.* This means that everyone understands that whatever is shared and discussed among the group stays with the group.

Facilitators should make it clear from the outset that the purpose of the activities and information sharing is for people to understand each other better without judgment.

Take a Break

When emotions run high, people's bodies react. Our muscles tense up, adrenaline flows, our heart rate increases, and our breathing quickens. These responses often cause people to be more likely to say or do something they will later regret. When a facilitator observes things getting heated and discussions turning unhealthy, a useful strategy is to pause the conversation and give everyone space to calm down. During the break, a facilitator can suggest people try some breathing exercises to relax their body, go for a walk, or anything that allows their body to calm down so they can self-reflect on what happened. They can ask themselves questions such as these:

- What triggered me?
- What need am I trying to fulfill?
- What strategies did I apply to fulfill this need?

When people feel they are ready to continue the conversation, a facilitator can help the group by encouraging them to apply active listening, suspend any judgments, and be curious. To ensure everyone feels heard, the facilitator can take a round-robin approach to ensure everyone has an opportunity to express themselves. In a virtual environment, speakers may be more comfortable sharing their thoughts if everyone else has their cameras off.

Those who do not want to say anything have the right to pass. A facilitator should use paraphrasing to ensure clarity and ensure that people feel listened to. After the group has shared and reflected on their triggers, needs, and strategies, they can discuss what is required to fulfill these needs and what strategies they may choose to apply in the future. This does not automatically mean every need will be met. Participants should be prepared to accept this.

At the end, to emphasize reflection and for the group to have closure, the facilitator can ask each person one at a time to answer a check-out question, such as "What's my biggest learning or insight from today?"

Empathy Mapping

An empathy map is a tool for people to capture and make sense of what they know about others, resulting in building more empathy. Scrum Teams can use empathy maps to understand the users of their products, other stakeholders, or members of the Scrum Team.

By filling in an empathy map for a fellow team member, people can build a deeper understanding of each other. An empathy map typically includes who the subject is, what they see, hear, feel, and think during an experience, and what their pains and desires are. Figure 4.3 shows the empathy map canvas.

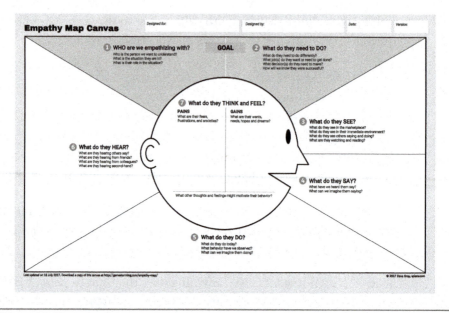

Figure 4.3 The empathy map canvas.

Participants can fill in an empathy map collaboratively. One way to facilitate team members building empathy maps for each other is for everyone to focus on each team member in turn for a short timebox, such as five minutes, while the rest of the Scrum Team asks a team member questions and fills in the empathy map as they go.

The Scrum Team should regularly revisit its empathy maps as new insights emerge.

Personal Mapping

Personal maps are an idea from Management 3.0.[4] A personal map is like a mindmap, but the focus is on people. They enable people to learn more about each other, thus helping build empathy among the team.

People can create their own personal map about themselves, but in Management 3.0 it is recommended that team members create them on each other's behalf. By creating a personal map for someone else, participants have

---

4. Appelo, Jurgen (2010). *Management 3.0: Leading Agile Developers, Developing Agile Leaders.* Addison-Wesley Professional.

to make an effort to understand and therefore build empathy with them. An example of a personal map is shown in Figure 4.4.

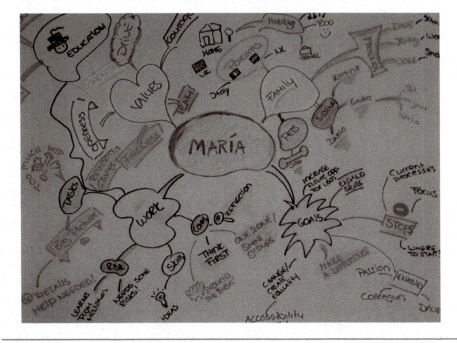

Figure 4.4 An example of a personal map.

The steps to create a personal map for someone else follow:

1. Start with an empty sheet of paper or a blank virtual canvas, and write down in the center the name of the person who is the subject of the personal map.

2. Write categories around the name. These might include education, hobbies, family, pets, and ambitions, among others.

3. Write relevant things around the categories based on what you know about the other person. At this point, you may realize that you do not know the person as well as you thought you did.

4. Organize some face time with the person, and ask them questions to get to know them better. Use the insights of this discussion to update or expand the map further.

5. Present the personal maps to the rest of the team.

Team Member User Manual

A team member user manual is another tool for team members to get to know each other. Each team member creates their own personal manual and adds information they believe others should know about them to improve how to interact and work together as a team. This may include preferred ways of communicating, working hours, collaboration style, and so on. An example of a team member user manual is shown in Figure 4.5.

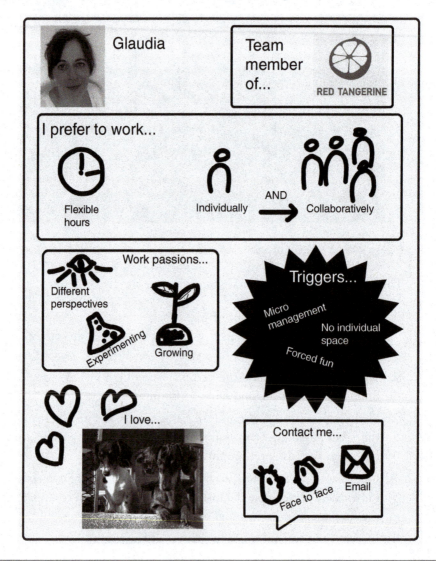

Figure 4.5 Example of a team member user manual.

A facilitator can arrange a session so that team members can share their manuals with each other. What follows are the steps to facilitate the creation and sharing of a team member user manual:

1. Participants prepare their own team member user manual. The facilitator can provide a sample template, but it is important that they emphasize to the participants that they can create their own team member user manual any way they see fit.

2. The facilitator should set the context for the creation of the team member user manuals, explaining that the purpose is for the team members to get to know each other better. The facilitator should emphasize that no one should feel obliged to share something they are not comfortable sharing.

3. The facilitator arranges a session for the team members to share their team member user manuals. Participants hang up their user manuals on the wall or in a virtual space on a virtual whiteboard.

4. Each participant shares their user manual with the group and answers questions from the rest of the group.

Personal team member user manuals can also be a great tool for onboarding new team members.

Empathy Buddy Exercise Using Feelings and Needs Cards

A facilitator can use feelings and needs cards and the empathy buddy exercise[5] as a tool to help people practice active listening and empathize with each other.

1. The facilitator gives a set of feelings and needs cards to the participants, which is usually just a pair of people. The feelings cards contain words like *apprehensive, confused, exhilarated, frustrated, hopeful, stressed out,* and *relieved*. The needs cards contain words like *belonging, kindness, harmony, security,* and *space*.

2. The participants review another set of cards that are called the empathy blockers. These are actions such as *correcting, denial, interrogating,*

---

5. To download a PDF of the feelings and needs cards, see www.malindaelizabethberry.net/uploads/8/4/7/8/84786408/deck_guide.pdf.

minimizing, and *shutting down*. These are behaviors that the participants will try to avoid during the exercise.

3. Each person has a set amount of time, such as five minutes, where they can talk uninterrupted. Or they can stay quiet if they choose to. The other person just listens.

4. During the timebox, the speaker lays down or highlights the feelings cards that match their emotions at that moment as they are talking.

5. In response, the other person lays down or highlights the needs cards that they believe are connected to the feelings cards indicated by the other person. The listener can clarify their intuition with statements or questions like, "Are you feeling uncomfortable because of the need for order?"

6. When a number of the needs cards have been selected, the speaker chooses those that most resonate for them.

7. The process ends with the listener asking, "What request do you have for yourself? What request do you have for me?"

8. The speaker and listener switch roles and repeat the process.

Explore and Support Diversity of Working Styles

People have different styles and patterns of working. For example, some thrive in collaborative working sessions, whereas others find it draining to work constantly with others and need time to reflect and process ideas on their own first, as we saw in the story with Bertram and Linda. There is a general assumption that the ideal work environment is one in which everyone is working and collaborating all the time. When teams force this to be the case, they drive away people who can potentially be great contributors, just not in the typical "teamwork" sense.

A facilitator can run a session for the Scrum Team to explore the members' diversity of working styles and help them understand and respect each other. This includes identifying working styles and characteristics that people use, that they appreciate, and those that may trigger them. It helps people reflect and empathize with others' preferences. The Scrum Team members may even go as far as writing policies into their team working agreement about how they will try to support everyone's working style and not repress anyone.

THE SCRUM TEAM WITH WEAK DECISION-MAKING

Team All Saints is in the retrospective of its first Sprint. "Time is up, team. Let's put our stickies on the wall," says Naomi, the team member who is facilitating the Sprint Retrospective. She and the rest of the team move up to the big whiteboard and start putting up their sticky notes in the columns What Went Well? and What Didn't Go Well? that Naomi had drawn on the whiteboard just a few minutes before.

"Wow, there are a lot of stickies in the What Didn't Go Well area!" she says. "So let's just start there. I'm just going to read them out from top to bottom, and we'll have a discussion on each one in turn. This one at the top says, *We didn't have a Sprint Goal.*"

Malik is the first to react. "I'm confused. The Sprint Goal was clear, we all agreed to it, and we met it."

"Really?" says Janaka. "We came out of Sprint Planning with the forecasted Product Backlog items for the Sprint, but most of them were unrelated to each other, and we ran out of time before agreeing what the Sprint Goal was. We never discussed it again. Even in the Daily Scrums we focused on the work and never talked about the Sprint Goal."

"It was clear to me," counters Malik. "We needed to have something for the user to interact with, meaning that we would have to build the infrastructure to enable us to show a welcome message from a data store to the user on the app."

Siobhan jumps in. "That's what you proposed in Sprint Planning," she says. "Remember, I wanted the focus to be on understanding our target users' needs."

"Naomi, if I remember correctly," Malik says, "you said, 'let's just go with the show a welcome message to the user for the Sprint Goal.'"

"Did I?" asks Naomi.

"Yes. That's what I remember as well," says Francois.

Janika adds, "That's not my recollection. I thought she asked us if anybody else had a suggestion for an alternative Sprint Goal. No one said anything."

"Well, that was your chance then!" says Malik.

"I was thinking, and then I didn't get the chance because we wrapped up the event."

"I'm so confused. I don't know what was agreed," mumbles Itope.

"Just because Naomi made a suggestion doesn't mean that is what we should have gone with, does it?"

"No, you are right, Siobhan. We should be making decisions as a team," says Naomi.

"So, how the heck do we do that?"

MAKING CLEAR DECISIONS

In the previous story, the All Saints lacked transparency in how they made decisions, resulting in confused team members who had different perceptions about what they agreed the Sprint Goal should be for the Sprint. Some thought the team had made a clear decision in Sprint Planning, whereas others were still thinking it through when they wrapped up the meeting.

In the story with team All Saints, Naomi had suggested a Sprint Goal and the participants had stayed silent. Naomi, as the facilitator, assumed compliance and ended the meeting. As team All Saints discussed the confusion in the Sprint Retrospective, it was clear that the team had experienced some tension. Team members had different understandings of the Sprint Goal, and some thought that the team had not decided on a Sprint Goal at all.

This shows the importance of transparency around what level of agreement is needed to carry a decision forward. To ensure alignment on decisions being made, a facilitator can use a variety of consent-checking and consensus-building techniques. This is where decision rules and decision-making tools come in, which we discuss next.

TRY THIS! DECISION-MAKING RULES AND TECHNIQUES

Scrum Teams need to make decisions all the time. They vary from determining what experiments to run to improve the team's effectiveness, to choosing which tools they will use, to deciding product solutions to meet the needs of their customers, to agreeing on Sprint Goals. A Scrum Team needs to have a clear indication of when a decision is reached, how it is reached, and whose input is required. This creates transparency, supports self-management, and helps with building agreements everyone can support. This is where decision rules come in.

Decision Rules

Without clear decision rules in place, a Scrum Team risks having discussions that drag on, those with loud voices getting their way, and time pressures rushing the team into making a decision or not making a decision at all. This can affect the Scrum Team's daily work, as we saw in the story with team All Saints, where team members were unclear what Sprint Goal they agreed on.

Not every decision is equal, as some decisions carry more risk than others. Context is key. A facilitator should help the participants decide which decision rules to use for different decisions. It is also important for a facilitator to understand how the choice of decision rules may affect the behavior of a group.

Next, we share the most common decision rules, with a summary in Table 4.1. We give examples of when to use each, potential downsides and challenges, and some techniques that teams can use to implement the decision rule. Scrum Teams may want to write which of these they will use under which circumstances into their working agreements. These are based on the writings of Sam Kaner[6] and Roman Pichler.[7]

- **Unanimous agreement:** Every person is in complete agreement and supports the decision.
- **Majority vote:** For a decision to pass, more than half of the participants must agree to it.
- **One person decides after discussion:** A single person makes a decision after asking for advice and talking things through with others.
- **One person decides without discussion:** A single person decides without discussion. This person carries out their own analysis and decides a plan of action independently of any consultation, advice, or discussion.
- **Delegation:** The person with final accountability entrusts the responsibility for making a decision to others. Those with the power to delegate should

---

6. Kaner, Sam (2014). *Facilitator's Guide to Participatory Decision-Making*, Third Edition. Jossey-Bass.
7. Pichler, Roman (2016). "Use Decision Rules to Make Better Product Decisions." Romanpichler.com. www.romanpichler.com/blog/decision-rules-to-make-better-product-decisions/.

ensure that they give decision-making authority to those who are the best
qualified people to make the decision.

Table 4.1 Common Decision Rules for Scrum Teams

Decision Rule	When to Use	Pitfalls	Sample Techniques
Unanimous agreement	• Decision needs strong buy-in from the team • Sustainability of agreement is important Example: agreeing to a Definition of Done	• Time consuming • Team members applying peer pressure, resulting in people agreeing to decisions they do not support	• Fist of five • Gradients of agreements scale • Feedback frames
Majority vote	• Speed is more important than the quality/durability of the decision, and making a decision is a better alternative to having no decision • Low-stakes decisions Example: where to go for team lunch	• Creates a win/lose situation • Risk of the minority feeling frustration and unwillingness to support the decision	• Show of hands • Roman voting • Anonymous vote • Polls
One person decides after discussion	• When a decision-maker wants to maintain control over their decision • When a decision-maker wants to leverage the collective intelligence and experience of others in the Scrum Team • To avoid decision by committee Example: Product Owner deciding on the order of the Product Backlog	• Can cause low buy-in or no buy-in at all if people feel their input is ignored • Less feeling of shared responsibility	• Open-ended questioning to gather ideas • Techniques for unanimous agreement and majority vote can be used to gauge opinion

Decision Rule	When to Use	Pitfalls	Sample Techniques
One person decides without discussion	• Low-risk decisions • High-stakes scenarios where immediate action is needed • When the decision resides with a domain-specific authority	• Decision-maker may not have all required information • Risk that others can disagree with the decision or have it forced upon them, causing low buy-in	N/A
Delegation	• There are better-qualified and more experienced people to make the decision • When decision-making causes unnecessary dependencies and delays Example: Product Owner delegates adding details to particular Product Backlog items	• People delegate to avoid making tough decisions themselves • People appear to delegate decisions but are unable to let go and interfere • People delegate to someone who is not qualified or does not have the experience to make the decision	N/A

Decision-Making Techniques

Teams can use various techniques to support the decision rule they have chosen. Here, we briefly explain a few decision-making techniques.

Roman Voting

Roman voting is a simple way for a facilitator to check agreement from a group. The practice takes its name from when it is said that Roman emperors would show a thumbs-up or thumbs-down to indicate whether a defeated gladiator would be allowed to live or die.[8] In the context of decision-making, participants can use it to show whether they agree with a proposal or not.

The facilitator makes sure that the proposal is presented and gives a countdown for everyone to cast their vote. Participants can vote in one of three ways:

• Thumbs-up: I agree.

• Thumbs-sideways: I am on the fence.

• Thumbs-down: I disagree.

---

8. Whether these gestures were actually used is the subject of much scholarly debate.

Fist of Five

With the fist of five technique, a facilitator can quickly ascertain the level of agreement felt by a group of participants as a whole.

A Scrum Team can use it, for example, to gauge the team members' level of agreement with a proposed item for their team working agreement or to ascertain the Developers' level of confidence in meeting a Sprint Goal and completing the forecasted Product Backlog items for a Sprint. However, the real power of fist of five is that it can trigger a conversation that everyone participates in about what assumptions they might have made or where there might be ambiguities.

To facilitate a fist of five, the facilitator first presents the topic. They ask everyone to hold up their fist, and after giving a countdown, everyone reveals their score by holding up a corresponding number of fingers accordingly:

- 5 fingers: I am in complete agreement.
- 4 fingers: This sounds good to me.
- 3 fingers: I am in the middle; I am okay to go along with it. Maybe there is something better, but maybe there is not.
- 2 fingers: I have some concerns.
- 1 finger: I do not like this.
- A closed fist: I totally oppose this.

After the vote, the team discusses the results.

As an alternative to using hands to vote, a facilitator can create a gradient agreement scale from 1 to 5 on a physical or virtual whiteboard where people can move a sticky note with their name on it on the scale.

Feedback Frames

Feedback Frames[9] are a simple way for people to anonymously vote on what they think about a presented option. Voting is on a scale of agreement. It is secret and anonymous, and all participants' votes are equal.

---

9. For full details on feedback frames, see https://feedbackframes.com/.

Feedback Frames are traditionally a physical tool. They have a number of slots in which participants can drop tokens without revealing their votes to anyone else. The slots range from one end to the other, representing different levels of agreement:

- Strong agreement
- Agreement
- Neutral
- Disagreement
- Strong disagreement
- Not sure

Figure 4.6 shows an example of a Feedback Frame.

Figure 4.6 An example of a Feedback Frame.

A Scrum Team can use Feedback Frames when it creates a team working agreement, for example. A session might look like this:

1. The facilitator starts by setting the scene and making sure that everybody understands the purpose of the session. A good way to do this is to present the open-ended question that the Scrum Team aims to answer. For example, the question might be: What are the rules that we want to agree to on how we will work together?

2. Everyone individually drafts ideas in response to the question.

3. Team members form groups to discuss their ideas, which they combine and consolidate. Each idea is written on a separate card or a sheet of paper.

4. Team members share their ideas with the whole group and combine duplicate or similar ideas.

5. The facilitator places each idea in front of its own Feedback Frame. Each Feedback Frame has the same number of tokens as the number of Scrum Team members.

6. Everyone drops a token in each Feedback Frame in one of the slots to indicate their level of agreement with each idea. Optionally, each person signs a sheet of paper at each Feedback Frame to show that they have voted. This provides a way to audit that the number of votes equals the number of signatories so that everyone has voted and that no participants have voted more than once. Another option is to leave space at the Feedback Frame for people to leave comments about the idea.

7. After everyone has cast their vote, the facilitator can reveal the results. Everyone should then be able to see the levels of agreement for each of the ideas.

Some virtual tools offer features such as a private mode, where participants can vote anonymously before a facilitator reveals how everyone voted. That way a facilitator can replicate the concept of Feedback Frames in virtual environments.

The secret scoring of Feedback Frames avoids groupthink and provides anonymity for the participants in how they have voted.

Dot Voting

Dot voting is another quick and simple way for a group to democratically make a decision. In contrast to roman voting, fist of five, or Feedback Frames, all of which test individuals' agreement with a single option one at a time, dot voting is a facilitation tool that gives people the opportunity to choose one or more options from a large pool. Dot voting typically works like this:

1. Participants present options they came up with by writing them on sticky notes or index cards, for example, and posting them on a (virtual) wall. A facilitator allows time for participants to ask clarifying questions about the options.

2. Each participant is given a number of dot votes. These can be actual sticky dots, or votes can be made by using a pen or a marker (or the virtual equivalent). Advice on the number of votes varies. One approach a facilitator can use is to give each participant a number of votes that is approximately equal to the number of options divided by 4. For example, if there are 12 options for participants to choose from, the facilitator gives each person 3 votes.

3. Participants place their votes. They can use all their votes on one option or split them across different ones in whatever ratio they choose. Voting is done without conversation about the options.

4. Once everyone has voted, the group counts the votes and declares the "winners." The participants may decide that the three options with the highest number of votes are the ones to take forward.

5. In the case of a tie among the top options, the facilitator can propose to run another round of voting. The same number of dots are redistributed, but this time, options are limited to those that previously came to the top, such as the top three.

Although simple and quick, dot voting does have its critics. After some people have placed their votes, others may be influenced by what they have chosen, culminating in people voting along the same lines because everyone else has. The facilitator can adapt the dot voting process in these ways:

• The facilitator labels the sticky notes with the options participants can choose from, such as A, B, C, and so on. Then they ask each person to individually write down their choices in private. Once everyone has made their choices, the facilitator adds their dots to the stickies. This technique helps people make up their own mind without being influenced by others.

- Use a virtual tool to dot vote. Most virtual tools allow anonymous voting, which means participants cannot see each other's votes until the facilitator reveals the score at the end of the voting timebox.
- Ask people to vote in a certain order. For example, a person with the most authority in a group, such as a CEO, is the last person to vote. Or, for example, when people have three votes, you can ask them to vote in three rounds; each person casts one vote in each round, and in each round people vote in a different order.

Another challenge can be that participants are expected to review and understand all the options. When many options are available, it may be overwhelming and difficult for all participants to fully understand all of them. Dot voting can end with curious results because some similar options can cause vote splitting, or an enthusiastic minority might place all its dots on one item.

KEYS TO FACILITATING TEAM DYNAMICS

In this chapter, we shared some ideas and techniques for facilitating group dynamics to help a team explore differing perspectives constructively and with respect. We now look at some key considerations when facilitating group dynamics.

BUILD TEAM EMPATHY

A running theme in this book is that facilitation does not start and end with the facilitation of a meeting, workshop, or event. In the case of a Scrum Team, it involves ongoing facilitation from Sprint to Sprint to help the team grow as a unit and to build understanding and empathy for each other. However, it is really important that a facilitator ensures that people are not forced to divulge information about themselves that they would prefer not to share.

HELP GROUPS NAVIGATE CONFLICTING PERSPECTIVES

Many people feel uncomfortable expressing ideas or perspectives that conflict with those of others. However, some level of conflict is a good thing when it involves people challenging ideas constructively.

A facilitator should avoid prematurely steering a group toward a conclusion because this results in the group losing an opportunity for people to build a better understanding of each other, their needs, problems, and to explore resolution options more deeply. Conversely, when discussions get out of hand, when it threatens the health and safety of the group, a facilitator needs to step in and take action to stop things escalating before it is too late. Sometimes conflict can grow to such levels that it is not just detrimental but also irrecoverable. A facilitator should always be content neutral in supporting the team. For more on content neutrality, see the principles in Appendix A, "Facilitation Principles."

Part of navigating conflicting perspectives is coming out the other side. Once a group has explored all the ideas, created a shared understanding, and critiqued them, it needs to make some decisions. If members have put in the work to agree on decision-making rules upfront, this is easier, but it may still require discipline and courage to enforce. The main thing is that participants believe the process to be fair and inclusive, which means they were able to explore options and discuss reservations before a decision was made as a group.

POWERFUL QUESTIONING

A facilitator is there to steer, not to solve. The facilitator should be working to challenge people's thinking and reveal issues, not resolve them. That can happen by employing facilitation techniques that encourage participants to challenge each other's thinking. A facilitator can pose powerful questions that are open-ended to help people do their best thinking and encourage them to express their thoughts out loud. An open question—one that cannot be answered with a simple yes or no answer—encourages dialogue and new thinking. These sorts of questions are built into many of the facilitation approaches that we have discussed in this book. The right question at the right time can get a group back on track toward its purpose. It sometimes takes courage to ask a powerful question, but knowing when and how to ask one is a key skill for a facilitator to have in their toolkit.

Depending on the context, a facilitator may choose to use directive questions, nondirective questions, or a mix of both. When facilitators ask the participants directive questions, they point the participants in a certain direction that they think is helpful. Examples are, "What should be our Sprint Goal?" or "How might we solve this problem?" These are useful questions, but when a facilitator needs to dig deeper, they can first paraphrase what a participant said and then follow up with a nondirective question. An example might be, "You are saying using X is the best way forward for the team…" followed by "So can you tell us more?"

CONCLUSION

Facilitation is part skill and part art that necessitates an understanding of human interactions in groups. This awareness helps a facilitator guide a team through a process and pull on members' collective wisdom by drawing out each individual's opinions and ideas. However, sometimes these interactions spill into unhealthy conflict for a variety of reasons. As we discussed, it is best for a facilitator to be mindful and mitigate this type of conflict from occurring in the first place.

The facilitation techniques that we detailed in this chapter can help facilitators manage the unpredictability and complexity of group dynamics so the group makes better decisions. The techniques we describe are only a start, but they are useful in helping groups build shared understanding, empathy, and accountability.

Whatever technique a facilitator applies when conflict takes place, it is essential that they stay neutral and not take sides. Instead, they must listen actively and let people talk openly without judging. A facilitator can help by paraphrasing during the conversation to clarify their understanding of what people shared to ensure that what is discussed is clear.

When an unhealthy conflict arises, a facilitator should acknowledge and deal with it sooner rather than later because the longer it festers, the worse it can get. Also, at no moment in time should a facilitator provide a solution for a team or team members, even when they are in conflict. Facilitation focuses on how people participate in the process of learning or planning to achieve a purpose, not the answer.

FACILITATING PRODUCT BACKLOG REFINEMENT

Product Backlog refinement includes breaking Product Backlog items into smaller ones.

A Scrum Team should break down Product Backlog items and deliberately order the Product Backlog so they can work on what they believe is most valuable for their product. Refining the Product Backlog can sometimes feel to Scrum Teams like a distraction from doing the actual development work, but without it their Sprint Planning will be more difficult. They can end up desperately looking for Product Backlog items to bring into the Sprint, without a shared understanding of the value of those items. As a result, the Scrum

Team can end up working on items in the Sprint that do not contribute to making much progress toward the Product Goal.

Scrum Teams refine the Product Backlog at any time during the Sprint as an ongoing activity in parallel to the development work. They can employ various strategies to refine their Product Backlog, which includes the Scrum Team splitting Product Backlog items into multiple smaller ones, adding details such as acceptance criteria, and sizing the items. Refinement is a collaborative activity with some separate responsibilities; the Developers are responsible for sizing, and the Product Owner is responsible for ordering.

Facilitation skills and techniques can help with Product Backlog refinement and the collaborations across the Scrum accountabilities. Let's look at some examples.

THE SCRUM TEAM EXPERIMENTING WITH DAILY PRODUCT BACKLOG REFINEMENT

Patrick, Martina, Volodymyr, Soma, and Dwight use Scrum to publish a newsletter in their small town every month. It is time for their regular Product Backlog refinement. In the past, they held a two-hour meeting every week to do Product Backlog refinement as a team, but at their previous Sprint Retrospective, Soma suggested that they try something else. During this Sprint, they will do a little Product Backlog refinement for up to 30 minutes every day, straight after the Daily Scrum.

Everyone gathers around the Product Backlog, which is made up of a number of index cards that the team has stuck to one of its office walls.

Patrick speaks first. "We usually start refinement with a reminder of the Product Goal. I'm sure we won't need to do this every day, but because this is the first time we're refining the Product Backlog in this way, I'll remind everyone now. Our Product Goal is to create a sustainable publication that informs and brings the local community together. Now that we have reminded ourselves on that, shall we start with any new items we need to add?"

"I've got something," says Dwight. "I got a call late yesterday with a potential story that could go into next month's issue. Apparently, someone in our town has a cat that looks like Ed Sheeran! I added a Product Backlog item with high-level details to the bottom of the Product Backlog until we could talk about it."

"Excellent! That's the kind of local feel-good story we need," Patrick says.

The team members continue their refinement. There are no other new items to add, so Patrick suggests that all of them have a quick look at the Product Backlog and discuss the order of items. The item at the top is to write an article about the proposed new parking garage for the town center. Everyone agrees that this is still the most compelling upcoming story, so it should stay high in the Product Backlog.

Volodymyr points out an item farther down the Product Backlog. "I think we should bring this one up," he says. "If we don't get sustainable income, the newsletter is doomed!" The Product Backlog item in question is one that was added three months ago, right at the start of the team's initiative. It offers people the option to subscribe for copies of the newsletter to be delivered to their door. "It will generate sustainable income," Volodymyr argues.

After further discussions, everyone agrees that this Product Backlog item should be something the team works on soon, so they move it near the top of the Product Backlog. They also move up the new story from Dwight, so it is highly likely they will pull it into the next Sprint.

Martina notices a Product Backlog item near the bottom of the Product Backlog, one about moving away from the current distributor. "Now that the distributor knows it is going to get regular business from us, it is going to give us a 20 percent discount for printing and distributing the newsletter. So we might as well stick with them." Everyone agrees, and they tear up the relevant index card and put it into the recycling bin.

Next, starting from the top of the Product Backlog, Patrick suggests that they look at adding more detail to the Product Backlog items. The top one, for the story on the car park, is already well defined.

The team instead focuses on the Product Backlog item for the subscription because it currently only has the following text: As a member of the local

community I can subscribe to the newsletter so that I receive a copy regularly.
The team has a discussion and adds the following acceptance criteria:

- I can subscribe to a free trial period of 3 months.
- I can choose to subscribe to a paid subscription for 6 months or 12 months.
- I can pay securely for the subscription.
- I can add my delivery address.
- I will receive physical issues of the newsletter at my delivery address.

"We have a lot to think about for this one, such as that last acceptance criteria," says Martina. "We will have a lot of work figuring out how to send the paper to people's homes." Everyone agrees. Patrick points out that their timebox for refinement is up.

The next day, the team has no new items to add to the Product Backlog. The team decides to continue refining the subscription Product Backlog item. Everyone agrees that it will be too much work to do in one Sprint so they decide to work on splitting it into multiple, smaller items.

Patrick reminds everyone that they don't need to work out all the details. "We just need to capture what it is we want to achieve into something we think we can do in a Sprint. We can work out the details of how we achieve it in the simplest way in Sprint Planning and during the Sprint."

The team splits the Product Backlog item into several smaller ones. The members discuss the order of the smaller Product Backlog items they have just created and agree that at the next refinement they will add more details. With that, they wrap up the day's Product Backlog refinement.

FACILITATION OF REFINING THE PRODUCT BACKLOG

The previous story demonstrated one example of a Scrum Team refining the Product Backlog. The Scrum Team carried out multiple activities as part of refining its Product Backlog. It added new Product Backlog items and removed others. It also changed the order of the Product Backlog. In addition, it looked into certain Product Backlog items and added more detail, such as acceptance criteria. The team members discussed whether items could fit into a Sprint and worked on splitting Product Backlog items into smaller ones.

Patrick provided some lightweight facilitation by giving the team's sessions some structure. He started the first session by reminding everyone of the Product Goal. He then guided them, one at a time, through different steps of Product Backlog refinement, from adding new items to breaking others down and adding more detail. He stepped in and warned the team that Product Backlog refinement is not about analyzing every item and coming up with detailed solutions, but instead understanding the required outcomes enough so that the team can define Product Backlog items that they think they can do within a Sprint.

TRY THIS! TIPS FOR PRODUCT BACKLOG REFINEMENT

Product Backlog refinement is not a defined event in Scrum. Scrum Teams have flexibility in how they manage their Product Backlog without being constrained by the rules of Scrum. With this flexibility comes some uncertainty for many Scrum Teams about what exactly they should do. While avoiding being prescriptive, here we share some facilitation tips for you to think about for Product Backlog refinement.

Refine the Product Backlog Collaboratively

Here are two examples of how Product Backlog refinement might look in a Scrum Team. First, a Scrum Team's Product Owner, or delegate (such as a person with strong analysis skills), writes detailed Product Backlog items and orders the Product Backlog without involving the rest of the team. Second, every Scrum Team member helps to adapt the Product Backlog, and the team seeks a consensus for all decisions.

In the first example, teamwork and collaboration are absent during refinement. Good facilitation of Product Backlog refinement includes encouraging collaboration across the Scrum Team. Collaboration between the Product Owner and the Developers is particularly important as they discuss aspects such as value, viability, dependencies, and effort—all things that, when intertwined, are factors in the Scrum Team's decision-making.

At the other extreme, involving every single Scrum Team member in Product Backlog refinement provides great transparency for the team, but it may be overkill. A Scrum Team may be happy to have a subset of the team refine the Product Backlog as long as their work is transparent and other team members can engage if they feel they have something to contribute.

A facilitator can help the Scrum Team think about who needs to be involved in Product Backlog refinement. Examples of how different Scrum Team members may be involved in refining a Product Backlog item at different times include:

- Any person can add Product Backlog items, capturing what the item is at a high level, as we saw with Dwight in the previous story.
- To further refine the Product Backlog item, a couple of the Developers might work together with the Product Owner to add acceptance criteria and develop some scenarios and examples.
- The whole Scrum Team may later be involved in reviewing the Product Backlog item and make a final agreement if the item is appropriately sized and it has enough details to deem it ready for a Sprint.

Some Scrum Teams may even extend collaboration on the Product Backlog refinement to include stakeholders. Although the Sprint Review is the formal opportunity for stakeholders to give feedback and influence adaptations to the Product Backlog, a Scrum Team does not have to restrict it to this. A facilitator can help a Scrum Team think about its stakeholders and how to use techniques to involve them in the management of the Product Backlog.

Every Scrum Team might have its own set of preferences. Capturing them in a team working agreement to make them transparent might also be helpful. We discussed team working agreements in Chapter 1, "Facilitating Alignment."

Focus Conversation on Why and What; Postpone How

In the story, Patrick pointed out that the team would not be able to work out all the details for a Product Backlog item upfront. The team can work out the implementation details in Sprint Planning and during the Sprint. This can be an uncomfortable shift in mindset for many people. People do not like ambiguity, and it is human nature to jump into problem-solving mode and draw conclusions before they really understand the problem. Product Backlog refinement is not where the Scrum Team solves problems.

Refinement's purpose is to build enough understanding of the problem, represented by a Product Backlog item, and split it down so that the Scrum Team has reasonable confidence that it can solve it in a Sprint. When Scrum Teams start discussing implementation, they can spiral into all kinds of details and hypotheticals. This can be wasteful because it is speculative, and things may change in the interim between refining the item and starting work on the item in the Sprint. A facilitator should help the Scrum Team focus on understanding the problem and encourage the team members to worry less about the implementation details until the Product Backlog item is selected to go into a Sprint.

THE STAKEHOLDERS WHO WANT IT ALL

Some Product Backlogs become monstrous and scary!

A few individuals are meeting to define what they want to have in the hotel they are investing in. They are adding items to the Product Backlog.

"Besides the pool, we should have a jacuzzi. Guests would love that!" says Vikram enthusiastically.

"Okay," says Ahmet. "I'll add it to the list."

"And why not have a steam room and sauna?" says Özlem.

"Good idea!" says Vikram. "Ahmet, add that to your list."

"Ahmet," says Emre, "please read aloud what we have so far."

"Well, the hotel will have forty rooms, its own restaurant, a separate piano bar, a parking garage, conference rooms, a gym, a pool with a jacuzzi, and a steam room and sauna," Ahmet replies. "You know, I appreciate the investment from all four of you in this project, but I'm not sure all this is going to be possible with the budget, especially if we want to open by the end of the year."

"Wait!" cries Vikram, "I thought of something else. It should also have a rooftop bar!"

"Good idea, Vikram," says Amaad. "Ahmet…"

"I know… put it on the list." Ahmet scribbles in his notebook. "Look everyone, this is turning into some Product Backlog. We won't be able to have all of it."

"You are using this Scrum thing with your team of architects and builders. You said it would be effective at helping deliver value for the money we are putting into this new hotel!" says Vikram.

"Well, yes," replies Ahmet, "but what I meant was, with Scrum, we will work on the most valuable things. We will have to prioritize. Remember that I said a condition of us working together was that I was going to be the Product Owner and have the final say. I just need help from all of you to help me decide what is most important."

"The rooftop bar!" says Vikram quickly.

"We definitely need to have the restaurant," says Emre.

"And the jacuzzi, steam room, and sauna," Vikram quickly adds.

"Yes, definitely," Özlem says. "Also, our guests will need parking, so we need the garage."

"We certainly need to include the conference rooms because we want to attract businesses as well as tourists," says Amaad.

"Everyone, stop!" cries Ahmet. "You're just listing everything again. What are the most valuable things?"

Ahmet's investors look at each other for answers. Vikram breaks the silence. "All of them!" he says.

KEEPING THE PRODUCT BACKLOG LEAN AND FOCUSED ON VALUABLE OUTCOMES

The job of a Product Owner is tough. At some point, Product Owners are going to disappoint at least one of their stakeholders as they make trade-offs between different Product Backlog items. Although the Product Owner makes the final decision on the ordering of the Product Backlog, collaboration with the stakeholders and the rest of the Scrum Team is important to support good decision-making, and effective facilitation can help with this.

We saw in the story that Ahmet was faced with a group of stakeholders who wanted more and more, risking the Product Backlog turning into a giant, uncontrolled monstrosity. It is beneficial to have stakeholder enthusiasm and abundant ideas for the new product, but just as important is talking about how the ideas fit in with the vision, desired benefits, and outcome the product should achieve. In the story, no one mentioned a Product Goal or a vision for who the new hotel would serve. Instead, the investors kept throwing in features they wanted without much thought about what outcomes they were trying to achieve with them.

A Product Owner may have their own opinions of what the Scrum Team should focus on. However, by facilitating conversations with the stakeholders, they can better understand what is really needed and why in the form of desired outcomes. This offers better clarity for the Product Owner and helps them make decisions that will deliver the most value.

The Product Owner makes these decisions transparent in the Product Backlog. When Product Backlogs become full of noise and grow so large that they become unwieldy, transparency becomes clouded, making it more complex for the Scrum Team to deliver value.

The Monstrous Product Backlog

I was a Scrum Master for a team working on a company's flagship product. On my first day, as I was getting to know the Scrum Team, I asked to see the Product Backlog. They opened the electronic tool and showed me a list of nearly 500 items. I couldn't hide my surprise at such a big backlog. Except that wasn't even the full story. What I was looking at was referred to as "the active part of the Product Backlog." The full Product Backlog had almost 10,000 items in it.

Any ideas that stakeholders had, any comments made in the Sprint Review or in other team interactions, any bugs that were raised (often in duplicate), any technical changes that the Developers wanted to make—all these things and more were constantly added to the Product Backlog. It was more a stream of consciousness than a true Product Backlog and, of course, it was impossible to manage effectively or have any notion of where the most valuable items were.

—David Spinks

TRY THIS! LEAD CONVERSATIONS TOWARD OUTCOMES USING EVIDENCE AND EMPIRICISM

Bringing everyone back to the Product Goal is a first step toward shifting the conversations to outcomes instead of output (features). Here are some techniques to aid you with this.

Facilitate the Development of a Product with a Lean UX Canvas

Building a new product is exciting, and often there is no shortage of ideas about what can be incorporated, as we saw in the story of the hotel. Ahmet's stakeholders focused on the features that the product should include without taking the time to reflect on what they were trying to achieve with the product and who it was for. Instead of creating a list of features, take an empirical approach and use hypotheses of value to guide a Scrum Team on what it should work on next.

The following questions can help a Scrum Team explore the direction it can take:

- What are we trying to achieve as a business?
- Who are we building our product for?
- What do our users want to achieve?
- What are their needs?
- What is stopping users from achieving their goals?
- How might we help them?
- How will we know our users have met their goals?

Although a Scrum Team and its stakeholders can use various techniques to explore these questions individually, using the Lean UX Canvas to facilitate discussions around these questions brings focus and some extra structure. The Lean UX Canvas is shown in Figure 5.1.

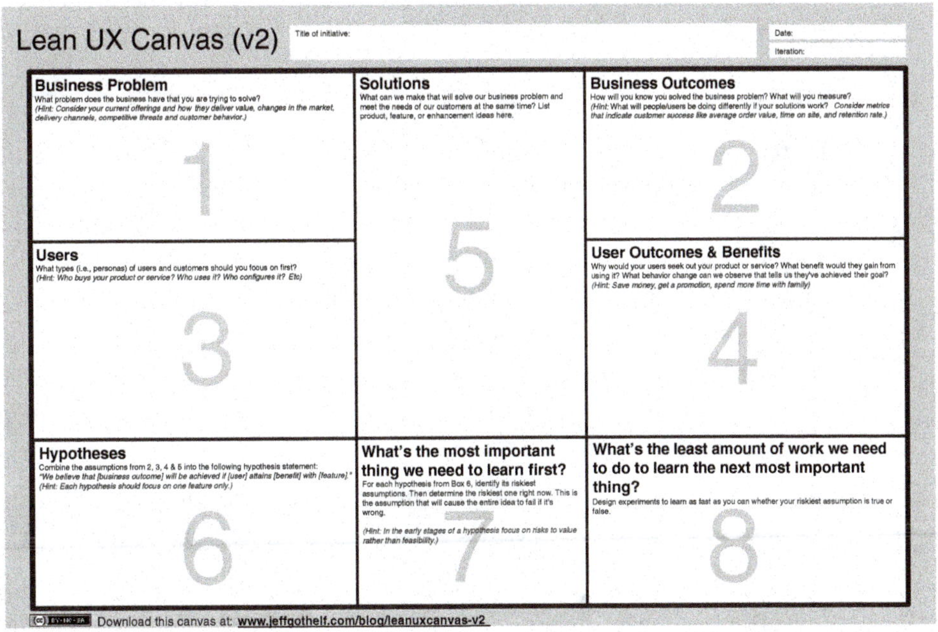

Figure 5.1 The Lean UX Canvas. Author: Jeff Gothelf. Source: https://jeffgothelf.com/blog/leanuxcanvas/.

License: Creative Commons Attribution-NonCommercial-ShareAlike 4.0 Unported (CC BY-NC-SA 4.0), https://creativecommons.org/licenses/by-nc-sa/4.0/.

When facilitating sessions using the Lean UX Canvas, we recommend integrating various techniques that have their origin in UX and design thinking. For example, empathy maps and personas help to build understanding and empathy with customers and users. We discuss empathy mapping in Chapter 4, "Facilitating Team Dynamics." Also, Scrum Teams can use problem statements to make the problem transparent that the product is being developed to solve. In addition, teams can use How Might We questions to stimulate motivation and innovation to solve them. We describe How Might We questions in Chapter 7, "Facilitating the Sprint Retrospective." Techniques such as worst possible ideas that we discuss in Chapter 1, and crazy 8s which we discuss in Chapter 4, unlock ideation and problem-solving. The participants in facilitated discussions around the Lean UX Canvas can bring all these together in hypotheses. The Scrum Team and the stakeholders use hypotheses to stimulate thought on what work the Scrum Team should undertake next to learn the most important thing. This is work to prove or disprove the hypothesized value so that when it comes to actually building features for the product, they can do it based on empirical evidence that what is being done is valuable.

Thirty-Five

Thirty-five, from Gamestorming,[1] is a technique that involves rating all group ideas. It is facilitated like this:

1. Participants write down their ideas on individual sticky notes or index cards. The participants could have generated these ideas using another technique in a previous session.

2. Each participant chooses a card that they believe is the most valuable. If the card they want to select has already been chosen, they look for the next best choice.

3. When everyone has a card participants form pairs, and for a short timebox of perhaps three minutes, they discuss what is on the cards in their hands. By the end of this timebox, they divide seven points between the two cards, based on the relative merits of each, and they write their scores on the

---

1. Gray, Dave, Sunni Brown, and James Macanufo (2010). *Gamestorming: A Playbook for Innovators, Rulebreakers, and Changemakers*. O'Reilly Media; 1st edition.

back of the card. Points can be divided between the options any way that the pair sees fit (4:3, 5:2, 7:0, and so on).

4. Each person swaps their card with their partner's. Then everyone forms new pairs for another round of scoring.

5. This is repeated for five rounds, so each person works with others to allocate a total of 35 points.

6. At the end of these scoring rounds, participants add up the totals on the back of the cards.

7. As a group, they can then sort the cards into an order based on the final scores.

Thirty-five is a useful facilitation technique that can be used to facilitate a session between the Scrum Team and its stakeholders to help inform the Product Owner about the ordering of the Product Backlog.

The Liberating Structure, 25/10 crowd sourcing technique is similar to thirty-five, although it has a few different rules, such as pairs giving each card a score out of 5.

Buy a Feature

The buy-a-feature technique was presented in the book *Innovation Games*.[2] In it, participants are given play money and come together to "buy" the features they want. Some of the items are priced so that no one person can buy those features on their own, leading the group to have to negotiate with each other and agree on top priorities.

Buy a feature can help the Product Owner understand what the stakeholders think is valuable. The items in the Product Backlog are given a price that can be set based on the Developers' sizing, but it does not have to be. It works well with 12 to 20 items and a group of 4 to 7 stakeholders, with each given a certain amount of play money.

---

2. Hohmann, Luke (2006). *Innovation Games: Creating Breakthrough Products Through Collaborative Play*. Addison-Wesley Professional.

The Product Owner may present the different Product Backlog items and their cost and then open the floor for the stakeholders to negotiate with each other to buy the features that are most important to them as a collective.

The learning for the Product Owner and the rest of the Scrum Team comes from observing the conversations between the stakeholders and their reasons for thinking certain Product Backlog items are valuable. These "why" conversations are what are really important. A Scrum Team that understands what stakeholders would like to achieve with certain features might be able to devise a better way to achieve the outcome. The stakeholders may even come up with ideas for splitting Product Backlog items into high-value smaller ones so they can "spend" their money more wisely.

WHEN THE USER EXPERIENCE IS FORGOTTEN

"Oh my," cries Katherine. "This is really annoying me now!"

"What *now?*" calls her partner Karol from the kitchen.

"This darn website. I'm trying to book our flights for our vacation. They don't make it easy!"

Karol walks into the living area of the apartment. Katherine is seated on the couch with her laptop on the coffee table in front of her. "Show me," says Karol.

"Well, first of all I wanted to compare options out of JFK, Newark, and LaGuardia. But I only have the option to search from one departure location."

"So just open another tab."

"I tried that," Katherine sighs. "When I do another search in another tab, the site is updated with the same result as what was on the first tab. It doesn't let me look at the two results side by side."

"Ugh. That is annoying."

"Anyway, I just ended up writing everything on paper. I found the flight I wanted to book. But then it automatically added check-in baggage, a meal, seat choice—all of which you of course have to pay more for! So, I had to go back and take all these extras off."

"I hate it when they do that."

"Yeah. So I removed all the extras and then went through to pay. And guess what?!"

"What?"

"It doesn't let you book without an account. When I created my account, the site lost the flight details I wanted to book, and now I have to start all over!"

"Oh no!"

"At least I have an account now. I'm signed in, so let me search for the flight details again and just get this done." Karol walks back to the kitchen as Katherine concentrates on her laptop.

"Oh, I don't believe this!" Karol hears Katherine shout from the next room. "You'll never guess what happened! Now it says there are no seats left!"

"No way!" Karol yells back.

"They must still be locked from when I was trying to book just now. For crying out loud! Who created this website?"

KEEPING THE USER FRONT AND CENTER

Many Scrum Teams focus on building and delivering features for their products. That is good unless they forget one crucial aspect: the end user! That is how products become bloated, overly complicated, and difficult to use. Lots of Scrum Teams write individual Product Backlog items as user stories, which can focus minds on the user, but teams often miss out on how to validate the assumed value. They also tend to forget about the bigger picture of the user's whole experience with the product.

The user story format focuses on the who, what, and why—who has a need, what they need, and why they need it. Various syntaxes are employed for user stories. An example is: *As a <type of user>, I want <something to be achieved>, so that <benefit is realized>*.

Scrum Teams can benefit from approaches to refining the Product Backlog that consider the outcomes that users are looking for from using the product.

TRY THIS! FACILITATING USER-CENTRIC PRODUCT BACKLOG REFINEMENT

The Scrum Team and the stakeholders should keep the end user of the product front and center when developing and refining the Product Backlog. This section discusses a couple of tools you can use to emphasize the focus on the end user of your product when facilitating Product Backlog refinement.

The Experience Now-Next-Later Roadmap

Unlike many other types of roadmaps that teams may use to plan out the delivery of features, this lightweight now-next-later roadmap focuses on the experience that the Scrum Team wants the user to have when using their product over time. This helps the team center on the user, giving clarity for near-term action and vision for the long-term desired user outcomes. One way to facilitate the creation of the experience now-next-later roadmap is to do the following:

1. Invite Scrum Team members and real end users of the product as participants.

2. Present the product or product idea.

3. Break down the group into smaller groups, and ensure that each small group has Scrum Team representatives and end users.

4. Ask participants to discuss in their groups and write down what they want to be able to achieve with the product on a sticky note. Participants should add their stickies to a board or a (virtual) wall. Remind participants that they should not add solutions or features but instead concentrate on what they, as a user, can do with the product.

5. Participants share the insights of user needs that they gathered so far with the whole group. They discuss, ask questions, and remove duplicates.

6. The facilitator or the participants draw three columns on the board or virtual wall and name the columns *Now*, *Next*, *Later*.

7. Participants order the insights into the appropriate columns. For example, when a team starts building a new product, it moves the stickies that represent the user's basic experience needs for the product into the Now column.

An example of the experience now-next-later roadmap is shown in Figure 5.2. The Scrum Team focuses on refining the items in the Now column in its refinement sessions. The advantage of this approach is that the Scrum Team is more likely to be focused on the why from the onset.

Our User Can...

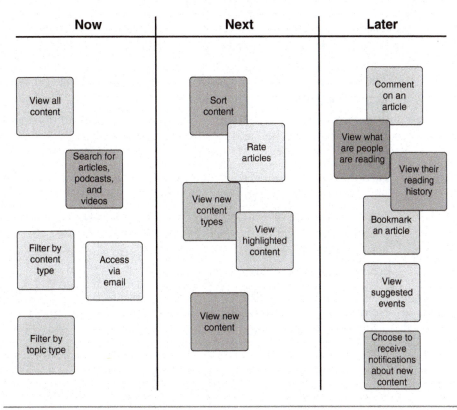

Figure 5.2 An example of the experience now-next-later roadmap.

The team regularly updates the roadmap when it learns more about the users and their interactions with the product.

Story Mapping

One of our favorite methods for focusing on outcomes is called story mapping, or to give it its full title user story mapping, a technique created and pioneered by Jeff Patton.[3]

---

3. Patton, Jeff (2014). *User Story Mapping: Discover the Whole Story, Build the Right Product*. O'Reilly Media.

Story maps describe a user's journey to reach a goal. This helps focus on what the user is trying to achieve and prevents teams from getting lost in debates over what features should be present and which should not. An example of a story map is shown in Figure 5.3.

Here is one way to facilitate a story mapping workshop that can be carried out with the members of a Scrum Team and their stakeholders:

1. The facilitator or an appropriate participant kicks things off with an introduction and shares the objective of the workshop. They should discuss what product participants will be focusing on in the session, the target user (user type), and the desired business benefit for the organization.

2. Participants start to map out the "narrative flow" or "backbone" on a (virtual) wall from left to right. These are the activities, at a high level, of the steps of a typical journey that the target user takes. These steps are ordered left to right by the sequence of what the user does. Participants may discover other types of users who complete similar journeys as they create their narrative flow.

3. Under each activity, participants add "user tasks" for what needs to happen for the user to be able to finish the step. For example, if the user wants to make payment, a user task could be "enter credit card details."

4. Participants can refine the user tasks where needed, such as when splitting some user tasks into smaller ones and adding detail. This is a great time for participants to explore and share their ideas and the opportunities they see for the product.

5. With a narrative flow in place and user tasks to complete each step for their user(s) in place, the participants order the user tasks under each activity by importance.

6. Participants then discuss which tasks a user absolutely must complete for each activity and visualize this by drawing a horizontal line across the story map. Everything above the line indicates what, at a minimum, the user needs to be able to do to reach their goal. This forms the basis for the participants to think about and identify the minimum set of features that their product needs to provide for that user.

7. Participants identify further horizontal divides across the story map to plan and visualize future versions and releases of the product.

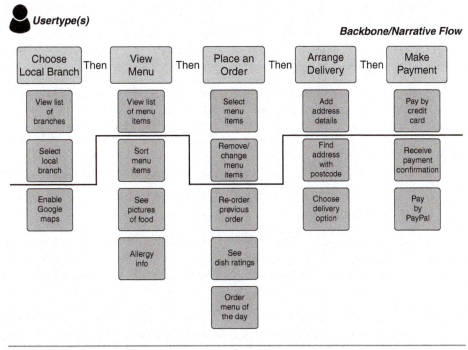

Figure 5.3 An example of a story map for ordering food online.

In our experience, the best story maps are those that the whole Scrum Team and stakeholders create collaboratively. The Scrum Team can add further detail to each of the user tasks, and these essentially become Product Backlog items. The story map itself is a great way of representing the Product Backlog. As such, it is continually revisited and evolves over time.

Scrum Teams that use Roman Pichler's product canvas can integrate their story map into the product canvas in the "big picture" section. We discussed Roman Pichler's product canvas in Chapter 1.

THE SCRUM TEAM THAT IS OBSESSED WITH ESTIMATING

Leo takes a long look at the clock on the wall. More out of agitation than anything else, he then looks at his watch. Unsurprisingly, it confirms what he already knows. *We have been at this for nearly three hours, and we have refined only two stories,* he thinks.

"Temi," says Brad, "you've gone for an estimate of 13 points again, even after the conversation we just had. Why?"

"I understand what everyone is saying," Temi replies, "but this bit of tech is still completely new to *us.*"

Alex jumps in, "Like we said earlier, we have all the documentation that explains how to integrate with it. If we follow the instructions, we should have no problems."

"*If,* Alex? *Should?* That sounds pretty speculative. Look, I'm just saying this is something we haven't done before, so we don't know what could happen. And we're going to have to test everything again to make sure it all still works."

Alex responds, "We've all thoroughly read the documentation. As we said in the last refinement session, nobody had any technical concerns. And we can all help with the testing. It's not like we need to test new functionality. It's just verifying everything we have already."

"Alright," says Brad, jumping in. "Now that we've just had *another* conversation about this Product Backlog item, let's do another round. Everyone, let's go to the cards."

Leo reaches for his 5 card for the third time for this Product Backlog item. As he does so, he glances again at the clock and sees that he and his four teammates have now been discussing this same story for more than an hour. He already knows that Temi will still go for a 13, and his teammates will go for a 5 again.

"Everyone have a number?" Brad asks. "Okay... three... two... one... reveal!" he calls, somehow still enthusiastically. Everyone holds up their cards. Leo was right. This time he can't disguise his frustration and lets out a huge sigh. The stalemate continues.

"We're spending so much time on this," Leo says. "I know the conversations we're having are useful, but there must be a better way…"

FOCUSING ON VALUABLE CONVERSATIONS THAT LEAD TO SHARED UNDERSTANDING

Leo and his team appear to be using the popular Planning Poker®[4] technique to size their Product Backlog items. Many Scrum Teams use this technique alongside some kind of relative size unit, such as story points or t-shirt sizes. However, these techniques are not part of Scrum. All Scrum says is that Product Backlog refining activities include sizing the Product Backlog items. The Developers who will be doing the work are responsible for this. The team in the story seemed to have misunderstandings about the purpose of sizing Product Backlog items. Some team members think items need to be sized so they can create an accurate estimate of the work. The use of the word *estimate* can reinforce that misunderstanding. Sizing helps Developers understand what is required and helps them decide on how much work they can take on during the Sprint.

We value any Product Backlog refinement approach that creates better transparency and understanding of Product Backlog items. In the story, instead of using Planning Poker® to create enough understanding to deem the item ready for the Sprint, Leo's team has fallen into the trap of endlessly arguing about the size of the item.

Scrum Teams should strike a delicate balance between doing enough refinement to ensure items are understood and ready for a Sprint and spending too much time striving for perfection. This can include Developers trying to reach total consensus on the size of an item or trying to understand everything that will be involved with doing the development work. We encourage Developers to embrace empiricism, the Scrum value of courage, and accept that some unknowns are always likely to emerge once the work has begun, no matter how much refinement they have done.

---

4. Planning Poker is a trademark of Mountain Goat Software.

TRY THIS! DOING JUST ENOUGH SIZING TO GET PRODUCT BACKLOG ITEMS TO READY

Many Scrum Teams' focus during Product Backlog refinement centers on sizing Product Backlog items. Whatever technique Developers use, they should build an understanding of the Product Backlog items through discussion, asking questions and challenging each other's and the Product Owner's assumptions. Stifling conversation or rushing a team to get to a size is poor facilitation.

Developers often size in story points using Planning Poker®, and when facilitated well, we believe it is still a powerful facilitation approach. What we like about it is that it invokes conversations that lead to better understanding of the work. In Planning Poker®, the Developers individually estimate the relative size of Product Backlog items using a set of Planning Poker® cards and, once revealed, the Developers discuss their differences. This leads to surfacing any assumptions or misunderstandings that the Developers may have, creating better shared understanding. The conversation is more important than the actual number the Developers agree to.

Developers sizing every Product Backlog using Planning Poker® can be time consuming, and some may even argue that it is arbitrary to size things with different story point values when dealing with complex environments and all the associated unpredictability that comes with it.

There are other alternatives to Planning Poker® and story points for sizing, and much has been written on them.[5] What follows are some alternative techniques. A facilitator should help the Developers explore the best approach for them for sizing.

Wall Estimating

Wall estimating is a technique that employs some of the white elephant principles that we discuss in Chapter 7. It works like this:

- Whatever relative size units the team uses, whether t-shirt sizes, story points, or something else, are drawn out on a wall, table, or a virtual space in separate columns.

---

5. For example, see Coleman, John (2022). "Talking About Sizing and Forecasting in Scrum." InfoQ. www.infoq.com/articles/sizing-forecasting-scrum/.

- A Developer takes one of the provided Product Backlog items and reads it aloud.
- The Developer then places the item in whichever column they think is a fair reflection of the relative size for that item and gives their reasoning.
- None of the other Developers speak; they are practicing active listening so that they get the opportunity to really understand the opinions of their peers.
- The process continues, each Developer taking a turn to place Product Backlog items and giving their reasons while the rest of the team listens.
- After a couple of rounds or so, Developers can choose to take the next item from the list, or they can use their turn to move any one item that has already been placed, again giving their reasons for doing so.
- If all items have been placed and a Developer is happy with where they all are, they can pass on their turn. Once all the Developers pass, they are done.

Wall estimation does not enable breaking down items, adding details, and so on, and it does not tease out assumptions and misunderstandings in the same way that Planning Poker® can. However, it is great for helping Developers size a number of Product Backlog items quickly, while still creating transparency and understanding between them, and encouraging active listening.

Right Sizing

Scrum only prescribes that Product Backlog items be sized and ready for the Sprint—namely, that the Developers have reasonable confidence that they can finish the Product Backlog item within a Sprint. It is for the Developers to determine if they have sufficient understanding of Product Backlog items to say that they meet this concept of "ready" through their involvement in refinement activities. A simple way to gauge the Developers' agreement of whether a particular Product Backlog item fits within a Sprint, is by carrying out a roman vote. Depending on the decision-making rule, the proposal either passes or fails. For more on roman voting and decision rules, see Chapter 4.

If the Developers decide that a Product Backlog item is too big and does not fit within a Sprint, the Scrum Team needs to break it down into smaller chunks. A Scrum Team can do this in many different ways. It can explore a variety of techniques for breaking down Product Backlog items during Product Backlog refinement. One resource to help with this is a poster from The Liberators: "10 Powerful Strategies to Break Down Product Backlog Items."[6]

KEYS TO FACILITATING EFFECTIVE PRODUCT BACKLOG REFINEMENT

Scrum does not prescribe how Product Backlog refinement must be conducted. It should be facilitated with the purpose of generating transparency and shared understanding. The following are some key considerations for facilitating effective Product Backlog refinement.

FACILITATE FOR COLLABORATION

When Scrum Teams refine the Product Backlog, they gain a deeper understanding of the problem space in which they are working. Collaboration between the Product Owner who has the vision for the product and the Developers who will do the work to fulfill the vision is key. Involving stakeholders—which might include customers and end users—in Product Backlog refinement can also be really valuable. Refinement should be facilitated in a way that is collaborative and gives everyone a voice to ask questions and share thoughts.

The Scrum Team loses an opportunity for creative thinking as a whole if a Product Owner or a delegate creates Product Backlog items in isolation and then merely presents them to the rest of the team. This is particularly true if the Product Backlog items are presented as ready-made solutions for implementations instead of hypotheses of value.

Product Backlog refinement does not always need to involve the whole Scrum Team at the same time. It does not have to only take the form of a meeting,

---

6. The Liberators. "10 Powerful Strategies to Break Down Product Backlog Items." https://shop.theliberators.com/products/experiment-10-powerful-strategies-to-break-down-product-backlog-items.

where the whole Scrum Team sits down together, looks at the Product Backlog items in turn to add details, breaks them down, and sizes them. Refinement involves any work that is done to the Product Backlog items to help get them ready to be pulled into a Sprint. This might involve one or more members of the team. It might involve specialist skills such as carrying out user research, stakeholder collaboration, feasibility analysis, risk analysis, business or system analysis, or high-level architecture or design, to name a few. Ideally, this is carried out with involvement from the rest of the team as much as possible, and when it cannot be, the results should be reviewed as a team.

Alternative Approaches to Product Backlog Refinement

In my time working with countless Scrum Teams, I have experienced many different ways of carrying out refinement. Quite commonly, it has been the whole Scrum Team coming together in a meeting, perhaps for one afternoon during the Sprint, and working on the Product Backlog. In other teams there have been people specially skilled in analysis or user research, for example, and most of their work could be called Product Backlog refinement. The key is what they were doing was shared with the rest of the team for transparency. It was even better when other Developers got involved with some of this work.

I've had other teams in fast-paced changing environments where refinement would be done every day, straight after the Daily Scrum for up to 10 minutes, and the whole team would discuss new information or requests, and we would immediately adapt the Product Backlog.

Other variations of Product Backlog refinement that I have used with teams include the so-called three amigos, in which a specialist from each area of the team, such as an analyst, coder, and quality assurance person, refine together with the Product Owner and later share the adapted Product Backlog to the rest of the team for feedback and discussion.

When it comes to Product Backlog refinement, I always encourage Scrum Teams to do what works for them. If what they are doing is not working, they should simply try something else.

—David Spinks

PERFECTION IS THE ENEMY OF GOOD ENOUGH

In an effort to maximize their understanding, some Scrum Teams spend many hours discussing and dissecting Product Backlog items, imagining all sorts of scenarios of what might happen when they do the work—often for the purpose of perfecting their sizing.

Often team members have different levels of comfort when it comes to ambiguity. This can become especially apparent when facilitating Product Backlog refinement. Some team members are comfortable with little detail and may get impatient with others who insist on exploring everything there is to know about a Product Backlog item. Here, the facilitator needs to ensure a good balance, allowing everyone to have a voice and keep focused on the topic without going into every single detail.

A goal of Product Backlog refinement is for the Scrum Team to get Product Backlog items ready for a Sprint. This means that the Developers are reasonably confident that they can complete the Product Backlog item within a Sprint. Developers agreeing collaboratively that they can finish an item within a Sprint is an act of sizing in itself.

MAKE DECISIONS TRANSPARENT IN THE PRODUCT BACKLOG

Facilitating collaborative interactions between Scrum Team members and stakeholders involves much more than facilitating what happens in meetings between the two parties. It includes ensuring that outcomes are shared, communicated, and made accessible. Scrum's vehicle for providing transparency of the decisions made as part of Product Backlog refinement is of course the Product Backlog.

Good Scrum Teams keep stakeholders informed of changes to the Product Backlog and Product Backlog items where relevant. We discuss stakeholder mapping and decision matrices in Chapter 1. They can be great tools for a Scrum Team to evolve strategies for different types of stakeholders. This could include deciding which stakeholders need to be made aware of results from Product Backlog refinement activities or identifying stakeholders to involve in Product Backlog refinement.

Some stakeholders will care about particular features and particular Product Backlog items, not least when it comes to Product Backlog ordering. Besides making the results of decisions transparent, it can help for the Scrum Team to be able to explain why certain decisions are being made.

FACILITATE SPACE FOR ONGOING STAKEHOLDER COLLABORATION

Stakeholder feedback need not only be about the latest Increment.

Sometimes stakeholders can pressure a Scrum Team to justify the order of the Product Backlog. A Scrum Team feeling the need to justify the placement of a particular item in the ordering in the Product Backlog should explore why the item is important to a stakeholder. The principle of healthy facilitation includes respecting different individuals' perspectives, and it might just be that the item is important to the stakeholder for a good reason. Instead of a presentation by the Product Owner explaining their decisions on the order of the Product Backlog, the Scrum Team can collaborate with the stakeholders and have an open discussion about whether they feel that items are in the right place.

Good stakeholder collaboration can be thought of as part of Product Backlog refinement.

CONCLUSION

Effective Scrum Teams invest in refining their Product Backlog to create a shared understanding of their work and goals because it helps them decide which work is most important to pursue that can fit into a Sprint.

In this chapter, we provided different facilitation techniques for a facilitator to encourage collaboration between the Developers and Product Owner as well as tips on how to boost a Scrum Team's understanding of the users and other stakeholders of their product. Both aspects are important for Developers to deliver value.

If your Scrum Team does Product Backlog refinement but Developers often disagree on what can be Done in the Sprint during the Sprint Planning event, they likely do not have a shared understanding of what the work is. The Scrum Team should consider regularly iterating on Product Backlog items as their understanding of them evolves. People think at different speeds and in different ways, as we discussed in Chapter 4.

FACILITATING THE SPRINT REVIEW

The Scrum Team and its stakeholders inspect a Done Increment as part of the Sprint Review.

The Sprint Review is a collaborative working session between the Scrum Team and its stakeholders during which they inspect the latest Increment. Typically this includes a demonstration. As a result of this inspection, they discuss what was achieved in the Sprint, any changes in their environment, and explore potential adaptations of the Product Backlog as the team works toward the Product Goal.

Although the Sprint Review is not the only time when the Scrum Team can interact with stakeholders, it is the prescribed event for the Scrum Team and stakeholders to discuss any new information that might affect what should be the next valuable items to work on for the product Increment. Information such as changes in the market or feedback from users along with other stakeholder feedback on the latest Increment results in the output of the event, which is an adapted Product Backlog that represents the team's plan going forward.

Picture the Sprint Reviews you have attended. Were they run-throughs of every Product Backlog item completed by the team that Sprint? Were they just demonstrations of the latest work by the Scrum Team? Were stakeholders disengaged? We have had our share of these types of Sprint Reviews also. In this chapter, we share how Scrum Teams can use facilitation to better navigate conversations and increase the effectiveness of their Sprint Reviews.

THE SPRINT REVIEW WITH LITTLE STAKEHOLDER PARTICIPATION

Members of Team Hurricane feel like they are finishing a good Sprint and are excited for the upcoming Sprint Review. Not only did they meet their Sprint Goal, they also completed all the forecasted Product Backlog items for the Sprint, and they pulled in an extra item and got that one Done too.

At the Sprint Review, Nicole, Hurricane's Product Owner, summarizes the Sprint Goal and gives an overview of each of the completed Product Backlog items. "Any questions?" she asks. She shrugs off the long silence and blank faces. She continues, "Francesca, I'll hand this to you now to demonstrate the result of all the work the team finished."

"Right. Let me share my screen," says Francesca, one of Hurricane's Developers. "Please jump in with any questions, comments, or feedback you might have. All the Developers from the team are on the call so we can capture any thoughts you have." For the next 15 minutes, Francesca's voice is the only one heard in the Sprint Review.

"And that's it!" says Francesca when she is done. She lets the silence hang for a few moments. "Hello? Is there anybody there? Hmm... is my internet down?"

"We're all still here!" Nicole says as soon as she manages to unmute herself. "Thank you, Francesca. What does everyone think? Any feedback?"

Silence.

"Are you happy? We are going to release this. Does anyone have concerns?"

"It looks good," someone says. Nicole is not sure whose voice it is but sees Ricky, one of the managers in the call center, nodding his head. It is hard to discern what the rest of the stakeholders think; some have their cameras turned off and are also on mute.

"If anyone would like to speak, you need to come off mute!" calls out Wolfgang, one of Hurricane's Developers and the team's Scrum Master.

Nothing happens.

"Okay. Well, that is the product Increment then," says Nicole. "I'm sharing the Product Backlog on the screen now. As you can see, nothing has changed since the last Sprint Review. Does anyone have any input on the ordering or content? I'm happy to go through anything again if needed."

The only response to the question is two people leaving the call.

"Well, thanks everyone. See you in two weeks at the next Sprint Review, I guess. Team Hurricane, do you mind staying on the call?" asks Nicole.

After all the stakeholders leave, Nicole looks at the other team members. "Thanks for running that, Francesca."

Francesca gives a thumbs-up and replies, "Is it me, or does anyone else feel that we are wasting our time with these reviews? We never get any feedback. None of our stakeholders say anything. We might as well not bother."

"I've been thinking the same," Wolfgang adds.

Nicole asks, "So what do we do to get more engagement and value out of our Sprint Reviews?"

GATHERING VALUABLE FEEDBACK AT THE SPRINT REVIEW

The feedback loops in Scrum help teams improve both their product and their way of working. Although it is not the only time to engage with stakeholders, the Sprint Review is the formal opportunity for the Scrum Team to gather feedback on its latest work from the stakeholders. This can include customers and end users. If nobody gives the Scrum Team feedback, or if the Scrum Team does not invite feedback, it misses an opportunity to review its progress toward its Product Goal.

Nicole asked the right question at the end of the story. Many Scrum Teams are tempted to drop or cancel Scrum events when they lack focus, purpose, and value, especially when participants are disengaged. However, by doing so they miss an opportunity to inspect and adapt. When Scrum Teams struggle with getting the value they seek from the Sprint Review, effective facilitation can help them structure it so they can receive the feedback they need.

A Sprint Review can feel lackluster for several reasons:

- The Scrum Team or stakeholders may not understand the purpose of the Sprint Review.
- The Scrum Team dives too deeply into details or technical aspects, losing stakeholder attention and their ability to contribute in a meaningful way.
- The event is facilitated in a way that offers little opportunity for stakeholders to interact with the team, and more importantly with the product Increment that is the result of the work of the Sprint.
- Sprint Reviews are consistently conducted without the right stakeholders attending or contributing in some manner. Often we see this happen when only internal stakeholders attend. Although internal stakeholders provide helpful information and ideas on how the Scrum Team can improve the product, they may not be the customers or end users who ultimately determine the product's value.

Whatever the reason, the Scrum Team should experiment with techniques and facilitation that put the appropriate stakeholders at the heart of the Sprint Review.

Preparing for the Sprint Review

I spoke with a Scrum Master who told me about how their team changed how they would prepare for the Sprint Review. One team he worked with had a few Sprint Reviews where the demonstrations went wrong. The team talked about this in the Sprint Retrospective and decided to take action. It set up a short session the day before the Sprint Review for team members to come together and decide what they were going to show and who was going to demonstrate it. The team added the details to a wiki page. This enabled the volunteers to get themselves ready for the demonstration, making sure they had the links and data on hand to avoid clumsy delays. The demonstrations went much more smoothly after that.

Another of the Scrum Master's teams found it useful to decide during the Sprint which Product Backlog items it would demonstrate and tag them in the Sprint Backlog so it could identify them easily. This team also got into the habit of adding the demonstration notes to the item during the Sprint—it just became part of the work to develop and test the item.

—Glaudia Califano

TRY THIS! STAKEHOLDER ENGAGEMENT THROUGH CONTRIBUTION

Here are some ideas for facilitating the Sprint Review to help transform stakeholders from being passive spectators to becoming involved and engaged. The aim is to put stakeholder feedback and input on the product Increment at the center of the event, helping the Scrum Team plan its future goals.

Invite the Right Stakeholders and Engage Them Before the Sprint Review

To get the most value out of a Sprint Review, the Scrum Team needs to make sure that it invites the right people at the right time. The Scrum Team should deliberately invite those who can provide valuable feedback by considering the product and where it is in its lifecycle and the Product Goal. Understanding who to invite is an important aspect of facilitation because the interactions within the event very much depend on the participants.

In Chapter 2, "Facilitating Sprint Planning," we discuss the stakeholder invite as a facilitation technique for the Scrum Team to craft its Sprint Goal. The result of this activity, which envisioned the outcome of the Sprint during Sprint Planning, can be used as the opening of the invitation to the stakeholders for the Sprint Review. We have found that preparing stakeholders for the Sprint Review sets up better interactions. The team might include preparatory questions for the stakeholders to think about, such as "What do you hope to get from the Sprint Review?" and "What valuable contribution can you bring?" The team can let the stakeholders know that contributions can relate to anything that concerns the product, such as the Product Goal, the Sprint Goal, the Increment, market conditions, customer behaviors, and so on.

When the team gives stakeholders context before the Sprint Review, asking them to think about how they can contribute, they improve the chance of higher engagement during the event. A Scrum Team thrives on the feedback from stakeholders, so those who contribute to the Sprint Review with feedback bring value. By prompting stakeholders to ask themselves what value they will bring to the Sprint Review and how they can contribute to making the product better, the team is helping stakeholders decide for themselves whether they should attend. Other open-ended questions for potential attendees to reflect upon include these:

- How would you like to help the team increase value, decrease waste, and manage risk?
- How can you participate in the Sprint Review to help the team make sustainable, measurable progress toward the Product Goal?
- How can the team know if they are receiving and giving value from and to the attendees in the Sprint Review?

These questions can also be revisited at the start of the Sprint Review as part of making connections and sharing expectations. Inevitably, some people may still attend the Sprint Review who cannot provide direct input or valuable feedback, which can distract from the event. As a facilitator, learn why they are there. They may attend because they want to show interest in the team's work or are curious about the progress of the product. If the Scrum Team finds that interested yet not necessary participants continue to attend the

Sprint Review and it is okay with this then, as a facilitator, experiment with creative techniques that allow them to participate but ultimately do not distract from the purpose of the event.

Sprint Reviews with Participant and Observer Roles

I worked with a Scrum Team that was a few Sprints into a new initiative. The participants would start their Sprint Reviews, excited to share what was Done during the Sprint and collect feedback so they could move forward, but they would often end the event a little discouraged.

At the review, a mixture of people would show up—some customers, some managers, and colleagues from other Scrum Teams. The Scrum Team interacted with the customers and collected feedback, but often awkward moments surfaced when the team posed questions to the whole group. Most attendees, with the exception of the customers, would be multitasking and working on other things. This was obvious because we were all attending virtually with cameras on, so you could see people looking somewhere else or typing.

This really distracted the team and was demotivating them. They felt that it also gave a poor image to their customers who were attending. However, the Scrum Team learned that the managers and their colleagues wanted to attend the Sprint Reviews because, while they clearly didn't have input or feedback to provide, they were curious about what the new initiative was and how everything was going. They thought they were being supportive by attending.

The team decided that it didn't want to ask people not to attend their Sprint Reviews, but it did want to remove the awkwardness and distractions. So it started sending out brief updates for the company newsletter on what its Sprint Goals were. The team also asked the Scrum Master to remind everyone about the purpose of Sprint Reviews.

For a few Sprints, at the start of each Sprint Review, the Scrum Team would welcome everyone and then announce that some attendees were there only to listen. Those people were politely asked to turn off their cameras to avoid distracting those who were there to engage and the person facilitating. This worked out for them. It was an easy and creative solution.

—Patricia Kong

Facilitate Making Connections and Share Expectations

Prior to the Sprint Review, ask attendees to consider one or two questions that we provided in the previous section or other questions you find appropriate.

In the Sprint Review itself:

1. The facilitator reminds everyone of the Product Goal and the Sprint Goal to provide focus.

2. As a connection exercise the facilitator asks participants, including members of the Scrum Team, to discuss in pairs how they would answer the questions they were asked to consider prior to the Sprint Review, such as "By the end of the Sprint Review, what is the best outcome you would hope for?" and "What valuable contribution can you bring to achieve this outcome?" Each person has two minutes to share their answers.

3. Each person finds a new person to pair with. Again, they share their answers for two minutes each.

4. Repeat for a third round.

This activity can be used as a warmup, and it helps to promote participation and engagement from everyone from the beginning of the Sprint Review. Also, by sharing ideas on how to contribute in multiple pairs, people may build on each other's ideas and perspectives, and they may feel more compelled to act in the way they say they will.

This activity can be used standalone even if the Scrum Team did not send a stakeholder email invite with the questions in advance. It can be followed up with further promotion of stakeholder participation by putting stakeholders in the driver's seat.

Put Your Stakeholders in the Driver's Seat During Sprint Review

Instead of members of the Scrum Team talking about what they worked on during the Sprint and demonstrating the results, this facilitation technique, as the name suggests, involves putting the stakeholders in the driver's seat. Whether the team and stakeholders are working together in person or virtually, this approach gets stakeholders involved beyond watching demonstrations by getting them to use the product.

The Benefits of Having Stakeholders Interact with the Product

We had two main stakeholders for the product of one of the first Scrum Teams I worked with. The Scrum Team and these stakeholders were new to Scrum. Everyone was open to implementing the mechanics of Scrum, but they seemed uncomfortable with the Sprint Reviews. Each time, the team was nervous about the event, and the stakeholders watched us demo functionality without giving much away. They offered little feedback, and we were really unsure if our work was meeting their expectations.

After about three Sprints of this happening, we tried something different for the Sprint Review. After the usual introductions, where we highlighted the Sprint Goal and the Product Backlog items that were part of the Sprint, we asked one of the stakeholders to volunteer to use the presentation laptop and try out the latest product Increment of the software. One of the Developers guided them through it. As the stakeholder went through the application, they made mistakes, asked questions, were uncomfortable, but also seemed delighted at other parts. The level of interaction was transformed, and we continued to use this approach for most Sprint Reviews going forward. The Sprint Review changed from something that the Scrum Team was nervous about to a place of mutual learning. We learned so much more about our stakeholders' needs, and they learned a lot about the product as it evolved.

—David Spinks

Chartwriting

Have someone with a view of everything capture the ideas and feedback in real time!

Sam Kaner explains chartwriting in his book *Facilitator's Guide to Participatory Decision-Making*.[1] Chartwriting, also known as scribing, is the practice of capturing people's comments. It should not be confused with taking meeting minutes. The primary purpose of chartwriting is not for record-keeping, but as a way to increase participation and engagement. When people see that their ideas and feedback are being captured by someone in the group in real time where everyone can see them, they are more likely to feel heard. Sometimes people find it difficult to let go of an idea and are unable to move

---

1. Kaner, Sam (2014). *Facilitator's Guide to Participatory Decision-Making*, Third Edition. Jossey-Bass.

on, such as in a Sprint Review when a stakeholder has a strong opinion. Chartwriting can change their behavior. Seeing their thoughts captured can free their mind for other contributions, increasing further engagement and participation.

The facilitator can do the chartwriting, but it may be helpful for someone else to do it so that the facilitator can focus their attention on the group and its interactions.

Whoever is doing the chartwriting should take the following guidelines into consideration:

- Refrain from making assumptions; instead, write down the contributor's exact words when possible. If a sentence is too long or complex, paraphrase or summarize it, but ensure that the contributor has agreed that the shortened version is a reflection of what they want to say.
- Treat all contributions and contributors equally.
- Take a neutral stance, and refrain from judgment. It is up to the group as a collective to decide which ideas and feedback are valuable.
- Ensure what is captured is visible to everyone. For example, when recording on flipchart paper, hang the output on the wall so that pages are visible to everyone at all times.
- Learn chartwriting techniques and tools, such as the use of different letterings, colors, formats, and icons.

Perfection Game and What? So What? Now What?

Most Scrum Teams demonstrate their work and then ask for feedback in an open forum during a Sprint Review with a question like, "So, what does everyone think?" This approach may exclude people who are anxious about how their feedback may be taken. The question is also broad, which can be positive, but it may be unhelpful in generating focused feedback for the Scrum Team. Some facilitation techniques that you can experiment with to mitigate these risks include the perfection game and What? So What? Now What?

For these activities, the facilitator needs to prepare a shared space where stakeholders are invited to leave their feedback. This can be on the wall or in a virtual tool.

In the perfection game the feedback wall has three prompting questions along the lines of these:

- On a scale from 1 to 10, where 10 represents perfection, how would you rate the latest product Increment?
- What did you like about it?
- If you did not score it a 10, what would be needed to make it perfect?

Often when people are asked to rate things, they give a top score without much consideration. Asking people a question about what is missing to make it perfect prompts deeper thinking and unveils feedback and ideas that may have otherwise remained hidden.

Nothing Is Perfect!

I was involved in the development of a new training course. We ran a few beta classes, primarily to get feedback on what people thought of the class and to learn how we could make it better. At the end we asked people to rate the class from 1 to 10. We kept getting scores of 9s and 10s, which was great for our egos but didn't really tell us anything. We changed the feedback mechanism for the next classes and used the perfection game. The classes started scoring 7s and 8s even though nothing else had changed. But we actually got really useful comments about why they were not scoring 10s. The perfection game really made people think about how the class could be made better.

—Patricia Kong

Another type of feedback wall where participants display their feedback is the What? So What? Now What? technique from Liberating Structures. These three questions are used as prompts:

- What? What stood out for you?
- So what? Why was this important to you?
- Now what? What follow-up actions should there be?

On the feedback wall, a facilitator can create different areas or columns with these three questions and invite participants to consider their answers and post them on the wall in the appropriate area. What are important are the reflections, the shared transparency of the responses, and, of course, the consideration of the follow-up actions after the session.

During a Sprint Review, the prompt of So What? can be used to have stakeholders think about how they might use the latest Increment, and Now What? can be used for the stakeholders to think about what the Scrum Team can do next to build upon what is important to them.

The perfection game can also be used in a Sprint Retrospective where the facilitator can ask the Scrum Team to rate how the Sprint went and what was missing to make it perfect. Similarly, What? So What? Now What? can be used in the Sprint Retrospective for a Scrum Team to reflect on its processes and tools, for example.

THE SPRINT REVIEW WHERE NOTHING IS DONE

Team Strike Force has been working hard over the last Sprint and the whole team is feeling under pressure. Team members collectively feel progress is being made, and they know that they are learning a lot—about Scrum, working with each other, their product, the users of their product, and the expectations of their stakeholders. However, they have a sense of trepidation as they gather for their latest Sprint Review. They had a few challenges this Sprint and don't quite have a Done Increment.

Agnes, one of the Strike Force Developers, leads the way into the meeting room ahead of the rest of the team. The main stakeholders for their product—Gem, the company's Chief Operating Officer and Daria, the Chief Finance Officer are already in the room.

Agnes sets up her laptop while Darren, one of the other Developers on the team, briefly welcomes the attendees.

"Agnes, are you ready to show what we've been working on?" Darren asks nervously.

"Yes," says Agnes. Before anyone says anything else, Agnes runs through a presentation, showing the results in the user interface of the work-in-progress application. "As you can see, it is working, but we've only verified it in Internet Explorer. We didn't have access to the range of mobile devices we wanted to test on. And our machines are locked from using any other browser."

"And, unfortunately, we didn't have time to run stress tests to be sure that the site will still be stable with the new feature with our usual volume of visitors," Darren adds.

"Okay," says Daria. "It looks fine, though. So I'm happy to sign this off."

"Me too. Go ahead and release it!" says Gem.

"Hold on," says Matt, the team's Scrum Master. "The Sprint Review is not a stage gate and—"

Gem cuts him off. "So this will be in production by the end of today? This Scrum thing is great!"

"Well," says Agnes, "I just want to make it clear again that we only tested in Internet Explorer and we didn't run any stress tests. We need to finish all this testing for us to consider the work Done."

"But you did test it?" asks Daria.

"Yes, but that was only functional testing on Internet Explorer to see if it worked. It is not really Done."

"It looks done to me!" says Gem.

Darren chimes in, "We won't be comfortable releasing it until we have finished all our testing."

"I'm sure it will be fine!" says Daria. "Scrum is all about taking risks, right? Just catch up with the testing in the next Sprint. We want this in production by the end of today."

The members of team Strike Force feel overwhelmed and stay quiet.

HELPING STAKEHOLDERS UNDERSTAND THE PURPOSE OF THE SPRINT REVIEW

To avoid confusion and uncomfortable situations, the overall guidance from Scrum is *not* to show work at the Sprint Review that is not Done. We saw in the story that Team Strike Force was pressured to release an Increment that was not Done. Scrum is not about taking risks as Daria stated, but quite the opposite. It is about managing and controlling risks. Undone work should not be released because of the risks involved: poor quality, the potential impact on users and customers, and loss of transparency on the actual progress being made.

Some education may be needed for stakeholders of Scrum Teams to understand Scrum, and good facilitation of the Sprint Review can go a long way. To make it a more valuable event, the Scrum Team should garner feedback on the latest Done work and focus stakeholder attention on value, challenges, and risks. When the Scrum Team is transparent about its challenges, it may even discover that some of its stakeholders can help mitigate risks and remove impediments.

Many Scrum Teams or their stakeholders do not want to spend time discussing the team's challenges. But in avoiding such conversations, the fundamental issues that prevent real progress from being made are not transparent, storing up problems for the future. Undone work accumulates, quality drops, trust erodes, and stakeholders and customers become unhappy.

TRY THIS! STAKEHOLDER COLLABORATION OVER STAKEHOLDER ATTENDANCE

Stage gates, milestones, and progress reports are traditional management tools used to demonstrate the progress being made and the current state of affairs. In the absence of any of these in Scrum, companies often revert to using the Sprint Review as a mechanism to fill the gaps. When stakeholders approach the Sprint Review with this traditional mindset, a Scrum Master has a teaching opportunity with them about the framework and empiricism. Until then, a facilitator must guide conversations back to what really matters during the Sprint Review: Done, value, feedback, risks and adaptation. The conversation may feel uncomfortable. The following ideas can help.

Transparency of Done and Undone

Many Scrum Teams are tempted to show and discuss partly completed work in the Sprint Review for different reasons, such as to get feedback on what has been completed so far or just to show that they have been working. However, when a team shows incomplete work, they risk confusing stakeholders about the true progress being made. Scrum is clear about the importance of being transparent about what is Done and what is not.

Our guidance is to simply state the Sprint Goal and the forecasted Product Backlog items for the Sprint at the start of the Sprint Review and make it clear which ones were Done and will be inspected as part of the product Increment and which ones were not.

We always recommend that teams keep stakeholders engaged during the Sprint. Remember that the Sprint Review is the one prescribed opportunity for a Scrum Team to meet with its stakeholders, but this does not preclude interactions during the Sprint that could include showing progress of work and getting feedback as the development work progresses.

Whoever is facilitating the Sprint Review should make clear that only those items that meet the Definition of Done will be formally inspected, and the Sprint Review is the opportunity and invitation for stakeholders to give feedback and influence the adaptation of the Product Backlog.

Make Challenges Transparent

When long-standing systemic issues beyond the Scrum Team's control prevent them from delivering valuable work, the Sprint Review can be a good place to make these transparent. A facilitated discussion can help everyone understand the problems and the risks involved, and a Scrum Team may even be able to get help from influential stakeholders to resolve impediments.

During the Sprint Review, set some time aside to facilitate a timeboxed discussion between the Scrum Team and stakeholders about which work was not completed and why. This is important information to share and learn from for the future.

One way to do this is to write down on a separate sticky note or card each challenge that the team ran into when trying to complete the work of the Sprint that is still left unsolved. These can then be posted on a physical or virtual board for everyone to see. These should be long-standing challenges that the Scrum Team identifies and cannot deal with itself, with a risk that they will prohibit future work from being completed.

By making these systemic challenges transparent, and specifically at the Sprint Review, help or a solution could be offered by one or more of the stakeholders to resolve the issues. For example, in the case of Team Strike Force, one of the stakeholders might happen to be the head of procurement. The stakeholder might be keen to see a particular feature Done that would help their procurement team make better deals with its suppliers; in that case, they may do what they can to influence the process to get the team mobile devices to test on. Or someone from security might be able to do something about the access restrictions to other browsers on the Developers' machines.

Risks and Their Impact on Longer-Term Forecasts

At the Sprint Review, a perfectly valid conversation between the team and stakeholders is around long-term planning. Typically, internal and external stakeholders want to have some idea of what the future looks like, however uncertain. In the Sprint Review, the Scrum Team resets stakeholder expectations based on new learning. Adjustments to the Product Backlog and future plans can be made in collaboration with the stakeholders, with the latest understanding of how the Scrum Team is progressing.

Some may consider such long-term thinking as inherently anti-agile. However, a Scrum Team needs to have direction so that it aligns with strategic goals, and this is provided by the Product Goal in Scrum. A path to chaos is disregarding what the future might hold and failing to monitor the progress toward a strategic goal. Therefore, we believe it is important to share the latest updated forecasts for transparency, consideration of progress toward the Product Goal, and as a conversation starter.

Many times, the conversation stops at the point of a forecast being produced. However, from an Agile perspective, this is where the conversation should begin. The forecast can be used to facilitate a conversation with prompting questions such as these:

- Where are the risks and impediments that might cause the forecast to be wrong?
- What are the implications if the forecast is wrong?

This mindset helps to shift thinking from adherence to a plan to driving improvement.

KEYS TO FACILITATING AN EFFECTIVE SPRINT REVIEW

We have explored some uses of facilitation techniques for the Sprint Review and how they might help with some of the common challenges with the event. This section looks at some of the key factors to consider when facilitating the Sprint Review.

CREATE A LEARNING SPACE

Some terms associated with Scrum become so ingrained into the culture and language of so many teams that people come to believe they are actually part of the Scrum framework. The end of Sprint demo and the show and tell are a couple examples of names that people use to describe a meeting near the end of the Sprint where the work of the Sprint is shown.

Demonstration, demo, and show and tell all imply a one-way conversation. People come to the event, interpreting it to be a place where they will passively see a presentation of the latest version of the product.

As well as reviewing the Increment, create a collaborative learning space in which stakeholders and the team can learn. The Sprint Review is the opportunity to share learning, which could be product development challenges, feature usage, changes in customer behavior or expectations, shifts in market conditions, or anything else that may require changes to the plan going ahead in the form of adaptations to the Product Backlog.

ENABLE INTERACTION AND COLLABORATION

The Sprint Review is a collaborative working session between the Scrum Team and its stakeholders. In our experience, the more stakeholders are inspired to contribute to the Sprint Review the better.

Ensure stakeholders are aware of the Sprint Goal before the Sprint Review and prompt them to think about how they will contribute to the event. One of the main purposes of the Sprint Review is to garner feedback, and nothing beats putting the product into the stakeholders' hands so they actually experience it for themselves. Rather than following a script, task them with using the product, and just observe them. Is the product intuitive for them? Do they have a good experience? Does the product solve a need? How might the product be improved for them? As a facilitator, work with the team to make stakeholders part of finding ways to improve the product. Try to make it an engaging, valuable, and collaborative session so that ultimately the Scrum Team can update the Product Backlog based on valuable feedback and the latest information available as they work toward the Product Goal.

ENGAGE THE RIGHT STAKEHOLDERS AT THE RIGHT TIME

To create an engaging session where everyone participates, you need to make sure you have the right people at the Sprint Review. Inviting the right people at the right time is essential for both stakeholders and the Scrum Team. The Scrum Team relies on valuable feedback, and stakeholders without a stake may not be the right people to have at the event. Having the wrong people is likely to cause low engagement, and they and the Scrum Team may be left wondering why they are there at all. Work with the Scrum Team to decide how to facilitate these types of sessions. Should reviews be invite-only? Should they be open but with constraints?

Stakeholders is a broad term, so what does it mean to be a Scrum Team's stakeholder? For us, the answer is *anyone who is impacted by, or anyone who has an influence on, the product of the Scrum Team.*

Not all stakeholders are equal. Some need to know a lot of detail about the Scrum Team's product and the progress that the Scrum Team is making. Others only care about certain aspects around the product, such as financials, and are less concerned about the product itself. The Scrum Team is responsible for how it collaborates with all its stakeholders, and this may well include doing much more than just inviting all stakeholders to the Sprint Review. We discuss stakeholder maps, decision matrices, and the how long has it been tool in Chapter 1, "Facilitating Alignment," as techniques to guide a Scrum Team's engagement with its stakeholders.

FOCUS ON GOALS AND VALUE

Stakeholders want to know that progress is being made and the Scrum Team is doing valuable work. Often, the default behavior of stakeholders leads them to look at the output of a Scrum Team—the tangible work completed and the speed at which it was completed (velocity). This is relatively easy to measure. However, Scrum is not a tool intended for producing output. The word *value* appears 25 times in the 2020 version of the *Scrum Guide*. Variations of the word *delivery* appear only 4 times, and one of those references the delivery of value. Successful Sprint Reviews are focused on validating valuable progress toward the vision. In other words, the Scrum Team is delivering value to customers to meet their desired outcomes. That is why it is important to start a Sprint Review with a reminder about goals.

The Product Goal is a step toward fulfilling the product vision, so reminding attendees in the Sprint Review about how meeting the Sprint Goal is a step toward the Product Goal helps to set context and focus on value. The feedback that stakeholders give in the Sprint Review, with the sharing of new-found knowledge about customer behaviors, the product in the market, and changing business conditions, helps the Scrum Team and its stakeholders validate whether value is being delivered and they are progressing toward the Product Goal.

When facilitating a Sprint Review, include some time for inspection of value metrics. Examples are usage of new features that were released in the past month, number of downloads, customer satisfaction, and other data that can be considered to be valuable for the Sprint Review and that measures the progress toward the Product Goal.

Facilitating the Sprint Review is not just about keeping to the timebox and making sure the work from the Sprint is demonstrated. A facilitator of the Sprint Review should ensure participants understand the purpose of the event and drive them to the outcomes—namely, a shared understanding of the latest product Increment and any new information that informs adaptations to the Product Backlog. Facilitating also involves preparation and follow-ups if needed. Everyone should be leaving the Sprint Review understanding the direction that the Scrum Team is heading in.

CREATE A HEALTHY SPACE FOR EVERY VOICE

A facilitator should use the principle of healthy facilitation that we discuss in Appendix A, "Facilitation Principles," when designing a Sprint Review, especially when considering how feedback will be shared. Not only is this important for the Scrum Team so that it can receive feedback constructively, but it is also important for the stakeholders to know that their feedback and ideas are appreciated. Many teams demonstrate their work and then invite feedback in an open space, which is not the most inclusive way of sharing ideas and feedback. Some stakeholders may not be comfortable being put on the spot, and others may need a little time to reflect.

Besides inviting open conversation in a group, we suggest a few other techniques for sharing thoughts, ideas, and feedback. One example might be a gallery walk, which we discuss in Chapter 8, "Facilitating Beyond a Single Scrum Team." Another example might be giving personal reflection time with a feedback wall (which can be a physical wall or virtual space) where people can add cards with their thoughts. When people see their thoughts are being captured in some way, they feel more listened to. Trust and collaboration are then further enhanced if people see their feedback go on to be incorporated into Product Backlog items in the Product Backlog.

CONSIDER THE WIDER MARKET

A product with no demand is irrelevant to the market and an irresponsible investment. Discussing and sharing new understanding of the current market and business conditions is an often overlooked part of the Sprint Review.

These discussions might include how previous versions of the product are performing in the market, the actions and performance of competitors, and feedback from customers including requests, positive reactions, and complaints. This can then be the basis to identify the gap between where the product is currently and how well it satisfies customer needs compared to its full potential, which in turn can drive the direction of the Scrum Team's next efforts.

CONCLUSION

The Sprint Review is the key inspect and adapt event for a Scrum Team's product. Scrum Teams often ask us how to get stakeholders to attend their Sprint Reviews and how to facilitate them better so that the event is more engaging. A simple action they might try is to solicit feedback directly from stakeholders on how to improve their Sprint Reviews.

As we discussed in this chapter, Scrum Teams risk losing stakeholders' attention and inputs about the product and the Product Goal when the Sprint Review is used as a status update to stakeholders, or the conversations are mostly centered on activity, output produced, and Product Backlog items completed. Likewise, the Scrum Team misses an opportunity to engage with stakeholders in a conversation about value and learn what might be missing from the product when the event is facilitated in this way. As a facilitator, encourage the Scrum Team to be clear about its goals and the objective of the event. Sometimes stakeholders need a reminder and context setting. Also, ask questions to initiate conversation and curiosity from stakeholders before, during, and after demonstrating the Increment.

A second common dilemma Scrum Teams have is what to do in the Sprint Review when they do not have a Done Increment. A facilitator can help the team discuss this situation in its Sprint Retrospective and observe whether it is a recurring pattern. In the Sprint Review itself, a facilitator should be sure to reset expectations for stakeholders and work with the team to make transparent what work was Done and what work was not. The *Scrum Guide* states that teams should only show work at the Sprint Review that meets the Definition of Done. When a team shares work that is not Done, they risk giving a false impression of progress. However, in our experience, this misses an opportunity for the Scrum Team to get feedback on the progress that has been made during the Sprint that can help them move forward. If a Scrum Team decides to solicit feedback on incomplete work, the facilitator can make it clear that when the Sprint Review is finished, stakeholders are invited to stay with the team and give feedback on work in progress that the team would like to discuss.

FACILITATING THE SPRINT RETROSPECTIVE

Inspect what went well, what did not, and what to improve.

The Sprint Retrospective is the closing event of the Sprint. It is an opportunity for the Scrum Team to reflect on its performance and look for ways to improve its ways of working. This can include anything that affects the Scrum Team's effectiveness, such as how the Scrum Team communicates and relates with each other as well as its stakeholders. The Scrum Team can also discuss how it ensures quality in its work and the effectiveness of the current Definition of Done, tooling, processes—in fact, anything that helps or hinders the team from achieving its Sprint Goal and producing value each Sprint.

A lot of information is widely available on how to run Sprint Retrospectives, yet many teams still struggle with this event. The reasons can vary, from unresolved frustration, teams that feel like they are plateauing, to mistaking fun activities for collaboration. When effectively facilitated, Sprint Retrospectives can help a Scrum Team dramatically improve its effectiveness, but in reality, teams often miss the point. In this chapter, we look at some examples and some ideas of how to improve these dynamics.

THE SCRUM TEAM PLAYING THE BLAME GAME

Ashley, the Spartan Army's Scrum Master, kicks off the team's Sprint Retrospective. "Let's cut straight to the chase," she says. "Why didn't we meet our Sprint Goal this time?"

Linus speaks first. "Well, to start off with, we practically lost a whole day after Karl broke the build."

"Don't blame me! At least I was prepared to work on the difficult task. If I remember correctly, no one else wanted to pick it up! Maybe if the user stories were clearer, we wouldn't end up having to go around in circles so much during the Sprint."

"Oh, so it's my fault?!" says Isaac.

"Well, you are the Product Owner. You should make sure the user stories are clear."

"Really? Because you didn't say anything in Sprint Planning. You and everyone else pulled it into the Sprint."

"It's only because there was nothing else ready for us to do."

"Okay, so we need to get better at agreeing what Product Backlog items we bring into a Sprint. I'll record that as an action item," Ashley says. "What else?"

Ken answers. "I had to cram in all my testing at the end of the Sprint. There was no way I could do it all in the last two days. People are getting their work to me too late."

"Well," answers Linus, "if you didn't insist that we finish a whole user story before starting testing, you would have something to do! Can't you take smaller changes?"

"And then have to repeat my testing? I'm busy enough playing catch-up with the testing left over from the previous Sprints."

"Why don't you learn how to automate your tests?"

"Why don't *you* learn how to code better? The number of bugs I find…"

Linus is sweating, and his face flushes a deep shade of red, as if he is boiling from the inside. The rest of the Spartan Army team stay quiet.

"Hey!" calls Ashley before anyone else can say anything. "I'm glad we are all getting everything out on the table. This is a good retrospective!"

Linus crosses his arms and sarcastically says, "Is it *really*?"

KEEPING THE SPRINT RETROSPECTIVE CONSTRUCTIVE

No, it was not a good Sprint Retrospective. Although healthy conflict, where team members explore their differences, can build understanding and empathy between team members, a facilitator needs to act before conflict becomes unhealthy and detrimental to the team. What we saw in the Spartan Army's conversation was blame, anger, frustration, embarrassment, and other such emotions that lead to unhealthy conflict, which ultimately hinders a Scrum Team from progressing.

The Spartan Army's Sprint Retrospective started with a lot of tension because the team did not achieve its Sprint Goal. Ashley, the Scrum Master who was also facilitating the Sprint Retrospective, was quick to confront the team as to why this happened. Listening to the conversations, it appeared as if the team had lots of potential improvements that it could explore. Automating testing, improving the quality of the content of the Product Backlog items, investing more in Product Backlog refinement, and taking shared responsibility are just a few of the improvements that could benefit this team. However, the Scrum Team was caught in a cycle of negativity, emotions were running high, and the event was not constructive. Instead of focusing on what the team can practically do to make things better, it was playing the blame game. People tend to play the blame game when they fear that owning their mistakes or taking responsibility for an error could negatively affect the way they are perceived. Strong facilitation is needed here. The facilitator needs to be able to balance a dynamic that allows the team members to challenge each other constructively, hold each other accountable, but also recognize when to step in if people resort to personal attacks.

Individuals can fall easily into the pattern of putting blame on others instead of examining what they can improve on as a team. The Sprint Retrospective is the prime time to reflect on this behavior. This is why it is important for a facilitator to strive for a positive and outcome-driven event from the start.

Fostering Psychological Safety

For the Sprint Retrospective to be effective, everyone on the team needs to participate openly and respectfully. This can only happen if psychological safety is present in the team.

Amy Edmundson refers to psychological safety as a belief that a person will not be punished or humiliated for speaking up, sharing ideas or concerns, asking questions, or making mistakes. It refers to team members believing that they can take risks without being shamed by other people. In psychologically safe Scrum Teams, the team members feel accepted and respected.

A lot of research has been conducted on psychological safety as a topic in group dynamics and team learning research. These three principles, by Amy Edmundson in her book *The Fearless Organization*,[1] are ones we think apply well for Scrum Teams:

1. Frame the work as a learning problem, not an execution problem.
2. Be humble. Acknowledge fallibility.
3. Be curious. Model curiosity and ask lots of questions.

---

1. Edmonson, Amy (2018). *The Fearless Organization: Creating Psychological Safety in the Workplace for Learning, Innovation, and Growth*. John Wiley & Sons Inc. Or see www.youtube.com/watch?v=LhoLuui9gX8.

TRY THIS! REGROUPING AND ADJUSTING PERSPECTIVES

Setting a positive and constructive environment for the Sprint Retrospective event from the outset encourages everyone to approach it from a place of openness and learning. A positive tone does not mean that everyone puts on a smile and fake cheerfulness; it means acknowledging situations and each other respectfully, while being open and curious to learning. Here are some ideas to help teams rediscover their purpose as a team.

The Prime Directive

Norm Kerth describes the Prime Directive in his book *Project Retrospectives: A Handbook for Team Reviews*:[2]

> *Regardless of what we discover, we understand and truly believe that everyone did the best job they could, given what they knew at the time, their skills and abilities, the resources available, and the situation at hand.*

The Prime Directive is a way of guiding and setting the tone for positive and outcome-driven Sprint Retrospectives.

Setting Expectations for the Sprint Retrospective with the Prime Directive

Whenever I work with a team that is new to Scrum, or it needs a refresher, one thing I do in the Sprint Retrospective is discuss the Prime Directive.

I simply show it at the start of the retrospective and encourage a discussion between the team members to explore what it means to them.

The Prime Directive helps me set the scene that we, as a team, should assume that everybody is trying their best and has good intentions, whatever the outcome. Using the Prime Directive has helped me instill a positive culture and establish the understanding that the Sprint Retrospective is a place where, without judgment, the team can reflect and pursue how it can improve in its ways of working.

—David Spinks

---

2. Kerth, Norm (2001). *Project Retrospectives: A Handbook for Team Reviews*. Dorset House Publishing Co. Inc., U.S.

In parallel to the Prime Directive, a facilitator can remind everyone of the Scrum values and their working agreement. In particular, the Scrum value of respect can be used as a North Star. For more on this, see Chapter 3, "Facilitating the Daily Scrum." We discuss working agreements in Chapter 1, "Facilitating Alignment."

Stepping Out of the Content and Reflecting on the Process

Who is to say that Ken's concerns about the number of bugs was right? Or that Karl was wrong about the user stories? It is not the job of the facilitator to decide; a facilitator should simply help the team work through its discomfort so that everyone can move confidently into the next Sprint with agreed improvements toward their way of working. The facilitator can do this by focusing on the facilitation principle of process, which we discuss in Appendix A, "Facilitation Principles." The principle of process is not concerned with a group's ability to adhere to schedules, predefined steps, and rules, but about encouraging an inclusive and collaborative process in which everyone has the courage to fully participate—something that Ken, Karl, and the other team members clearly needed.

Stepping back from the Sprint Retrospective discussion or any tense interaction in a group to reflect on how everyone feels proceedings are going can help team members move forward in a more participatory way. To start, a facilitator prompts the group to step out of the content of the discussion and state their own observations. For example, the facilitator could say, "I notice that people are blaming each other" or, "I notice that there are some frustrations in the group." At this point, it is important that the facilitator uses statements to express observations.

The facilitator can then ask the group questions to validate these observations, like, "Does anyone else feel the same about this?" or, "Has anyone else noticed something similar?" A facilitator can also encourage the group to reflect on the team's behaviors and what is being said with prompts such as, "How do you feel about this?" or, "What is your response to this?" The group can then explore its different perspectives.

The purpose of asking people to step back and reflect on the process and behaviors instead of the content is not to solve the problems of the group or to get everyone to agree. Rather, a facilitator uses the tactic to raise awareness and build empathy. With better self-awareness and understanding of the group dynamics, people are better placed to return to the content of the discussion they were having.

The How Might We Question Format

Procter & Gamble introduced the How Might We (HMW) format in the 1970s, and it was later adopted by the design company IDEO. The technique is popular in design thinking, and it can be used by any teams solving complex problems. Team members reframe their challenges into problems that can be solved collaboratively with HMW questions. They mentally shift to a proactive approach to solving problems.

HMW questions:

- Suggest that a solution is possible (How)
- Offer team members a chance to answer the question in a variety of ways (Might)
- Encourage a collaborative approach and team accountability (We)

An example of using the HMW technique is in the Sprint Retrospective when the Scrum Team has repeatedly struggled to achieve its Sprint Goals. Here is a suggestion on how to use it:

1. The facilitator first reminds the Scrum Team members of their Sprint Goal, emphasizing that it is a shared goal for the whole team to collectively achieve in the Sprint.

2. The Scrum Team starts by uncovering the problems and gaining insights into what stopped it from achieving the Sprint Goal. Each team member writes down on sticky notes what they believe blocked or hindered the team from meeting the Sprint Goal. Examples might be, "No time for testing" and "Too many outstanding bugs."

3. Team members add their sticky notes to a (virtual) wall, and the team groups duplicates or similar items together in an affinity map. We discuss affinity maps in Chapter 1. The team should summarize in one sentence the problem that each group of sticky notes represents. An example might be, "Work did not meet quality expectations as defined in our Definition of Done."

4. Before reframing the problems, the facilitator should remind the team members to avoid writing their HMW questions with solutions already baked in.

5. The team now creates its HMW questions. It could use 1-2-4-all to do this, followed by a dot vote to identify its top three How Might We questions to tackle first. For more on 1-2-4-all, see Chapter 2, "Facilitating Sprint Planning," and for more on dot voting, see Chapter 4, "Facilitating Team Dynamics."

6. From there and with a fresh perspective, the Scrum Team can discuss and generate options to answer its top HMW questions and generate action items.

In the story with the Spartan Army, one of the problems that the Scrum Team had was quality issues. An example of a HMW question to avoid is one that includes a suggested solution. For example, "How might we implement more automation?" restricts the team to one solution, but there could be many other potentials ways the team can improve quality. A better HMW question is this: "How might we ensure quality in our product so that it meets our Definition of Done within a Sprint?" By phrasing the HMW in this way, team members can come up with a variety of options on how they can improve quality and still deliver value within a Sprint.

THE TEAM MEMBERS WHO BELIEVE NOTHING WILL CHANGE

Scrum Teams sometimes feel like external forces are pulling the strings.

John and Daniel arrive in the meeting room.

"Well, thank you for joining us," Clint says sarcastically.

"Sorry," replies John with equal sarcasm. "Daniel and I were actually doing something useful."

Clint lets the last comment go. "Well, we were all just individually capturing what went well and what didn't go well during the Sprint. Come and grab a sharpie each and some sticky notes. I'll add an extra two minutes to the timer, just for you two."

"Oh, this again…" groans John.

John and Daniel join their colleagues at the table. Clint announces that the two minutes are up and asks everyone one by one to stick their notes onto the wall under one of the two headers he has prepared: What Went Well? and What Didn't Go Well?

"Don't forget to stick any duplicates together!" Clint reminds them.

Daniel is up first, followed by Julie. Miguel and Rohan go next. Clint adds his own notes. John and Nikki both stay seated.

"There's not a lot here," says Clint. "Oh, well. Let's go through them. This one under What Didn't Go Well? seems to have the most duplicates. Let's see… *Access to environments.* This came up last time, didn't it?"

"Yes," says Julie, "and the retrospective before that!"

"There's no point talking about it. The operations team is not going to change its policy, no matter how many times we ask," John says.

"Right," says Clint. "Let's move on then. This one says, *We failed the Sprint because we don't have enough people.*"

"Yes, that was me. We still haven't replaced Ida since she left," says Rohan.

"Indeed. But we all know about the recruitment freeze. There's nothing we can do," says Clint. "Moving on… Did anyone put anything on the board that we can come up with an action for?" The whole team stares at the board.

"I have an idea," offers Nikki. "Since we can't do anything else, why don't we organize a team outing? We haven't hung out in a while."

"Good idea! Okay, let's wrap up," says Clint.

"Well, that was a waste of time… again," John mutters to Daniel on the way out of the room. "Why do we even still bother with retros? Nothing ever useful comes out of them."

GETTING VALUE OUT OF THE SPRINT RETROSPECTIVE

Scrum Teams are challenged to identify impediments and come up with improvements in the Sprint Retrospective every Sprint. Teams soon discover that many of the things that are reducing the team's effectiveness are part of their wider environment, and it often appears as if the improvements that the Scrum Team can make by themselves are limited. The same issues are raised again and again at the Sprint Retrospective and nothing gets done about them, leading the team to perceive the Sprint Retrospective as a waste of everybody's time.

A Team Taking Ownership of Its Improvement

I was working with a new Scrum Team that felt like its management was unsupportive of it and of agile in general. During one Sprint Retrospective, after the members listed potential improvement items, I noticed that they were marking several of the sticky notes with either a black *X* or a red *O*. When I asked what that meant, the Scrum Master told me that the black *X*s were items that the team was already aware of because they had come up in every other retrospective and were issues for management to solve. The red *O*s were new items for management to address. Only one item was unmarked, and it was about coffee.

The Scrum Master added all the new items to a list called "The Organizational Backlog," and the team proceeded for the rest of the retrospective to grumble about how it couldn't get better as a team because none of the managers were doing their jobs and removing the impediments on the Organizational Backlog.

What I quickly realized that this team needed first was not for managers outside the team to remove impediments, but for the team to work with management to make goals transparent, to make clear what the team is empowered to change, and most importantly to shift the mindset of the team to take ownership of its improvement.

—Patricia Kong

TRY THIS! CHALLENGE THE SCRUM TEAM TO OWN IMPROVEMENT

Here are some facilitation techniques to try if the Scrum Team feels as if it has little control over making changes in its environment or is not getting value out of its Sprint Retrospectives.

Circles of Concern, Influence, and Control

The circles of concern, influence, and control is a model introduced by Steven Covey in his book *The 7 Habits of Highly Effective People*[3] in which he distinguishes between proactivity and reactivity. The model is helpful for groups to focus on what is achievable and to challenge their perceptions about what is beyond their control.

One way to facilitate a Sprint Retrospective using the circles of concern, influence, and control is to first draw two concentric circles on a physical or virtual whiteboard space. The inner circle is labeled Circle of Control and the outer one is labeled Circle of Concern. Members of the Scrum Team are then invited to add things that are affecting their performance. Items that they feel the Scrum Team *cannot* do anything about are placed in the outer circle of concern, and those that they feel the Scrum Team *can* do something about are placed in the inner circle of control.

The Scrum Team can then focus on designing improvement actions for the items that are in the central circle of control. It should address the most impactful ones as soon as possible; however, it should not ignore the items in the outer circle of concern. In this exercise, the facilitator must guide the team to discuss and understand whether these things are actually outside the Scrum Team's control. The team members can discuss if there is anything they can actually do to influence or even take control of the issues. The facilitator draws another circle between the circles of control and concern. This is the area referred to as the circle of influence, where the team might be able to influence others into taking action. A conversation can then be facilitated to explore which items from the circle of concern can be moved into the circle of

---

3. Covey, Steven R. (2004). *The 7 Habits of Highly Effective People: Powerful Lessons in Personal Change* (15th anniversary edition). The Free Press.

influence, or even into the circle of control. An example of the circles of concern, influence, and control is shown in Figure 7.1.

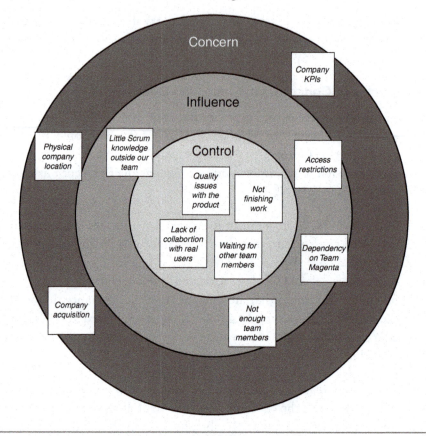

Figure 7.1 An example of the circles of concern, influence, and control.

In the story, Rohan raised a concern that the team had reduced capacity after one of the team members left the company. Because of a recruitment freeze, the team said nothing could be done about it. The team also pointed to an impediment of access restrictions. Again, the team claimed that nothing could be done about the issue because the restrictions are a company policy. At this point, the facilitator should guide people away from apportioning blame or acting helplessly, and help people think about how they can constructively improve the situation instead. Following a discussion about what is actually inside or outside a team's circle of control, people often discover that they are able to make improvements and have a lot more influence over things than they realize.

Instead of allowing the discussion to center on a particular problem or solution, such as "We don't have enough capacity; we need to get more people!", a facilitator should refocus the group on questions that encourage more creative thinking, such as:

- How can we adjust the way we plan and manage our work following the change in team make-up?
- What skills are we missing on the team?
- What is our plan to acquire those skills? Could we learn them?
- What can we learn from why this person left so we reduce the risk of it happening again?

Similarly, instead of feeling blocked by a company policy, a facilitator can prompt a discussion with questions such as these:

- What can we do to earn the trust required for the operations team's policy to be adjusted?
- How can we show the impact that the policy has on us being able to meet our Sprint Goals and produce a valuable Done Increment each Sprint?

This exercise is meant to shift a team from feeling powerless and paralyzed to feeling proactive and positive about its ability to remove barriers to success. The goal is for the facilitator to guide the team away from a mindset that rejects and closes down possibilities.

Discussing a Scrum Team's circle of influence can lead to productive conversations of where the team needs to strengthen communication channels and form partnerships and alliances. Although the Scrum Team may not have direct influence over something, this will help the team learn who does, which further grows their circle of influence if they work on those relationships.

Scrum Teams that are more aware and curious of what is actually possible through using a technique like the circles of concern, influence, and control often find that they become more proactive as a team over time, which enlarges their circle of influence. The circles of concern, influence, and control is a living artifact that can be revisited periodically in Sprint Retrospectives.

Delegation Poker

Although Scrum defines the accountabilities of the Developers, Product Owner, Scrum Master, and the collective Scrum Team, some context-specific decisions may need to be made, but it is not clear from the Scrum framework alone who should make these decisions. In addition, organizations have their own hierarchies and policies, blurring even further where decision-making authority lies. The result is that the Scrum Team might be unclear on what decisions it is actually allowed to make.

Delegation poker is a tool from Management 3.0[4] that can be used to facilitate a conversation between a Scrum Team, its stakeholders, and management to make transparent where decision authority lies. Note that delegation poker is about where decision-making authority resides; it is not for actually making the decisions.

An example of how delegation poker might be facilitated is as follows:

1. Start by gathering all the decisions that require a discussion on whether they should be delegated. This might be anything from who makes hiring and firing decisions to what type of coffee is available in the office. It can be done collaboratively between the Scrum Team and relevant stakeholders, which could and should include management.

2. Facilitate a session involving anyone affected by the potential delegation decisions, such as managers and team members.

3. The facilitator or a participant reads each delegation decision aloud.

4. The participants then choose one of the delegation cards in secret, with the card they choose reflecting how they believe the decision should be delegated. When ready, everyone reveals their cards.

---

4. Appelo, Jurgen (2010). *Management 3.0: Leading Agile Developers, Developing Agile Leaders.* Addison-Wesley Professional.

5. The facilitator then encourages a conversation on the results, such as by asking the people with the highest and the lowest cards to explain their reasoning for their choice first.

Optional rules include what is called the highest minority and the lowest minority. These involve the person with the highest number or lowest number, respectively, to be discounted and excluded from the conversation. These rules are to cater for cases such as team members who think everything should be delegated, there are those who just want to be told what to do all the time, or there are managers who do not want to give up control.

The delegation cards can be defined in a Scrum context as follows:

Tell: Management will tell the Scrum Team what it has decided.

Sell: Management makes the decision and will try to convince the Scrum Team that it is the right decision.

Consult: Management decides after consultation with the Scrum Team.

Agree: Management and the Scrum Team make the decision collaboratively.

Advise: The Scrum Team makes the decision after consultation with management.

Inquire: The Scrum Team makes the decision and managers ask the Scrum Team to inform them.

Delegate: The decision is fully delegated to the Scrum Team.

Over time, delegation poker can be used regularly as other pending decisions come to light or the impacts of previous delegation policies are better understood.

THE SCRUM TEAM THAT THINKS THERE'S NOTHING LEFT FOR THEM TO IMPROVE

Team Baboom are in their 89th Sprint together. Team members work well together, usually meet their Sprint Goals, produce a Done Increment each Sprint, and have few quality issues with their product. Their stakeholders are satisfied because they feel the team is producing value, customers are happy, and they trust Team Baboom to do the right thing.

Karim, a Developer, takes a turn to facilitate the Sprint Retrospective. Given the amount of time that Baboom has been together, its Sprint Retrospectives are feeling a bit stale, and the team struggles to find ways to improve.

"I have an idea for this retrospective," Karim tells his fellow team members as they all arrive on the conference call. "It's a bit different, but I hope it will help us challenge ourselves and our use of Scrum." Karim shares a link to the electronic whiteboard that he has prepared.

"You'll see on the whiteboard I have a set of cards, and each one has an element of Scrum. For example, this one," Karim clicks on one of the cards and moves it around slightly, "says *The Daily Scrum*. This other one says *Definition of Done*," he says, clicking and moving around one of the other cards. "You'll see that we have all the elements of Scrum, the accountabilities, the events, the artifacts, and I included cards for our complementary practices.

"To the left is a scale from least valuable to most valuable. Now, what we are going to do is take turns, me included. When it's your turn, pick one of the cards and read it out loud to the group. You then place it somewhere on the scale depending on how valuable you think that part of our process is to us. You also need to give a brief explanation about why you placed it where you did. It is really important that the only person who speaks is the person whose turn it is. Everybody else listens.

"On your turn, you also have the choice to move one of the cards that has already been placed on the scale, again, giving one or two sentences of explanation about why you are moving it. If it's your turn and there are no more cards to place and no cards you want to move, you pass. We keep going until everyone passes. I hope that makes sense. Are there any questions?" After a few seconds of silence, Karim continues, "Shall we?"

Davenesh volunteers to go first. "*Sprint Retrospective*," he reads out. He moves the card to the bottom of the scale, next to the Least Valuable label. "I think Sprint Retrospective is the least valuable element here. We have been doing Scrum for so long that we don't have any improvements left."

"That's not true!" Jyotana cries. "We still have the odd quality issue—"

Karim jumps in, "Thank you, Jyotana. But remember, only the person whose turn it is gets to speak. It is not about them justifying their decision, but us understanding each other's perspectives. The rest of us just listen. If you disagree, you can choose to use your turn to move the card somewhere else on the scale."

The team continues to take turns adding cards. For the first couple of rounds, most cards are placed with what Karim perceives are superficial reasons. On her turn, Jyotana moves the Sprint Retrospective about a quarter of the way up the scale away from the Least Valuable side with the statement, "I think we still get some value from our retrospectives." Karim begins to doubt the value of the exercise. But as the cards to be placed start to run down, things start to get interesting.

"I'm moving our peer review process from here near the top, down to near the bottom," Saska says on her turn. "We always have to wait for a lead to become available. Pretty much always everything is fine. I do think we need to have reviews, but only allowing them to be done by leads slows us down."

Nobody says anything, but Karim senses a change in the atmosphere.

It is Sai's turn next. "Actually, I'm glad Saska said that. I'm going to move this peer review card all the way to the bottom. I feel like I'm constantly interrupted to do reviews, and everything I check is always really good. I trust the team, and I think the rule of only me or Davenesh doing them isn't a good one."

It is back to Davenesh. "I'm moving the Sprint Retrospective up. I know I put it near the bottom earlier. But this thing about the peer review, I think we have just found something we need to talk about as a team." Davenesh holds his hand up to his camera to give Karim a virtual high-five.

CHALLENGING SCRUM TEAMS THAT HAVE REACHED A PLATEAU

We saw Karim use a facilitation technique called white elephant to encourage the team to look at themselves and what they do in a new light. We explain how you can facilitate using this technique later in this chapter. Like Team

Baboom, many Scrum Teams that have been together for many Sprints eventually experience a plateau, whereby they struggle to identify areas for improvement. The Scrum Team might feel that it is as effective as it can be, or, more likely, it has become complacent.

In this case, the aim of a facilitator is to challenge a team to challenge themselves. A Scrum Team might achieve its Sprint Goals and deliver a Done Increment most Sprints, but how can it get to a place where it meets its Sprint Goal and can deliver *multiple* Done Increments *every* Sprint? The team might have good quality with few problems, but what can it do to ensure *no* problems with its product Increments? Stakeholders and customers might be satisfied, but how can a Scrum Team move them to being delighted? How does a Scrum Team even know what the customers of its products are thinking? Do team members understand who their customers are, what their needs are, and whether their product solves these needs? What can the Scrum Team do to understand these things more? Retrospectives should be facilitated so that the Scrum Team learns to ask these kinds of questions of itself to drive it to the next level of improvement.

Generally, in a Scrum Team's early days, it has lots of ideas and actions for improvement. Team members are learning to gel as a team and finding out how to best approach their work. Facilitating the Sprint Retrospective is a case of organizing and prioritizing which improvement actions to implement next. But as the team progresses, the easier improvements have been actioned, and things get harder, including for the Scrum Team to identify and articulate areas for improvement. Facilitation then becomes about exploring the diverse perspectives of the team and comparing opinions on what is working and what is not. Facilitators adapt their techniques and employ different skills accordingly.

TRY THIS! LEVERAGE DIFFERENT PERSPECTIVES TO PURSUE AWESOMENESS

Given the complex nature of their work, Scrum Teams benefit from exploring each member's thinking, but they often struggle to really listen and build a shared understanding of each other's point of view. If this is your experience, your objective as a facilitator is to create a space that allows the participants to explore the differing perspectives and promote active listening.

Events or meetings can be facilitated in several ways that enable everyone's voice to be heard while encouraging full participation and active listening from those involved. In the context of the Sprint Retrospective, the team should not forget the purpose of pursuing improvement. Here, we explore some approaches for leveraging the different perspectives of the team and pursing awesomeness.

White Elephant

The phrase *white elephant* can be traced back to Thailand (previously known as Siam).[5] White elephants were rare and considered sacred, so they were highly valued. However, they were expensive to keep because they required special food and were protected from being used as working animals. The story goes that the kings of Siam would give the gift of a white elephant to anyone who was out of favor with them as a blessing and a curse. The financial burden of owning a white elephant could ruin the recipient.

A facilitator can use the white elephant approach to help a team explore what is low value, burdensome, or wasteful. Subsequently, the participants then agree which areas to tackle first for improvement. Although we showed in the story how white elephant can be used to facilitate a Sprint Retrospective, it can be used for anything from sizing or ordering items on a Product Backlog to exposing how effectively a Scrum Team thinks it understands and applies the different elements of Scrum. It is useful to create an environment that encourages everyone to actively engage so they can develop a shared understanding of their different perspectives.

The following are guidelines for facilitating a white elephant approach:

- Prepare a physical or virtual space with a sliding scale that gives some indication of "worst" to "best." For example, you might use Least Effective to Most Effective or Least Value to Most Value.

5. History Extra (2021). "Why Do We Say 'White Elephant'?" www.historyextra.com/period/victorian/why-do-we-say-white-elephant/.

- Prepare the items to be placed on physical or virtual cards, or sticky notes.
- Participants take turns choosing a card. On their turn, the participant reads the content of the card out loud to the group. They then place it on the scale where they believe it is most appropriate, giving their reasons.
- A facilitator may decide to timebox each person's turn, such as to one minute. If the participant does not place the card on a scale within this time, they must place the card in the middle of the scale.
- Only the team member whose turn it is can speak. They place the element wherever they believe is appropriate, and without external interference. It is important that other participants stay silent, do not pass judgment, and just listen.
- On their turn, participants can decide to move one card that has already been placed somewhere else on the scale, again giving their reasons. The facilitator should decide beforehand if this can be done at any time or if a certain number of cards need to be placed first.
- If a participant is content with where all the cards are placed, they can pass on their turn. The process continues until everyone passes. The facilitator might include the rule that if no decision is made within a minute on someone's turn, the participant's turn becomes a pass.

Figure 7.2 shows a result of a white elephant exercise. Facilitation with white elephant is great for people to understand each other's perceptions and opinions. The final placement of the cards is secondary to the increased understanding that the participants have of each other. The exercise gives everyone a voice, and it can reveal insights and new understandings that can be followed up with other facilitation techniques for the participants to explore further and come up with concrete actions.

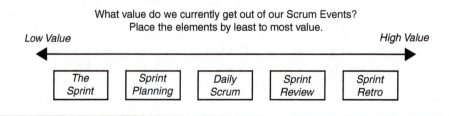

Figure 7.2 A result of a white elephant exercise.

Definition of Awesome and Improvement Boards

An idea for Scrum Teams to challenge themselves to greater levels of performance that comes from the Spotify Engineering Culture videos[6] is called definition of awesome.

When creating a definition of awesome, a Scrum Team defines what it means for them to be in their best possible, or awesome, state. It might include things such as "We always achieve our Sprint Goals and produce value each Sprint," "We can go from idea to building and testing an idea within one week," and "We learn if our Increments are valuable to our customers or not after releasing them." A team's definition of awesome provides a direction, not a destination. It is a lofty goal that is beneficial because it can help the team raise its standards.

If a Scrum Team can agree what awesome looks like to them, it can help them think of improvement actions. According to the Spotify Engineering Culture videos, teams use improvement tracking boards to visualize this to better track their improvement progress. This board would reflect the team's definition of awesome, its current biggest problem to solve, its next target condition, and approximately three improvement actions that the team is carrying out now or will next. An example of an improvement tracking board is shown in Figure 7.3. As actions are implemented, the team adds the next set of actions until it meets its targeted condition unless it finds the target no longer relevant.

The team can revisit its definition of awesome and the improvement board during Sprint Retrospectives where team members update the next biggest problem, the next target conditions, and new actions as the team and the environment around it evolve.

---

6. Tjernsli, Andreas (2018). "Spotify Engineering Culture Part 2." www.youtube.com/watch?v=rzoyryY2STQ.

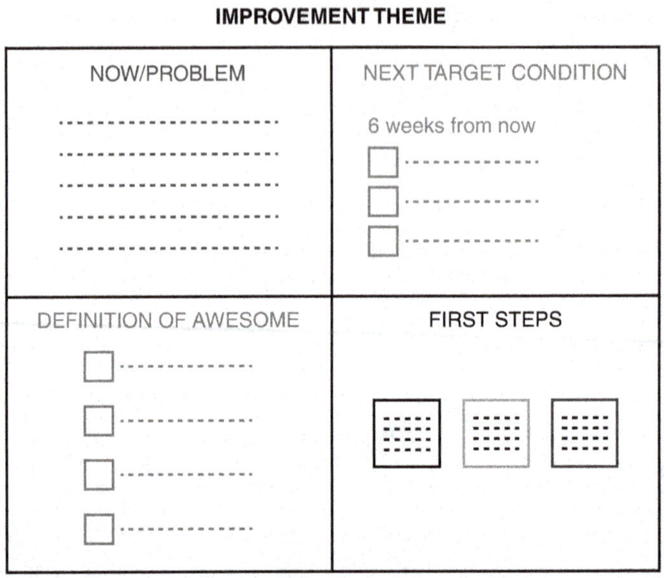

IMPROVEMENT THEME

Figure 7.3 Example of an improvement tracking board.

THE SCRUM TEAM DEALING WITH A MAJOR CHANGE

"I'm really worried," says Lance. "Michael was the heartbeat of this team. He was the one we all went to for help. Not only that, he was great at stakeholder management, he stuck up for us, and…" Lance is interrupted by the beeping of a timer. "Wow, my minute is up already! Here you go, Suzy. It's your turn." Lance pulls the small woolen alpaca finger puppet off his finger and hands it to Suzy, who is sitting to his left.

Richard starts the timer as Suzy slips the finger puppet onto her left forefinger. She spends many seconds just staring at it as the rest of Team Alpacas stay silent. Eventually she says a few words. "Michael is the reason I'm here. I learned so much from him, and he really helped me grow my confidence. I'm crushed. His departure was so sudden. On a personal level, it feels like we've lost a family member." She stays quiet for a few more seconds and then removes the finger puppet, passing it to Steve on her left.

"Me?" says Steve as he adjusts the finger puppet on the pinky of his right hand while Richard again resets the timer. "In a way... I think this could be a good thing. We're supposed to say what is really on our minds right? Well, in a way, I think we grew too dependent on Michael. I mean, we're supposed to be a team, right, but in one sense, he held us all back. He made all the big decisions; we would always have to go along with his ideas. Yes, he was brilliant, but I actually see this as an opportunity for other people to step up. Yes, it is a bit scary, but we can now grow as a team, which I think we weren't able to do before."

The timer sounds. "That's everybody," says Richard. "Thank you all for sharing. I think we all understand each other's thoughts and feelings a little better. Now we're going to go around again, but this time we should talk about what we've heard from everyone else. Then we'll open the floor for an open discussion about how we move forward. Alma," Richard waves the finger puppet in the air, "is back with me, so I'll start..."

DEALING WITH PROFOUND CHALLENGES

In the story, Team Alpacas were coming to terms with a big change in circumstances. One of their most valued team members has left the team, leaving the rest of them with concerns about a shortage of skills, leadership, and ideas in the future.

Difficult situations are a fact of life that almost all Scrum Teams encounter at some point. This could be a change of circumstances like we saw with Team Alpacas losing a valued team member, or other things beyond the Scrum Team's control, like company takeovers or new management policies. Scrum Teams often have difficult stakeholders, unrealistic expectations thrust upon them, or environments with limited understanding of agility. Scrum Teams face tough impediments, from dependencies on third parties to missing the skills in the team to get things to Done.

Scrum does not fix any of these things. Whether or not a team is using Scrum, these challenges are a symptom of the environment that Scrum Teams operate in. However, Scrum is designed for these difficulties to come to the surface, and the Sprint Retrospective event is the opportunity for the Scrum

Team to inspect itself and make adaptations to improve the situation. But that is where Scrum ends. It offers no answers on how to deal with whatever challenges the Scrum Team faces.

An effective facilitator enables Scrum Teams to dig deep and confront their challenges without stepping over personal boundaries. We saw Team Alpacas used a technique that we look at in more detail next, as well as some other approaches.

Try This! Taking Steps toward Resiliency and Improvement

Scrum Teams almost inevitably come up against some tough impediments or experience difficult situations. Here we share some techniques for a team to build resilience and empathy for how all team members are feeling and dealing with their situation.

The Check-In

A check-in is a personal approach to start a meeting. Although a check-in is a good way to begin an event or meeting, it is especially important when team members have experienced something that has affected them negatively. For example, they have just learned that one of the other members of the team suddenly left, they had a horrible Sprint where everything went wrong, or the organization went through major changes.

Checking in invites everyone to be present, seen, and heard. It allows people to share how they are feeling without being obtrusive. It helps to identify anything that may affect people's participation in the event. It allows people to connect with each other more deeply, and often, by getting outside factors off their chest at the start, participants can shift their focus and be fully present in the session. Additionally, by encouraging everyone to speak openly from the outset, a particular tone of openness is set. Often, once a person has shared their thoughts within the group, they are likely to be less hesitant to speak again.

The Subjectivity of Team Health Checks

With one Scrum Team I worked with, at the start of the Sprint Retrospective, I would ask the team members to score individually on a sticky note how well things were going on a scale of 1 to 5. I would then collect all the notes and reveal them. On one occasion, I got several scores of 4 and 5, but there was an outlier—a score of 1. We then went into a conversation as a team to uncover what I had assumed was an impediment that had not been raised.

I realized later that this form of health check was subjective and didn't always reflect how the Sprint went. The reason for the low score was that the company had announced that there would be no bonuses that year. One of the developers was really disappointed because they had made plans in their personal life based on getting a bonus.

I found that supplementing the health check with a check-in helped us understand everyone else's mood going into the rest of the Sprint Retrospective. It was not mandatory for people to explain why they felt a certain way at a particular time, but having knowledge of each other's feelings helped the team empathize with each other and understand each other's perspectives more.

—Glaudia Califano

A facilitator can conduct a check-in in several ways. One way is to use a round-robin approach, whereby everyone has an opportunity to take a turn to share. People who may feel uncomfortable or are resistant have a right to pass and can just observe. A facilitator can use the following as guidance for a round-robin check-in:

- Explain the purpose of the check-in and that everyone will have an opportunity to share anything that may be affecting their mood.
- Ask for a volunteer to go first. This person should make it clear when they have finished before the next person takes their turn. They can say, "That's all I wanted to share," or if they want to skip their turn, they can simply say, "Pass."
- If others in the group interject, the facilitator should respectfully remind the group that everyone should be given space to check-in without interruptions or judgment from others.

- After everyone has checked in, the facilitator can summarize what they heard to acknowledge what has been shared. For example, they could say something like, "From what I heard, many of you felt a lot of pressure this week, so let's consider this in our retrospective." The group is then better equipped to move on.

Check-In and Check-Out Questions

Many meetings can benefit from a check-in or a check-out, regardless of whether the participants have struggles or not. A check-in can be used as a structured way to give everyone an opportunity to share something at the start of the meeting to increase presence, engagement, and participation.

Here are examples of check-in questions:

- What is your current greatest challenge?
- What would you like to achieve in this meeting?
- What is your goal for today?
- What is something that made you proud lately?

A check-out round is a way to close a meeting, and it emphasizes reflection.

Examples of check-out questions are:

- What was your biggest takeaway from the session?
- What will you do differently next time?
- What has been your highest high and lowest low in this session?

Facilitators should be creative, adapt questions to the situation, and keep them fresh.

The check-in can be used at the beginning of the Sprint Retrospective or as a stand-alone activity. If a team wants to delve deeper into how they are feeling about a situation, the Liberating Structure conversation café is an alternative facilitation approach.

Conversation Café

A conversation café can be facilitated with one or more groups of five to seven people. It is best to arrange seating for everyone to face each other in a circle. Each group elects someone to act as the host. This person is also a participant, but they try to make sure that the six conversation café agreements are followed:

- Suspend judgment as best you can
- Respect one another
- Seek to understand rather than to persuade
- Invite and honor diverse opinions
- Speak what has personal heart and meaning
- Go for honesty and depth without going on and on and on

For conversation café, the participants need a talking object. In the rounds where it is used, only the person holding the object should be speaking. The rest of the group listens without interrupting the speaker. The facilitator ensures that the participants understand the six agreements and the theme. The conversation café proceeds over a series of four rounds:

1. First round: Each person in the group, in turn, takes the talking object and shares what they are thinking in response to the theme. Each person has one minute of speaking time.

2. Second round: Following the first round, each person takes the talking object and shares their thoughts and feelings, having listened to everybody else. This is again timeboxed to one minute per person.

3. Third round: The talking object can be kept and passed around, or discarded at this point, as the group has an open conversation. The conversation can last between 20 and 40 minutes.

4. Fourth round: The talking object is again passed from participant to participant for up to a minute each, for everyone to share their takeaways.

A conversation café can be great for a group to make sense of a difficult situation and to build empathy and understanding with each other as a collective. When people really pause and listen to each other to harness the wide range of perspectives, it is cathartic and, in our experience, often results in the emergence of innovative ideas.

To identify and create motivation for action, the conversation café can be followed up by delving into what is actually possible.

Discovering the Art of the Possible

Sometimes it seems as if it is impossible to make progress in a certain situation. A problem can seem daunting, and we do not know where to start. But once a start has been made and we see some progress, the impossible suddenly starts to feel possible. The secret is getting started.

A facilitator can encourage a group to look for the first possible steps that can realistically be achieved and will contribute toward realizing a full solution. A good prompting question to ask is, "If this was achievable, where would we start?" The first step can be something that someone or the team can do that does not need approval from someone else or requires tools they do not have access to.

Facilitating such a discussion helps people move away from a feeling of powerlessness, while encouraging them to discover how they can use their individual and collective power to come up with some initial steps, however small, to start to make a difference. The focus changes from what cannot be done to what can be done.

All ideas can then be shared and grouped on a (virtual) wall in an affinity map. The affinity map forms the basis for convergence and the extraction for insights as a group. Next steps can then be identified, agreed on, and carried forward. For more on affinity maps, see Chapter 1.

For a more detailed and structured approach to help a team discover the art of the possible, a facilitator can use the 15% solutions technique from Liberating Structures. Here, the prompting questions for people to think about are:

- What is your 15% solution?
- Where do you have discretion and freedom to act?
- What can you do without more resources or authority?

These are then explored over a series of different rounds:

1. First round: 5 minutes. Everyone records their 15% solutions to the challenge individually.

2. Second round: 6–12 minutes. Individuals take turns sharing their ideas in small groups of 2 to 4 people.

3. Third round: 5–7 minutes. Keeping to the same small groups, participants ask questions, clarify, and refine each 15% solution one at a time.

Root Cause Analysis

The fishbone diagram, also known as the cause-and-effect diagram or the Ishikawa diagram, was created by the Japanese professor and organizational theorist Kaoru Ishikawa to study the causes of a specific event. It can be used to facilitate a root cause analysis discussion. An example is shown in Figure 7.4.

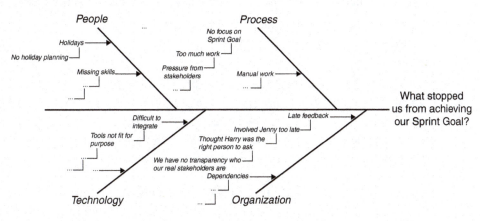

Figure 7.4 An example of a fishbone diagram.

To facilitate a discussion using a fishbone diagram, write down the problem, issue, defect, or circumstance in a shared space for all to see, such as on a whiteboard or in a virtual tool. Draw a horizontal line, extending to the left of this. From this main line, participants identify categories of causes. For each of these categories, the team can continue digging, exploring layers of cause and effect in search of the main root causes. The technique is sometimes synonymous with the 5 whys method, where the approach is to simply take a problem and drill down to the root cause by asking "why?" five times.

Sometimes improvement actions only address symptoms and not the root cause. With the deeper analysis of cause and effect from using a fishbone diagram and the 5 whys, the participants discover root causes of problems that can then become the target for improvement actions.

For example:

> *Why did we not meet our Sprint Goal?* Because we couldn't complete the key Product Backlog items.
>
> *Why?* Because there was too much work for us to do in the Sprint.
>
> *Why?* Because we had to spend a lot of time on manual regression testing.
>
> *Why?* Because as our product is developing, it is growing in complexity, and there are more and more features that we have to check manually.
>
> *Why?* Because we have no test automation.
>
> *Why?* Because we never invested in it.

This example shows that a team may identify an initial improvement action such as this: *Take less work into the Sprint*. However, this only treats the symptom and will result in the team achieving less and less each Sprint over time. The deeper analysis might reveal a much more effective improvement in the long term, such as starting to invest in automation testing.

Facilitating conversations around a fishbone diagram is a great way to dive into a topic deeply. However, as a facilitator, be aware that questions that start with "why" can sometimes feel like an attack and elicit defensive responses. Use judgment and care when wording the questions, and only use this technique when the Scrum Team is in a psychologically safe environment, in which team members feel like they can share, challenge, and discuss things with each other without feeling judged or being punished.

THE SCRUM MASTER FOCUSING THE RETROSPECTIVE ON FUN

"Your Scrum Master is here… It's Miller time!" Miller shouts, a little too loudly, as he joins the conference call. The rest of Team Pilsners stay quiet.

"So Pilsners, have I got another fun retro for you! I've been working on it all week, and I think you'll all really enjoy it!"

"So that's where you've been," Barry says. "I needed your help a couple of days ago. Some of the Team Jazz members contacted me saying they had a dependency on us. They wouldn't take no for an answer, so I stayed late to get the work done. I'm a bit annoyed that I had to do that actually."

"Let's not talk about that now, Bud. This is not the time to be looking at the past. This is the retrospective!" As if to reiterate the point, Miller shouts again, "It's Miller time!"

"Will you at least stop calling me Bud? My name is Barry."

"I know that, but remember we gave ourselves nicknames to fit with our team name."

"You mean that you gave us nicknames just to fit in with your actual name," Barry replies.

Miller ignores the comment and continues. "To kick things off, we'll have a fun icebreaker. I want everyone to take a picture of your feet and then upload the pictures to our chat."

"What! Why?" says Melinda.

"Because then we all have to guess whose feet they are!" says Miller.

"I don't get it," says Anne-Marie. "How will this help us? Are we ditching our product to start selling shoes or something?" she adds sarcastically.

"Haha, no," says Miller. "This is just for fun, Stella!"

"Oh! Why didn't you say so," replies Anne-Marie. "I'm sorry, I didn't realize we were here to have fun. This will be even more fun than our last retrospective, when you made all of us talk about our favorite pizza toppings. Look, Miller, we've got some really important stuff that I want to talk about… and stop calling me Stella."

"We'll get to that. Let's just do the activity. It'll help us connect. Get your photo uploaded." Miller waits while the team members upload their photos. "Right. Let's see…. So I see one pair of feet and… what is that? That's a table leg, isn't it? And this one… those are cat's paws… C'mon, everyone. I don't think you are taking this retrospective seriously!"

SERVE THE NEEDS OF THE TEAM

We saw in the story that Miller had an agenda to make the Sprint Retrospective about having fun, and this was according to what he thought of as fun. Although Scrum Teams can discuss ways to make their work more enjoyable in a Sprint Retrospective, the purpose of the event is clearly lost when it is facilitated purely to have fun. Especially when "fun" is forced upon the team.

Facilitators often use icebreaker and energizer activities to start the Sprint Retrospective and other meetings. Although these can be useful to make people feel comfortable in each other's company, they can lack a connection to the actual purpose of the session. Without this connection to a purpose, the activities can feel forced. The participants may become apathetic or resistant, not only to those types of activities, but toward the rest of the event and even to future events.

Miller was not focused on helping the Scrum Team fulfill the purpose of the Sprint Retrospective. Namely, to increase the quality of their work and their effectiveness. His comment, "This is not the time to be looking at the past. This is the retrospective!" shows that he was more interested in playing out his activities and he did not seem to understand the purpose of the Sprint Retrospective. He also acted more like some kind of entertainer, not a facilitator.

TRY THIS! HELP PARTICIPANTS CONNECT TO THE PURPOSE AND CREATE THEIR OWN AGENDA

A facilitator's role is not to entertain or to do what pleases themselves. A facilitator is there to guide discussions and interactions to achieve a desired outcome.

A facilitator can help a group of participants by making them feel at ease, but they must also connect them to the purpose of the session.

Although part of facilitation involves preparation, there is a danger that overdesigning a meeting might actually suppress what needs to be discussed. That is why it is important to focus on the purpose and be flexible in the format as discussions emerge. Here are some things to consider to keep meetings focused on the purpose and the needs of the participants.

Connect to the Purpose

In the story, Miller's activity of having the team guess whose feet were whose had no relevance to the purpose of the Sprint Retrospective or any of the challenges the team was facing. Team members were explicitly confused and frustrated. That is not to say that introductory activities should not be used, but they have to be relevant to be effective. To be effective, they should support the facilitation principle of process, and connect the participants to the purpose.

A team check-in as described earlier in this chapter is one such activity that can be used to start a Sprint Retrospective to get the Scrum Team connected to the idea of how things are going. The perfection game, as discussed in Chapter 6, "Facilitating the Sprint Review," is another such effective opener. Here team members could be asked to score how well they think the Sprint went from 1 to 10, where 10 represents perfection. They are asked what would be needed to be able to score a 10. This additional prompt focuses people to connect to the subject more deeply.

Retrospective formats that use imagery and metaphors are another way to connect team members to the discussions on how to improve. The sailboat retrospective format, from *Innovation Games*,[7] is just one example. A facilitator prepares a poster or image on a whiteboard of a sailboat, an island, the wind, the boat's anchor, and rocks. The team is asked to think about these as metaphors to prompt discussions. The sailboat represents the team and its journey to its goals, represented by the island. The wind helps the team

---

7. Hohmann, Luke (2006). *Innovation Games: Creating Breakthrough Products Through Collaborative Play*. Addison-Wesley Professional.

toward its goals. The anchor represents what is slowing the team down, and the rocks are potential risks that the team might encounter on the way.

Lean Coffee

There are not many problems that a good cup of coffee cannot help to make better! Lean Coffee is a helpful way to generate ideas for improvement during the Sprint Retrospective. The Lean Coffee website describes Lean Coffee as "a structured but agenda-less meeting. Participants gather, build an agenda, and begin talking."[8] Facilitating a Lean Coffee session consists of several steps:

1. Participants set up a board with three columns: To Discuss, Discussing, and Done Discussing.

2. Everyone individually writes their topics for conversation down on separate sticky notes or cards and adds them to the To Discuss column. The number of topics is limitless.

3. Each item is briefly introduced by its creator in one or two sentences.

4. Any items that are unclear should be quickly clarified.

5. Participants dot vote on the items that are of most interest to them. Typically, each person gets three dots, but this depends on the number of topics the group generated. For more on dot voting, see Chapter 4.

6. Based on the number of votes, the items are ordered in the To Discuss column. The item with the highest number of votes is pulled into the Discussing column.

7. The facilitator starts a timer. The group then discusses the item in the Discussing column for a predetermined short timebox, such as five minutes.

8. The facilitator signals the end of the timebox. A roman vote is held to see if the participants are interested in continuing the discussion. If so, the item is discussed for a further but shorter period, such as three minutes. Optionally, voting can be held again. The item does not move to Done until interest has waned for the majority of participants.

9. When the conversation is completed for an item, the card for it is moved to Done Discussing, and the session moves on to the next highest item in the To Discuss list.

---

8. Taken from the Lean Coffee website: https://leancoffee.org/.

10. At the end of the overall session, participants summarize and agree on takeaways and follow-up actions.

Lean Coffee is a helpful technique especially when a group has some quieter voices. Because everyone starts silently by generating topics for conversation individually and the team votes on what is discussed, there is more of a balance of topics generated from across the group. However, a facilitator still needs to pay attention to loud voices that can dominate the conversations.

Facilitating a Lean Coffee session is similar in person or online with the right conferencing and virtual whiteboard tools. Dedicated online Lean Coffee tools are widely available. Either way, we like Lean Coffee because the short timeboxes force people to be concise, and a bit of time pressure can help people be creative. Drinking coffee is entirely optional!

KEYS TO FACILITATING AN EFFECTIVE SPRINT RETROSPECTIVE

As we have seen in the scenarios of this chapter, Scrum Teams struggle with pursuing continuous improvement for various reasons. Although Scrum comes with the Sprint Retrospective as the event for the Scrum Team to inspect and adapt itself, Scrum does not describe how to actually run this event effectively. This is where appropriately selected facilitation techniques can help, with the following factors in mind.

CLARIFY INVOLVEMENT AS A FACILITATOR AND PARTICIPANT

In Appendix A, we discuss the facilitation principle of process and recommend that facilitators be content neutral. A Scrum Team should explore what effect this recommendation has on them when it comes to facilitating the Scrum events. In the Sprint Retrospective, the whole Scrum Team should participate, but whoever facilitates should be neutral. The options are to have someone from outside of the Scrum Team facilitate or have someone take a dual role.

Both options have trade-offs. A facilitator external to the team is likely to have not built up the same level of trust with the team as the team members have with each other, so the team might not be as comfortable being as open as usual. On the other hand, if a team member takes on the role of both facilitator and participant, they risk being biased or being viewed as biased during facilitation. This could look like they are leading conversations in a certain direction, which could confuse other participants and make them question the facilitator's neutrality. To avoid biasing the conversations, a facilitator should make it explicit when they are facilitating versus when they are participating. They can announce to the group when they are speaking as a facilitator and when as a participant.

A technique like Lean Coffee or conversation café can help. Using these approaches, a facilitator provides guidance on the format being used and keeps time but can take part in the discussions as a participant.

CREATE POSITIVE ENERGY

In the Sprint Retrospective, a Scrum Team discusses what went well during the Sprint and what did not. Typically, because the outcome of the event should be some actionable improvements, Scrum Teams tend to focus on what did not go well. When it feels as if a Scrum Team cannot take action, it has no control over things, or making improvements is daunting or seemingly impossible, the event can quickly become a breeding ground for pessimism, unhealthy conflict, or pity parties.

An effective facilitator should keep everyone's mind on the purpose of the event as the formal opportunity for a Scrum Team to collaborate and make things better. The facilitator should help people understand and empathize with each other, starting from a place where everyone assumes positive intent from others. This can help people imagine a better future and start the conversation about how to get there. Underlying good facilitation techniques for the Sprint Retrospective should be generating positive energy for the Scrum Team to explore what is possible. A Scrum Team may discover that there is more it can do to improve things than it realizes.

Facilitators should also draw attention to what is going well. Sometimes, Scrum Teams lose sight of the improvements that they have made, and bringing attention to these improvements can bring positive energy to the team as a whole. It can also build momentum and motivation for further improvement.

DON'T IGNORE THE ELEPHANT IN THE ROOM

The short iterations of Scrum combined with the challenge of meeting a Sprint Goal and delivering at least one Done Increment every Sprint quickly uncovers impediments that inhibit a Scrum Team from achieving these things.

Many Scrum Teams, particularly early on in their journey, focus on trivial issues. What went well? *We worked well as a team and communicated well.* What didn't go well? *We didn't get a Done Increment.* What improvement action can we take forward? *Start the Daily Scrum with a fun icebreaker.*

Or sometimes team members raise something uncomfortable. For example: *I don't think everyone is equally committed. I don't think our Definition of Done is rigorous enough. We are not being transparent about building a poor-quality product. Our forecasts are completely unrealistic.* The temptation is to skip past the comment to avoid conflict or a difficult conversation.

The real elephant in the room as to what is impeding the Scrum Team's effectiveness goes unaddressed because people feel uncomfortable talking about it. Good facilitation of the Sprint Retrospective should create an environment where difficult conversations can come out. Trust, and the Scrum values of courage, respect, and openness play an essential part in this. Conversations may still be uncomfortable, but to become a great Scrum Team, everyone has to become comfortable with some discomfort.

PROTECT THE HEALTH OF THE TEAM

Although good facilitation of the Sprint Retrospective encourages conversation around difficult challenges faced by the Scrum Team, this involves some level of conflict as the team navigates through building empathy and a shared understanding as it takes on its challenges. A certain level of conflict is a good thing. It means that members of the Scrum Team are challenging each other, leading to better understanding and ultimately better outcomes.

However, conflict beyond a certain point becomes detrimental to a team. When it turns into personal attacks and is more about personalities than the issue at hand, a facilitator needs to step in to protect the overall health of the team.

FACILITATE FOR THE SCRUM TEAM TO GET CREATIVE

If a Scrum Team wants to solve difficult problems, it needs to get creative. This involves deeper thinking, going beyond the obvious, and approaching problems with a proactive mindset so that it is possible to make some progress to deal with tough challenges.

Facilitation needs to allow inclusivity and promote participation. Facilitation of the Sprint Retrospective, perhaps more so than any of the other Scrum events, needs to create space for different personality types. Patience, understanding, and empathy can unlock some really creative ideas to solve difficult problems.

FRAME CHANGE AS EXPERIMENTS

Scrum is an empirical process, meaning that decisions are made on what is known at any given time, and knowledge grows through experience. By extension, what is decided can only be framed as a hypothesis as the best way to act—hence, why the Scrum events are designed to implement the empirical pillars of transparency, inspection, and adaptation. In other words, improvement actions should be considered an experiment, as something to try that the Scrum Team hypothesizes will lead to improvement, but they cannot know for sure until they try it.

Facilitating a Sprint Retrospective and framing improvement actions as experiments tends to generate less resistance to change than if changes are seen as something that is final. Facilitating the conversation around designing small experiments that can be rolled back if they are found to not be fit for purpose increases engagement because it makes people more prepared to give change a go.

CONCLUSION

The Sprint Retrospective is the event for the Scrum Team to inspect and adapt itself to improve its effectiveness. The team discusses what is working well and what is not, and it identifies improvement actions. However, as we've shared in this chapter, Scrum Teams underutilize the Sprint Retrospective for a variety of reasons: underwhelming participation, ambivalence, changing circumstances, poor facilitation, and so on. We hope that by sharing our own experiences with Sprint Retrospectives, and several facilitation formats and ideas, others can improve and remedy their situations.

Sprint Retrospectives are often associated with conflict in a team. Conflict is actually healthy when it is productive, but when team members hold off disputes and save unresolved conflict that has been affecting their morale until the Sprint Retrospective, or purposely avoid conflict, the facilitator must handle the situation and confrontations with care. A facilitator will be more successful in aiding the team dynamic by considering the facilitation principles that we discuss in Appendix A than with elaborate facilitation techniques. For help facilitating conflict, see Chapter 4.

For a Scrum Team to be effective, it must participate in its process and see that it works. When a facilitator helps a team identify areas for improvement in a Sprint Retrospective but fails to make transparent how and when to follow up on improvement actions, the Scrum Team falls short of reaching the outcome of the event.

A facilitator can help the Scrum Team by encouraging it to visualize and plan at least one improvement item as a candidate to go into Sprint Planning. By making in-progress improvement actions transparent on the Sprint Backlog the Scrum Team can evaluate the progress of the planned improvement(s) during the Sprint.

FACILITATING BEYOND A SINGLE SCRUM TEAM

8

Facilitating beyond a single Scrum Team can be an even trickier puzzle than with one.

So far, we have mainly focused on facilitation practices for one Scrum Team and its stakeholders. However, for various reasons, a facilitator might be helping a group larger than a single Scrum Team. For example, people from different teams might come together to learn about a specific topic, or teams might need to address the dependencies between them.

In this chapter, we explore facilitation beyond a single Scrum Team. Facilitators can also use some of these techniques with one Scrum Team.

Let's dive in.

THE SCRUM TEAMS WHOSE MEMBERS COULD BE SHARING KNOWLEDGE

Sean bumps into Giuseppina at the coffee machine. Both are Developers working in different Scrum Teams.

"Hey, Sean!" Giuseppina says as she waits for the machine to pour her coffee. "How are things with you?"

"Okay, I guess. I'm just having one of those days. Well, one of those Sprints, actually," he replies.

"How come?"

"We're working on implementing the company's new standard data storage system. I'm struggling to get it working with the same level of performance that we had with the old one."

"Oh, we had that issue," Giuseppina says. "We did that work for our app a couple of Sprints ago. We spent a whole Sprint investigating the issue, and we found that there are some really important configuration settings. I could show you what we did if you'd like."

"That would be great. Thanks, Giuseppina! I'm sure glad I bumped into you today. Who knows how long it would have taken us to figure it out for ourselves. Say, wouldn't it be cool if we could share tips like this between teams? We could save ourselves so much duplicated effort."

COMMUNICATING AND SHARING KNOWLEDGE ACROSS THE ORGANIZATION

Organizations that have autonomous cross-functional teams reduce dependencies and enable their Scrum Teams to get Product Backlog items Done because the team has all the skills to do so. However, without proper channels in place, a person who identifies with having a particular skill might feel cut off from others with that same skill. They might feel as if there is no one to develop ideas with on their particular specialty and grow concerned about keeping their skills sharp when they cannot bounce ideas off of others in the team. Also, if multiple Scrum Teams have similar problems or challenges, they may end up duplicating efforts to overcome those issues, as we saw in the previous story with Sean and Giuseppina.

Scrum is great for knowledge sharing and communication within the Scrum Team. However, additional practices are useful to meet the challenge of sharing information and maintaining good communication between teams and across an organization. Although town hall meetings, mass emails, and postings on intranet notice boards are efficient ways to broadcast to large groups, they are one-way communication tools that have limited impact. Two-way communication is more effective where people come together to discuss and share ideas and information, but it requires more effort and coordination. Facilitation can help.

TRY THIS! FACILITATE LEARNING ACROSS THE ORGANIZATION

The Sprint Retrospective is the primary means for a Scrum Team to inspect its effectiveness in delivering value and to make adaptations to improve what it does. However, in many organizations, Scrum Teams can speed up their improvement efforts by going beyond their own Sprint Retrospectives to share their learning and improvements. Organizations can coordinate knowledge sharing across organizational boundaries to improve the flow of information. Here, we share some facilitation ideas to help you support teams and the wider organization in scaling learning.

Communities of Practice

A community of practice is a group of people who come together to nurture particular skills and interests. It cuts across organization lines and helps people from across different Scrum Teams share knowledge and experiences, solve common problems, and develop skills. A community of practice has a focus on learning, sharing knowledge, and improving specific skills.

Typically, representatives from various teams start and evolve communities of practice. People should feel as if it is worth attending and choose to do so. Facilitation can help create communities of practice that are valuable and that become established. Ideally a member from the community of practice takes a leading role in facilitating it, or members decide to rotate facilitation.

Although communities of practice are organized around specific skill areas, membership should be open to anyone with an interest regardless of their current skill. Open communities of practice encourage people to pick up new knowledge and skills outside of their current area of expertise, which helps in boosting collaboration and developing empathy for others.

Lunch and Learn Sessions

Lunch and learn sessions are informal meetings typically held at lunchtime or scheduled breaks to share knowledge and experiences about a topic.

Lunch and learn sessions are typically open to anyone in the organization, and attendance is optional. Anyone can nominate a discussion topic or make a presentation. Lunch and learn sessions are informal and facilitation is usually lightweight, although a facilitator can add value by organizing discussion topics and helping people prepare.

Retrospectives at All Levels

Organization-level retrospectives help the entire organization continually improve. A facilitator can help build openness to, and acceptance of, retrospectives at every level of the organization. This may include facilitating retrospectives at the team, departmental, or executive levels, in which participants share challenges and identify improvements.

A facilitator can choose from many retrospective formats; however, whole department or multiple team retrospectives will likely have a large number of participants. This creates a huge opportunity for people to explore different perspectives, share common challenges, and be creative. However, it also creates a risk that a facilitator will lose control of the session because of the number of people involved. A facilitator can apply techniques to enable participants to surface ideas and insights while maintaining transparency for all, even in a large group. Techniques that help to facilitate large groups are discussed later in this chapter.

THE SCRUM TEAMS WITHOUT A SAY ON THEIR TEAM MEMBERSHIP

Jez, Angie, Zakaria, Inês, Abdul, and Sana meet on a conference call for the first time together. They have just been told that they are going to be working together in the same Scrum Team as part of an organizational restructure.

"I can't believe they arranged the teams like this!" cries Jez. "And have you seen the product they've allocated us to? There is going to be loads of user interface work, yet their rule of having one specialist skill in each team means I'm going to be overloaded!"

"Well, I'm going to be really bored," says Abdul. "It looks to me like there will only be one or two Sprints' worth of database work."

"And we don't even get to choose our own team name!" Angie says. "At least we didn't get called 'Team Brown!'"

"It's just dumb how they have done this," Jez continues.

"Did you see team Azul?" says Inês. "Putting James and Ashi together is not going to go well. They do not like each other at all."

"There are so many problems with this. We could have come up with better team structures ourselves," says Jez.

ORGANIZING AND STRUCTURING MULTIPLE SCRUM TEAMS

Organizing a large group of people into separate cross-functional Scrum Teams is challenging. Some organizations want to ensure that there are people with each skill on every team or they create skills matrices to inform them of how to divide people into teams based on mixing the current skills available as best they can. Where there are scarce skills, people are allocated across teams on a part-time basis in each. Other organizations simply create component Scrum Teams where managers divide teams along functional boundaries, resulting in specialist teams. Examples might be the marketing Scrum Team, the business intelligence Scrum Team, the user interface Scrum Team, the middleware Scrum Team, and so on.

Scrum provides little guidance on organizational structures other than that the goal is to have Scrum Teams that can produce value each Sprint, which includes them being able to produce at least one Done Increment each Sprint.

TRY THIS! SUPPORT SCRUM TEAMS TO ORGANIZE THEMSELVES

Besides cross-functionality, the other important characteristic of Scrum Teams is that they are self-managing. Allowing people to decide the composition of their Scrum Teams is highly empowering, it promotes self-management, and it is more likely to yield more effective results. People who have been allowed to self-manage into teams have higher cohesion, deeper trust, and more effective interconnections. Professionals who are closest to doing the work are best placed to decide how to do the work, which includes organizing the skills and people needed on a Scrum Team. This utilizes the knowledge of the people and avoids problems created by management pushing a superficial and constraining solution.

In addition to skills, factors such as experience, diversity, interpersonal relations, and the nature of the work all have a part in team effectiveness. As such, it should also be acknowledged that a perfect approach to composing Scrum Teams, or a perfect result, is rare, so Scrum Teams may need to work together and make adjustments to their team makeups in future Sprints.

Here, we share some tips and ideas that you can use to guide people in organizing their Scrum Teams.

Establish Boundary Conditions

When it comes to Scrum Teams forming themselves, management should participate in the process and not abandon employees without input and support. Management should recognize that they do not have all the answers and respect the expertise and the decisions that the Scrum Teams make within specified boundaries. A facilitator can run a session with those having decision-making authority together with representatives of people who will be on the teams. Collaboratively, they can decide the boundary conditions that Scrum Teams need to consider when they organize themselves. The following are examples:

- Teams must be between six and eight people, and the number of teams should not exceed ten.
- Each Scrum Team should have at least two people with two or more years experience in the company.
- All team members should be located within time zones of no more than three hours apart.
- Scrum Teams have analyzed the departmental Definition of Done and believe that they have the skills to meet it.
- Scrum Teams must be able to demonstrate that they can produce Done Increments in no more than three Sprints after formation.

Again, these are just examples. The types of boundary conditions will vary from organization to organization.

Facilitate Self-Managing Team Formation

A facilitator can help a group of people form themselves into Scrum Teams in a few ways. In our experience, no single approach works best, but we try to involve the people who will be part of the Scrum Teams as much as possible.

A facilitator needs to ensure that everyone involved understands each of the following aspects:

- The agreed boundary conditions
- The process that will be used for the team formation
- People's skills so that informed decisions can be made about the cross-functionality of the Scrum Teams
- The forecasted upcoming work around which Scrum Teams need to form

Facilitating Self-Managing Scrum Teams Formation

We have helped organizations facilitate the formation of Scrum Teams in different ways.

In one organization, around 100 people were involved in a team restructure as they moved to Scrum. The managers were open to experimenting with a session for these people to decide their own teams. We facilitated a session with the managers and representatives of people who would be part of the teams to decide the boundary conditions. We then held a virtual meeting with everyone involved. One of the managers talked about what work was coming up, set the context for what we were going to do, and described the boundary conditions for the teams. In a virtual space, we had a series of virtual icons representing different skills. We asked people to upload an image of themselves and add the icons that represented their skills to their image. We also asked people to add a sticky with some text to indicate their level of experience within each skill by ranking themselves from 1–3, with 1 being beginner, 2 being intermediate, and 3 being advanced.

The virtual tool allowed us to create a number of breakout rooms that people could move to by themselves. And that was it. It was up to the participants to go into breakout rooms, call other people in, leave and go somewhere else, and generally figure out how they were going to form their teams. Some teams formed quickly, some took a bit longer, and a few people were swapping in and out of teams when we brought up issues of some teams not meeting all the boundary conditions. But within about two hours, all the teams were formed.

People appreciated the opportunity to form themselves into their teams. The teams were far more cross-functional than they had been set up previously, with a lot fewer issues around dependencies. All of this meant that the time to deliver items of value was significantly reduced when it came to the teams doing the work.

—Glaudia Califano and David Spinks

Visualize and Reflect on Dependencies as an Ongoing Concern

When multiple teams work together, some of the biggest barriers to effectiveness are dependencies. Dependencies can cause significant delays, make planning much harder, and reduce organizational agility. Ideally, these dependencies should be minimized as far as possible. To understand the impact that dependencies might be having, a good first step is to build empirical evidence of the problems caused by the dependencies rather than relying on hearsay.

Visualization of dependencies should help everyone understand their true nature. This can happen in many ways, and Scrum Teams should experiment together to find out what gives them the transparency they need. When designing such a visualization, consider the following:

- Dependencies between Scrum Teams for particular Product Backlog items
- What the dependents are waiting on
- The length of delay caused
- Some data on how often dependencies occur between particular Scrum Teams and particular types of work
- Accessibility, such as use of color and size of elements on the visualization

Facilitators can use a visualization of dependencies as a conversation starter. They can invite a representative from each of the Scrum Teams to a regular session to review what the visualization is showing. The representatives should be people who are familiar with the work, who know about the dependencies they have on other teams, and know about the dependencies that other Scrum Teams have on them. Sometimes people who are not directly involved in the details of the work do not know enough about what is actually going on.

During this session, team representatives talk about dependencies that their Scrum Team has on the other teams, either immediately or with regard to work coming up in near-term Sprints. They can share what they think they need from other teams and when they need it. This can be made transparent on the visualization, and useful metrics on dependencies can be updated while the group is together.

The team representatives go back to their respective teams to share important insights and help their team adjust their plan. Team representatives can run this gathering as frequently as needed, depending on the environment. Examples might be once or twice a week, or once every two weeks. Teams should not wait for this meeting if dependencies need to be made visible and discussed, but frequent discussions happening outside the scheduled meeting between team representatives would suggest the meeting needs to be held more regularly.

To emphasize, the visualization of dependencies facilitates the conversation. Over time, the visualization and associated data may prompt conversations around team composition and any adaptations to team membership. A facilitator can help people explore the potential pros and cons of proposed changes and build agreement with the teams for any change.

Facilitating the Visualization of Dependencies in Component Teams

I was brought into one organization's IT department where dependencies were a particular challenge. Scrum Teams had been formed along preexisting organizational functional boundaries, meaning that component Scrum Teams existed: two for the website, one for middleware, one for data storage, one for business intelligence, and one for support and operations.

One of the website teams would select a Product Backlog item in a Sprint and start working on it. However, it wouldn't take long to discover that the feature the team was working on needed to access data from another system. So the web team would raise a request with the middleware team. The middleware team would be in Sprint itself, so the request would go onto its Product Backlog to be picked up, at best, in the following Sprint. When the middleware team picked up the item, it would need collaboration from the data storage team. However, it had already planned out its Sprint so this request sat in another Product Backlog, waiting to be picked up.

Each team had a "Definition of Done," but Done only meant completed at the component level. The teams had something called Done-Done, which was the extra step of integrating all the work.

The actual effort required to do the work from each team amounted to a few days. Yet, because of the lack of transparency and planning, it was regularly taking several Sprints to deliver a truly Done feature. These sorts of scenarios were happening again and again.

The first thing I did was help the teams visualize their cross-team dependencies and facilitate regular discussions with representatives from each team to bring better transparency and smarter planning. Just doing this changed the time it took to deliver features from several weeks to being able to start features and get them ready for release within a Sprint. The visualization and these meetings also kick-started conversations around how the teams were structured. Because team members were involved, they had a big say when the organization moved away from component teams to more cross-functional teams.

—David Spinks

THE CHAOTIC CUSTOMER REVIEW

Frasier is facilitating a large meeting where the product Increments of Team Sequiturs, Team Scrambled Eggs, Team Wings, and The Jack Russells will be reviewed with a sample of real end customers. The event is a great opportunity for the Scrum Teams to discuss and get feedback on their separate products.

Frasier is out of breath as he rushes to the door of the meeting room. He is late and rushes to push the door open. It opens a few inches before it hits something. The thud is followed by a surprised yelp.

"Sorry!" Frasier says when he realizes the "impediment" behind the door is a person.

"No worries," the man from behind the door says. "Standing room only now, I'm afraid." The two maneuver the door so that Frasier can enter the room. Frasier is shocked to see that the room is completely full of people. He squeezes past them as he makes his way to the front of the room, where Vijay from Team Sequiturs awaits with his laptop in front of the presentation screen.

"Thanks for coming, everyone! It's great to see so many people here. Let's jump straight into the demo, shall we? Vijay, please kick us off." Vijay looks at Frasier with a look of concern etched over his face.

"I need my adapter so I can connect my laptop to the screen."

"Darn it. Okay, let me go and get it." Frasier raises his voice to address the room. "Sorry everyone," Frasier says. "We'll get started in a few moments. Just a minor technical issue."

Frasier stumbles his way back through the throng of people. "Should have booked a bigger room, Fraze!" he hears a voice call out. He gets out of the door and runs at full speed to get to Vijay's desk. Other than Vijay's monitors, docking station, mouse, and a half-drunk cup of coffee, the desk is empty. Frasier looks in the drawers. The adapter is not there. He looks under the desk. Nothing. With no idea what to do, he runs back to the meeting room. Sweat now forming on his brow, he makes his way again to Vijay.

"It's not on your desk, Vijay. What do we do?" Frasier says in a panicked whisper.

"It's in my laptop bag. I left it at the reception desk."

"What? Why didn't you say that before?" Frasier again passes through the mass of people, runs from the room again, and eventually returns with Vijay's laptop bag, calling out more apologies as he re-enters the room.

A few minutes later, Vijay is all set up. They skip any introduction. "So, I am going to demo the updated administration screen."

There is an audible groan, and one voice calls out, "I'm not interested in that!" Another says, "Frasier, can you DM me when we get to the Team Scrambled Eggs stuff on the new promotion's functionality? I'm going to go and get coffee."

"Is that an option?" calls out another voice. "I'm getting coffee too. Frasier, also DM me when this bit is over." More people make it clear that they are uninterested in the admin screens and will return.

Frasier loses track of whom he is supposed to message when they are done reviewing the Sequiturs work. It hardly matters. When Vijay has finished showing the admin screens and people have given their opinions, which included a lengthy discussion on the color palette used, there is only 15 minutes left of the scheduled timebox to review the work of the other three teams.

PREPARING FOR A LARGE MEETING

The session in the previous story did not go smoothly mainly because of Frasier's lack of preparation. In brief:

- The room that Frasier booked was far too small. He had done no prior preparation regarding understanding the number of people who would be coming to the event.
- He had not ensured that the equipment to run demonstrations was ready.
- Some stakeholders were clearly uninterested in everything that was going to be discussed.
- There wasn't enough time to review all the Scrum Teams' work, and the meeting didn't start on time.
- Frasier wasn't even on time himself.

A facilitator who is unprepared creates the kinds of issues we saw in the story. And the larger the meeting, the greater the problems caused by the facilitator's lack of preparation. Facilitating a large group can be challenging enough without amplifying the problems with poor preparation. In any large meeting, facilitators are challenged to keep everyone engaged and contributing so that they achieve the meeting's purpose within the meeting's timebox. For more on facilitation preparation, see Appendix C, "Facilitation Checklist."

TRY THIS! DECENTRALIZED LARGE MEETINGS

Sometimes large meetings involving multiple Scrum Teams and their stakeholders are unavoidable.

Large meetings might become less effective as the number of participants grows. Some of the challenges can be reduced by decentralizing the meeting so that everyone's attention does not have to be on the same thing at the same time. In this approach, facilitators break the meeting into parallel sessions that focus on different aspects of the meeting's overall topic. Techniques for facilitating decentralized meetings are presented here.

The Science Fair/Science Expo

On-demand inspection at a science fair stall.

In a science fair or science expo, all the Scrum Teams gather into one place to provide on-demand inspection and give stakeholders the opportunity to visit areas of interest. The idea is that Scrum Teams make different areas available for inspection and feedback simultaneously. Scrum Teams' representatives at each station have discussions with whomever is interested and turns up.

Scrum Teams invite stakeholders to a big enough space that is appropriate to set up the required number of different stations, or they can run it as a virtual session using a tool that allows breakout areas.

Members of the Scrum Teams host at each station to facilitate, demonstrate, and guide stakeholders in interacting with the result of the work from the Sprint. Note that not all team members have to be hosts. To promote learning and understanding, other team members are free to visit other stations and act as stakeholders. Team members can decide to rotate the hosting so that everyone gets a chance to explore. Remember that the idea is to promote participation and collaboration, so hosts should avoid one-way presentations. The aim is to let stakeholders try the Increments, ask questions, discuss, and give feedback. The hosts are there to facilitate and guide. Index cards, a (virtual) feedback wall, or some other way to capture feedback should be available to record interesting questions or insights.

Participants should have the opportunity to move from station to station and be encouraged to move on if they are not doing it on their own. The facilitator can start the session by inviting participants to go to any area of their choosing. The facilitator can create a cadence, such as 15 minutes per round, and give a signal for people to take the opportunity to move on to other stations, or they can decide to stay where they are for another round.

An alternative format is to ditch the rounds and just have one big timebox, with people free to roam from station to station as they choose.

World Café

Group conversations are served with World Café.

World Café[1] is a divergent and convergent approach that facilitators can use with a large group of people. Participants have conversations at a series of "café" tables or in breakout rooms when facilitated virtually. The large group is broken down into smaller, roughly even-sized groups of a maximum of five people per group. Each small group is allocated to one of the tables.

The facilitator prepares a question or statement for each table. For example, perhaps they are facilitating a large group Sprint Review, and they decide to use the 4Ls questions after the latest Increment has been demonstrated. They divide the questions across four tables:

- **Liked:** What did you enjoy, and what did you like about the product?
- **Learned:** What have you learned about the product?

---

1. Brown, Juanita; Isaacs, David (2005). *The World Café: Shaping Our Futures Through Conversations That Matter.* Berrett-Koehler Publishers; Illustrated edition. Or see https://theworldcafe.com/.

- **Lacked:** What did you feel was lacking in the product, and what could be better?
- **Longed for:** What did you long for in the product, and what do you wish was present?

Each group explores and discusses the question at their table for a set time-box, perhaps 20 minutes. Optionally, the facilitator can help to ensure everyone has equal voice time by instructing the table groups to use a talking object. With this, only the person holding the object is allowed to speak. The group rotates the talking object to another person after a set timebox, such as every 4 minutes, or the person can pass the object on once they have had an opportunity to say all they want to say.

During the discussions, participants capture ideas and thoughts with doodles, sketches, or text. At the end of the timebox, groups rotate to another table and repeat the process, building upon the content left at the table by previous groups. The process continues for several rounds or until all groups have visited all tables.

A variation can be that one person stays behind each round to act as the table host. This person, at the start of the next round, summarizes what has been discussed at the table up to that point.

The next step is to invite all the participants to share their insights as a whole group.

A facilitator can use World Café for a variety of scenarios where a large group of people participates, such as inviting all Scrum Teams involved in a product to refine a shared Product Backlog, or it could be used for facilitating a multiple Scrum Team Sprint Review where different features or products are allocated to different tables for review and discussion.

Gallery Walk

Gallery walk is a technique that has less structure than World Café. It originated as a classroom-based approach to promote active learning and involves the facilitator posting various open-ended questions about a topic in different areas on the walls. Participants form small teams, or they can do the gallery walk as individuals, with each starting at a different area. They write their thoughts in response to the question at the station before moving on to the next station after a fixed time period, such as 3 minutes. The next team or individual reviews the inputs from the previous round(s), and they add their own thoughts in response to the question. This continues, and after everyone has visited all areas, people go back to their first station to review the responses. Finally, a discussion is facilitated as one big group.

Just as in World Café, within a large group all participants in the gallery walk have the opportunity to contribute, share, reflect, and build upon each other's ideas.

Shift and Share

Some might be familiar with the Liberating Structure shift and share, and notice its similarities with World Café and gallery walk. Shift and share has a greater emphasis on the presentation of innovations, and it has more structure to the session.

Scrum Teams can facilitate a shift and share as follows:

1. First they set up stations, each with one or more presenters.
2. The group of participants splits into the same number of small groups as stations available. These groups stay together throughout.
3. Each group rotates from station to station.
4. At each station, the presenters give a 10-minute presentation. Presenters can supplement their presentations with examples and invite participants to interact with product features.
5. A 2-minute timebox follows to allow for questions and feedback.
6. The groups then have 1-minute to rotate to the next station.
7. The groups repeat the process until they have visited all stations.

Making Insights Transparent to All

Facilitating the Sprint Review using practices such as those mentioned previously generates a lot of feedback, which is exactly what Scrum Teams want. At the same time, making sense of all this data can become a challenge in itself.

Whichever technique the facilitator uses, it is important that they enable the group to come back together as one to spend some time sorting through the feedback. One technique to use to increase transparency and help to organize a large amount of data is to create an affinity map. We discuss affinity maps in Chapter 1, "Facilitating Alignment." During the process of creating the affinity map, themes, patterns, and insights emerge.

Graphic Recording

Graphic recording is a visual technique that can be effective in actively engaging participants in conferences, meetings, and events. A facilitator can decide to partner with a graphic recorder who conveys and captures key messages through visuals in real time. Graphic visualization of key messages helps the group focus, follow along, and take in key messages faster. It helps to increase shared understanding, create a visual memory, and promote creativity. Furthermore, participants obtain a full image of a situation, improving decision-making. At the end of a session, the group has a visual summary that can be shared with all participants.

KEYS TO FACILITATING BEYOND A SINGLE SCRUM TEAM

A Scrum Team's challenges and problems are not bound within the team, so a facilitator may need to work with more than one Scrum Team. Here, we share some key considerations for facilitators to think about when it comes to facilitation in scenarios that involve people beyond a single Scrum Team.

PLANNING AND PREPARATION FOR BIG GROUPS

A facilitator always needs to plan and prepare, but this is especially true when it comes to facilitating large groups. If a session is going to be held at a physical location, the facilitator needs to ensure adequate space, not only for people to sit comfortably, but also for people to take part in activities. These activities might involve people moving around, sticking things on the wall, and looking at them together.

In a virtual space, the facilitator needs to think about the provision of virtual whiteboards with space for individuals and smaller groups if they plan to break people into smaller groups. The facilitator needs to think about setting up breakout rooms without delaying proceedings too much. This could be done in a break, or the facilitator could have a cofacilitator to help, as we discuss in Appendix B, "Adapting for Virtual."

In addition to planning for the physical or virtual space, facilitators should think about timing. With bigger groups, it is more challenging to find times that are suitable for everyone. Again, we advise focusing on participants' needs. Many facilitators schedule meetings where they can find a gap in people's diaries or to suit themselves. Meetings are often scheduled during people's lunchtimes or outside of people's normal working hours. It can be even more challenging when arranging virtual meetings with participants joining from different parts of the world and in different time zones. At the very least, the facilitator needs to make the purpose of any session clear, think about who really needs to attend, and seek feedback from participants about suitable times. The facilitator may not be able to please everyone, but they should do the best they can to accommodate everyone.

STRONG COMMUNICATION AND CONNECTION TO OBJECTIVES

When facilitating a big group, it is even more important that the facilitator clearly articulates the purpose of the session so that participants understand it. This helps prevent people from getting sidetracked and wasting time on discussions that do not contribute to the purpose. One way to help with that is to start with a connection activity.

In a workshop, for example, the facilitator can share the learning objective for the session and then ask people to form small groups to discuss what they know about the subject already. Or, if the purpose is to solve a particular problem, the small group discussion can center on why solving the problem is important. Connecting participants to the subject in this way can focus them on the objective going forward.

CLEAR SUMMARIZATION

Just as important as making sure the purpose is clear at the start of a large group session is summarizing at the end so that participants can get a feel for how well the objective was met.

Ideally, this should not come from the facilitator. We recommend having participants summarize what they think was achieved and what insights they uncovered. The facilitator can invite different participants to share thoughts. The facilitator might paraphrase what is said to check understanding but not decide the summary on behalf of the group and determine whether the objective was met. For more on paraphrasing, see Chapter 4, "Facilitating Team Dynamics."

PROVIDE REFLECTION, FEEDBACK, AND PARKING LOT SPACES

The larger the group size, the more complex it is to facilitate full participation. The facilitator can provide a reflection and feedback space so that all participants know there is a place for them to express themselves, even if they do not get the chance to share their thoughts in the main session. Participants can write their reflections and feedback on sticky notes and add them to the space during a session or even after a session has ended.

A facilitator can also use the space as a "parking lot." People often have thoughts or raise issues that are not directly related to the discussion being had or the objective of the session. Yet those thoughts and issues may still be valuable, and the participants do not want their thought to be lost. The facilitator can direct people to a parking lot space where they can capture anything they have on their mind. The items in the parking lot can be discussed later, at the end of the session, or they can be reviewed afterward with actions planned for suitable follow-ups. For example, the facilitator may arrange for the participant to have a follow-up conversation with interested and appropriate parties.

Facilitate Organizational Communication

In addition to facilitation of large group sessions, facilitators should be helping with communication at the organizational level. In many companies, communication to a particular team is through an individual such as a manager, team leader, Scrum Master, or Product Owner. This creates a bottleneck, reduces transparency, and increases the risk of things being lost in translation.

Limiting communication in this way can seem to be more efficient, but in complex environments, it is better that communication is more collaborative instead of having dependencies on individuals for it to happen between Scrum Teams or departments. With the right planning and use of facilitation skills and techniques, a facilitator can make this happen while keeping the communication focused and still relatively efficient when lots of people are involved. The main consideration, though, should be on facilitating conversations to make things transparent, catalyze improvements, and aid decision-making. This could be when Scrum Teams have impediments or dependencies, when there is value in sharing knowledge and learning, or in creating better transparency about what is going on across the organization.

Apply Facilitation Principles but Adapt Facilitation Techniques

A facilitator should fall back on the facilitation principles that we discuss in Appendix A, "Facilitation Principles," regardless of whether they facilitate for a small group, a Scrum Team, interactions with representatives from across Scrum Teams, or a larger group made up of people from multiple Scrum Teams and stakeholders.

Regardless of the situation, a facilitator should always aim to facilitate in such a way that enables participation. They should ensure that participants are guided with purpose through an inclusive and participatory process. This process, along with relevant information, artifacts, decisions, and ways these decisions are made, should be transparent. The facilitator works to maintain healthy interactions in the group. This approach likely requires the facilitator to adapt their facilitation techniques to the situation.

CONCLUSION

Facilitating beyond a single Scrum Team is a considerable topic, and we have only scratched the surface here. We have highlighted common scenarios, such as when individuals would like to share and learn from others with the same subject matter interests or, for instance, when dealing with cross-team dependencies. When facilitating across teams, large groups or sessions with multiple teams, facilitators should plan ahead, be clear with objectives, and find creative ways for attendees to connect with each other and the topic quickly. We have provided techniques and ideas in this chapter to help.

We have purposely avoided discussion of different scaling solutions because scaling Scrum is beyond the scope of this book. Our intention with this chapter has been to provide tips and ideas for facilitating the communication and knowledge sharing beyond a single Scrum Team that is often needed in organizations. Scaling Scrum is well documented elsewhere, including in the book *The Nexus Framework for Delivering Scrum*[2] in the Professional Scrum series.

---

2. Bittner, Kurt; Kong, Patricia; West, Dave (2017). *The Nexus Framework for Scaling Scrum: Continuously Delivering an Integrated Product with Multiple Scrum Teams* (The Professional Scrum Series). Addison-Wesley Professional.

MOVING
Conclusion
FORWARD

Moving forward rarely happens in a straight line!

Throughout this book, we have shared stories, based on our real-life experiences, of challenges that Scrum Teams struggle with on a daily basis. We have shown you how we have personally navigated and facilitated those scenarios in the spirit of giving you ideas that you can try when you encounter similar situations. No situation is exactly the same so you need to adapt the techniques we have shared in this book to your own situation and your own personal style.

What we hope this book has given you is a set of tools and techniques you can add to your own personal repertoire and purposefully adapt to your unique situations. Each scenario in this book includes techniques you can immediately experiment with in the detailed "Try This!" sections and things to think about in the "Keys to Facilitation" sections.

Before we leave you to put this knowledge to work, we offer you some final thoughts on how to get started, what to avoid, and how to continue your journey facilitating professional Scrum Teams.

GETTING STARTED

If you are like us, when you read a book, everything makes perfect sense until you try to apply it. To help you get over the first barrier, here are some things to consider:

- **Get to know the basics of the Scrum framework:** Thoroughly understanding Scrum and how to apply the Scrum values will help you be better equipped to guide a self-managing Scrum Team during its events and discussions.

- **Get to know the facilitation principles:** The facilitation principles will help you as a facilitator to guide a group of people to achieve shared outcomes in ways that are inclusive.

- **Know some facilitation techniques and when to use them:** This book describes more than 80 facilitation techniques. Becoming familiar with how and when to use them, and more importantly practicing them, will help you hone your facilitation skills.

- Experiment: Take time to experiment with a technique and see what happens. Understand that what works well one time may not work the next time, and vice versa. When things work well, celebrate, but do not give up when things do not work out the way you hoped they would. Understanding what worked and why, and what to do differently the next time, will help you to improve.

- **Observe others facilitating:** Are they demonstrating the different facilitation principles? How do they deal with silence or tense conversations? When do they use more structured techniques versus opting for more group conversation and open questioning?

- **Reflect on your own facilitation:** Did the techniques you used help you apply the facilitation principles? Was there full participation? Was the objective met? Were the conversations inclusive? Were you transparent about your process? Were discussions healthy?

- **Be flexible and kind:** Show grace to yourself and others.

- **Cofacilitate:** This allows you to learn on the job. Also, the extra support helps if things go wrong. In addition, cofacilitation offers more support and attention for the participants.

Becoming good at anything requires time, repetition, and learning from your mistakes. Do not give up when the result is less than you had hoped for. If you can learn from those experiences, you *will* get better.

WATCHING FOR COMMON FACILITATION MISTAKES

Learn from the mistakes of others. You can't live long enough to make them all yourself.

—*Eleanor Roosevelt*

The three of us cannot remember all the mistakes we have made as facilitators and professionals working with Scrum Teams, but we certainly remember the lessons we have learned. The stories and knowledge we share in this book are largely inspired from the mistakes that at least one of us has made in the past.

As a facilitator, you will experience uncomfortable situations and make mistakes. The impact is lessened when you keep the facilitation principles that we discuss in Appendix A, "Facilitation Principles," in mind. Here are a few things to keep an eye out for when facilitating and some suggestions on what to do if you get stuck.

TRYING TO DESIGN THE PERFECT SESSION

A facilitator will not find the perfect agenda or flow to an event or meeting. It does not exist. If you find yourself having trouble getting started with designing a session:

- Keep the purpose of the Scrum event or the session at the forefront of everyone's minds.
- Think about the context and the situation that the group is in.
- Get advice from other facilitators. Their perspective and support can confirm your approach or point you in another direction.

MISMANAGING TIME AND EXPECTATIONS

An effective facilitator does not facilitate a session exactly to their agenda. They do not want to stop healthy conversation just because a timebox has ended or make people feel like they are being ignored. However, facilitators should not ignore timeboxes. Timeboxes exist to help teams and participants focus on the task at hand.

At times, a group may go down a path that no one planned for but is worth exploring. Or maybe the team is following the agenda, but the group's needs are not being met. Here are some ideas to keep the participants on track:

- Make sure the desired outcome of the discussion is transparent and understood.
- Prepare. Have a plan and at least a loose agenda.
- Consider what occurred during the participants' last time or event together.
- Point out timing and where the group is in their discussion.
- Discourage individuals from monopolizing the conversation by asking for input from others.
- Ensure what is needed to make a decision is clear. In Chapter 4, we discuss the importance of having transparent decision methods. Ask if people need a refresher of the decision-making process that the group uses.

- If you have a cofacilitator, discuss both of your observations and what adjustments to make if energy levels are dropping or conversations are going off track.
- Get feedback in real time during a facilitated session by conducting a mini retrospective.

NAVIGATING GROUP DYNAMICS

Different types of conflict can exist in a Scrum Team. Throughout this book, we have discussed divergent and convergent methods to help a team navigate the situation where they need to maneuver through the Groan Zone and disagreement to collaboratively come to consensus. This conflict is healthy, necessary, and expected for everyone to participate fully in solving complex problems.

In Chapter 4, we addressed negative conflict in teams in detail. In general, negative conflict contains some key characteristics. Conflict can be negative if differences are ignored, expectations are not managed, an individual's needs are misunderstood, the disagreement focuses on assumptions rather than facts, or the individuals involved have no desire to find a solution.

Whatever the situation, the facilitator should not ignore the conflict. Sometimes people think that the tension will go away, but instead it festers when it is ignored and allowed to persist. The following are some ways to prevent misunderstandings or deescalate a situation:

- Acknowledge that everyone is human and humans are emotional beings.
- Stop people from continually interrupting each other. Be mindful that they may not be aware of their behavior.
- Paraphrase and summarize back to the group to improve clarity.
- Reduce confusion by asking individuals, "Can you repeat what you are saying using different words? What is at the heart of your concern?"
- Pay attention to tone and body language.
- Avoid rushing to a result. People think differently. Slow down.

- When people are voicing concerns, ask them what can be done to address their concern.
- Listen for agreement and acknowledge it in some manner, no matter how small. This helps to build both morale and clarification.
- Advise everyone to step back, take a break, and get some fresh air.

When you have had a rough time while facilitating a session, the last thing you want to do is keep playing it back in your head. It is easy to blame the situation or other people and hope things will go better the next time. You should resist that temptation.

Instead, take time to step away from your own emotions to do a little self-diagnosis. Would you do anything differently the next time? Would a different approach have been more effective? Discussing the situation with a peer or mentor can help you turn these unpleasant situations into genuine personal and professional growth opportunities.

IMPROVING AS A FACILITATOR

Facilitation is only helpful when it enables a purposeful and participative environment in which people feel safe to engage, learn, and collaborate. Facilitators help enable this environment by relying on their own creativity, empathy, some structure, and willingness to improvise along the way. Undoubtedly, at times you may find yourself in messy situations, and the best way to learn is through application.

In the spirit of continuous improvement, getting feedback on a facilitation process is a helpful way for a facilitator to learn and develop their skill. This book offers several ideas on how to get feedback, but a simple tip is to just ask others about your strengths and areas for improvement. From there, as a facilitator, you can inspect and adapt your approach as you move forward.

FACILITATION PRINCIPLES

The five facilitation principles[1] of participative, purposeful, process, transparency, and healthy are core to effective facilitation. Facilitators should draw on these principles when deciding which facilitation skills and techniques might serve a group best to achieve their objective. Facilitation principles are intertwined and support each other.

PARTICIPATIVE

Participative is *the* core facilitation principle. A facilitator should aim to get full participation from a group so that they get the benefits of all participants' skills, knowledge, and perspectives.

Full participation does not imply that all participants must speak. Rather, it means that people are intellectually and emotionally engaged and putting their energy into participating in group interactions. They receive opportunities to share their ideas and thoughts, while actively listening to others' perspectives. This enables ideas to surface and innovative solutions to develop

---

1. Adapted from "Principles of Meeting Excellence" from SeriousWork and Sean Blair.

from the group as a whole. Through this type of engagement, participants begin to build empathy for each other's perspectives, needs, and goals.

A group is more likely to take on shared responsibility when there is full participation. Individuals participate more when they feel involved and know that their voice is heard in a group because they identify with the larger collective and its successes as well as failures.

Conversely, if ideas, processes, and so on are forced, people participate less. They do not feel a sense of ownership and are likely unmotivated to perform at their best.

PURPOSEFUL

To be purposeful as a facilitator means to establish clear objectives.

Purposeful facilitation requires the facilitator and participants to have an overarching objective in mind that they are working toward, such as a Scrum Team creating a Sprint Goal. A facilitator should ensure a shared understanding of objectives so that everyone understands what the expected outcomes are of their collaboration.

Purposeful facilitation is important because it drives focus. Facilitators can quickly lose sight of the purpose of what they are facilitating. Consider the facilitator who tends to treat the Sprint Retrospective as a time for team-building activities, rather than as a time for the Scrum Team to plan ways to improve as a team, which is the true purpose of the event.

PROCESS

To achieve objectives, facilitators need to apply process. Process is the use of facilitation to guide a group of people toward the desired objective of the interaction in a way that is inclusive, fair, and open. This should not be confused with using a process to define step-by-step instructions to follow.

The following elements are important for a facilitator to consider when helping a group progress in a way that encourages collective participation and shared understanding:

- **Content neutrality:** Remaining neutral and not taking a position on the content or outcome of the discussion.
- **Process advocacy:** Advocating for certain processes and techniques that encourage an inclusive environment for full participation.
- **Support:** Managing facilitation with others to help prepare, facilitate, and implement follow-up actions.

Facilitators risk losing trust and credibility if they appear biased about a topic or person when facilitating. They should remain content neutral.

Facilitators who are knowledgeable about the facilitation process, principles, and different techniques can better help the participants in reaching their objectives during an event or meeting. They are better equipped to adapt their process more easily to enable a group to progress toward their desired objectives of the interactions in ways that are collaborative, inclusive, and leverage diverse perspectives.

Depending on context, sometimes facilitators need support. They can enlist one or more cofacilitators to help manage and adapt processes as things evolve.

TRANSPARENCY

Transparency exists when a group has a shared understanding that enables participants to have the same comprehension of a situation.

Shared understanding helps people collectively reach consensus, make decisions, and achieve outcomes. In complex environments, groups are highly likely to require facilitated collaboration and discussion sessions where participants are mindful and actively listen to one another to develop a shared understanding.

Facilitators should ensure transparency on the process and learning used to arrive at decisions as well as transparency of the decisions themselves.

Scrum Teams use artifacts like the Product Backlog and the Increment to support transparency for their work together. Other approaches that groups use to aid transparency include using a common language that is not overly complex, articulating items concisely, and supplementing text with visuals if it aids understanding.

HEALTHY

The healthy facilitation principle requires people to respectfully connect with each other on a human level.

A good facilitator understands that human beings are emotional life forms and that human interactions evoke different emotions. Facilitators expect people to experience negative feelings such as frustration, anger, judgment, blame, and disengagement. They know that if the process or issues causing them are not addressed, progress is impeded.

Therefore, a facilitator looks to build psychological safety in a team to create an open, inviting, and active environment where people eagerly contribute and empathize with each other. Moreover, when psychological safety is present, individuals can more openly collaborate and discuss conflicting perspectives.

It is important that a facilitator can distinguish individuals fairly discussing conflicting perspectives from destructive behaviors such as criticizing, shutting down other ideas, and seeking to form alliances. If these behaviors are apparent, a facilitator should address them as soon as possible to avoid them escalating into unhealthy conflict.

ADAPTING FOR VIRTUAL

This book is agnostic about in person versus virtual facilitation. Although we mention a few tips and differences between the two mediums, it is our belief that facilitators can adapt most facilitation techniques for virtual use, provided the right tooling is available, such as a good virtual meeting platform and virtual whiteboard space.

All the facilitation principles we have discussed in this book still apply whether facilitation is taking part in a physical or a virtual setting. For example, the facilitation principle of purposeful is arguably even more important in a virtual session when participants' attention is competing with background activities such as barking dogs, playing children, arriving packages, and the din of daily life. In addition, with the facilitation principle of process in mind, a facilitator needs to consider the fatiguing effects for people of sitting behind a screen in a meeting for long periods of time.

We leave it to the facilitator to get creative with circumstances and tools available while keeping the facilitation principles in mind. In this appendix we share some specific tips for facilitating virtual meetings.

COMMUNICATION AND COLLABORATION TOOLS

Virtual tooling has improved dramatically in recent years, and the growth of remote work has continued to feed improvements. Part of the facilitator's skill is finding the right tools and learning how to use them for the needs of the group they are facilitating.

In this section, we share some tips when it comes to virtual communication and collaboration tools.

KEEP IT SIMPLE

Choose tools that are intuitive and easy to use. Complex tools, although powerful, can get in the way of effective collaboration.

For most techniques that we discuss in this book, teams need tools that allow participants to connect with video, audio, and chat. Because many techniques we recommend in this book include divergent and convergent thinking and splitting participants into smaller groups, teams also need tools that allow them to create independent virtual breakout rooms in the same session. Additionally, teams need access to a shared collaboration space, such as an online whiteboard where participants can add content including virtual sticky notes, text, images, or free-form drawings.

INTRODUCE THE TOOLS

To reduce technical issues in virtual meetings, when sending out a meeting invite to participants, the facilitator should include information on the tooling that will be used. This is especially important for people who have not used the tools, or the organization's configuration of them, before. The facilitator can also help people prepare by giving them a way to try the tools before the meeting. Participants may also need short instruction videos or how-to guides for the tools.

When using virtual whiteboards, facilitators should test that participants can add content to the whiteboard. One way to do this is to ask participants to introduce themselves by using a virtual sticky note to give some details about themselves or write about what their expectations are for the meeting. They could even upload a picture. Facilitators can ask participants to do this before the session.

CONSIDER HAVING A COHOST

Virtual tools create additional meeting overhead. Having a cohost who helps with the technical aspects can free the facilitator to focus on the needs of the group.

When running virtual sessions, facilitators often break large groups into smaller ones for activities. The facilitator needs to deal with setting up breakout rooms for the groups, which can cause delays and be stressful when needing to do so in real time. Most virtual tools allow the facilitator to give permissions to a cohost which enables them to set up breakout rooms and allocate people to them. The cohost can administer the breakout rooms in the background while the facilitator addresses the group with guidance for the activity.

Cohosts can help by monitoring the chat window, should the tool selected have one. They can also troubleshoot technical problems that participants are having and help keep time.

VIRTUAL MEETING ETIQUETTE

As part of their working agreement, a team can discuss and agree on their virtual meeting etiquette. This can include how the team members expect each other to behave in virtual sessions. Maybe they are agreeing that they will not multitask, or they will raise a virtual hand to indicate that they want to speak so that people do not speak over each other. We discuss team working agreements in Chapter 1, "Facilitating Alignment."

BE INCLUSIVE AND RESPECTFUL OF INDIVIDUALS' NEEDS

A facilitator should strive for inclusivity for all. When choosing virtual collaboration and presentation tools, facilitators should treat accessibility considerations as essential requirements to create inclusive and accessible virtual interactions, meetings, and communication. They should check that their tool complies with international accessibility standards and the accessibility features it offers. Facilitators can ask participants what type of accessibility is needed as part of their meeting invite. This way, they can ensure that the right configuration is applied in the tool when the meeting starts.

MINIMIZING VIRTUAL MEETING FATIGUE CAUSED BY CAMERAS BEING ON

Various studies[1,2] show that video calls are mentally demanding and can cause physical exhaustion when people spend a lot of time on them. From a facilitation point of view, it may lead to a decrease in engagement and productivity.

People who facilitate commonly ask how they can ensure that participants turn their cameras on in virtual sessions. Many facilitators try to encourage team members to keep their cameras turned on at all times because it is a popular belief that this enables more engagement and inclusion and ultimately increases productivity. However, researchers have found that people who are constantly on video conference calls with their cameras on have increased virtual meeting fatigue. The results of one study published in the *Journal of Applied Psychology*[3] indicated that keeping cameras on during virtual meetings is more fatiguing than having them off. This fatigue results in less engagement and a reduction in voice.

---

1. Microsoft (2020). "The Future of Work: The Good, Challenging & Unknown." www.microsoft.com/en-us/microsoft-365/blog/2020/07/08/future-work-good-challenging-unknown/.

2. Shockley, Kristen M., Allison Gabriel, Daron Robertson, Christopher. C. Rosen, Nitya Chawla, Mahira Ganster, and Maira Ezerins (2021). "The Fatiguing Effects of Camera Use in Virtual Meetings: A Within-Person Field Experiment." *Journal of Applied Psychology* 106, no. 8, 1137–1155. https://doi.org/10.1037/apl0000948.

3. Ibid.

Furthermore, in the *Journal of Applied Psychology* paper, the researchers detailed causes for virtual meeting fatigue. Participants in a video call see many other people on the screen at the same time, which is a lot of information to constantly be taking in. Someone may glance off to the side, but as a viewer, our brain interprets that as the person looking at someone else on the screen. People feel they are being watched all the time, further increasing their cognitive load. Subconsciously, our brains are working harder, not just in interpreting what we are seeing, but also in how we present ourselves. These factors combine and result in greater fatigue when cameras are on in virtual meetings. Evidence such as this undermines the goals of a facilitator who insists virtual meeting participants keep their cameras on at all times.

This is not to say that facilitators should recommend that participants have their cameras off; rather, they should consider when it might be beneficial to have cameras on in a meeting and when it does not matter. Here are some tips on how a facilitator can help participants minimize fatigue caused by virtual meetings and camera use.

Reduce Screen Window Size

In a physical meeting, people look directly at the speaker. They take notes and may look around. However, the level of eye contact and the size of people's faces that appear onscreen is unnatural in virtual video meetings.

An easy way to mitigate this effect is to simply suggest that participants resize the window of the virtual meeting tool so that the other participants' faces are not so prominent.

Participants Turn Off Self View

In many virtual meeting tools, participants not only see others on their screen, but they also see themselves. Seeing yourself in real time during video calls can lead to increased self-criticism and stress. In short, it can be exhausting.

Most virtual meeting platforms have an option to switch off self view. Some also have the option for participants to replace the video of themselves with an avatar.

INCORPORATE PERIODS OF AUDIO ONLY

Nonverbal communication plays a big role when people interact with each other. People use facial expressions, hand gestures, nod or shake their heads, shrug their shoulders, and so on to express themselves. These nonverbal signals are harder to read through our video screens. Participants' minds need to make more of an effort to send and receive these cues.

A facilitator can mitigate some of the buildup of fatigue by scheduling audio-only periods, where they ask participants to turn off their cameras and turn their bodies away from the screen.

KEEP SESSIONS SHORT

Part of the preparation that a facilitator does for a meeting is to consider the amount of time participants will be able to invest, stay engaged, and contribute. This is especially true for a virtual meeting.

A facilitator can keep sessions short by taking these precautions:

- Adding extra emphasis on the facilitation principle of purpose.
- Giving participants prework. For example, a facilitator can send the Scrum Team members a preparation activity before the Sprint Retrospective that involves individual reflection. The team members can then discuss their insights on this together in the event.
- Limiting the number of tools and keeping them simple for participants to use.
- Splitting larger groups into smaller groups for activities.
- Limiting attendees to those who really need to be there. If necessary, sessions can be recorded with consent from the participants, or minutes can be taken and shared with others afterward.
- Spreading sessions over multiple days.

BREAK DOWN CONTENT AND ACTIVITIES

A facilitator can encourage an ongoing level of engagement by breaking down content and activities so that people are not doing the same thing for long periods of time.

For example, instead of running three long blocks in one session, consisting of a one-hour presentation, followed by a one-hour discussion, and then finishing with half an hour of Q&A, the facilitator can plan for more granularity. They can break these blocks into smaller chunks, each of which encompasses smaller sections of presentation, discussion, and questions.

TAKE REGULAR BREAKS

A facilitator should allow for regular breaks. According to a study carried out by Microsoft,[4] fatigue begins to set in 30–40 minutes into a virtual meeting. Allowing numerous short breaks and encouraging people to stretch and move away from their desks helps keep participants engaged and the meeting productive. Break times can vary. For example, a facilitator can send people for short micro-breaks of 5 minutes, and at other times the facilitator can suggest longer breaks of 15 minutes or more.

RESPECT PEOPLE'S TIME

A facilitator and participants demonstrate respect for each other by enabling meetings to start and end as scheduled. To mitigate the risk of delays, a facilitator can open virtual calls 10 minutes before the scheduled start time for people to join and test their sound, camera, or any other technicalities. This, together with introducing the tools they will be using in the invitation, increases the chances that a meeting can start on time.

Respecting time also includes taking people's locations and their time zones into account. Remote working has enabled teams to form with members from different parts of the world. A team can agree on times they can meet virtually as part of their team working agreement.

---

4. Microsoft (2020). "The Future of Work: The Good, Challenging & Unknown." www.microsoft.com/en-us/microsoft-365/blog/2020/07/08/future-work-good-challenging-unknown/.

CREATE SPACE FOR CONNECTION

Building connections is an important part of facilitation. It sets the tone for a session and gives everyone the opportunity to speak from the onset. In a physical setting, participants have multiple opportunities to connect all the time. For example, they bump into each other in the office, or they go and grab some coffee together and have a chat.

In a virtual space, participants do not have the same opportunities to connect. They have to rely on the facilitator to create time and space for people to make connections. Facilitators can run a structured connection activity, for example, by asking participants to check in, as we discuss in Chapter 7, "Facilitating the Sprint Retrospective." Alternatively, a facilitator can simply open the call 10–15 minutes before the official start time and invite participants to come early. The facilitator ensures that the meeting starts on time, but people have space to chat.

SHARING WITH THE WHOLE GROUP

We described many activities in this book in which facilitators ask participants to explore something in smaller groups, such as in pairs, and then come together to share their insights with the rest of the group. In a virtual environment, the facilitator can send people in smaller groups into breakout rooms. However, when the smaller breakout groups are asked to share their insights with the whole group, often a period of silence and awkwardness results because participants are unsure who should speak for their breakout group. We recommend that the facilitator asks participants to decide in their breakout rooms who will represent their breakout group when they are back in the main room.

MAKING DECISIONS VIRTUALLY

Decision-making techniques are covered in Chapter 4, "Facilitating Team Dynamics," where we described tools such as roman voting, fist of five, feedback frames, and dot voting. These require physical action from participants, such as holding up a number of fingers.

Replicating these actions in virtual environments can take several forms:

- Participants can simply hold their hands up to the camera.
- Participants can use chat functionality to enter their roman vote or fist of five score and reveal it after the facilitator counts down.
- Participants can use virtual reactions, such as emojis and thumbs up or down.
- Participants can move a sticky note marked with their name on a 1 to 5 gradient agreement scale that a facilitator creates on a virtual whiteboard.
- Participants can vote anonymously in a tool that offers a private mode feature and then learn how everyone else voted.
- The facilitator can set up online polls to allow participants the benefit of anonymous voting.

THE POWER OF SILENCE

Many people feel uncomfortable with silence. Some facilitators push participants to speak when there is silence in a meeting for a few seconds, or they fill the silence themselves because of the feeling of awkwardness. Regardless of whether someone facilitates in a physical setting or a virtual one, we recommend against doing this.

A rule of thumb is to leave the silence hanging even longer in virtual environments—up to 10 to 15 seconds—before asking the group if they have any new thoughts. A facilitator leaving space for people to think and reflect is an important technique to give everyone the opportunity to express themselves. Silence often indicates that people are thinking. In a virtual setting, people may be leaving silence because they do not want to interrupt each other, and it can be difficult for people to pick up on whether others want to reply.

Those facilitators who are uncomfortable with silence may want to distract themselves by counting in their head.

TAKE IT TO THE TEAM!

The Scrum Team can discuss their preferences for virtual meetings, such as use of cameras, as part of their team's working agreement. In some situations, team members may feel cameras should be on, whereas in other situations, it is fine to have them switched off.

Another example the team can agree on is how often to take a break. It can experiment to find what works best for them.

HYBRID FACILITATION

We previously discussed facilitating virtual meetings and interactions. Today, many organizations work in a hybrid way, with some employees working in the office and from home at different times.

Hybrid meetings involve some participants being present physically in the same room, while others join the discussion virtually. These types of meetings are challenging and rarely work optimally.

A facilitator can remind the team that whatever the meeting structure, full and equal participation is expected from everyone. The most straightforward way to do that is to create an equal environment for all participants. For example, whether people are in the office or working remotely, everyone joins a virtual meeting from their own device. That way, the experience is the same for everybody.

FACILITATION CHECKLIST

Facilitation does not start or end with the event or meeting itself. It can involve a fair amount of preparation and follow-up. Here, we share some of the most common elements that a facilitator has to think about when preparing to facilitate a session and following up afterward. Although this list is by no means exhaustive, it is thorough. Feel free to add steps that you find necessary, especially after facilitating a session.

PREPARATION

Effective facilitation requires a certain level of planning, organization, and attention to detail. Why, when, who, how, and where to facilitate are all questions that a facilitator may want to explore before a session. Preparation allows a facilitator to frame clear goals and objectives, and create an environment that encourages participation, collaboration, and meaningful interactions among participants during the session itself.

"I do find that there's a fine balance between preparation and seeing what happens naturally."

—Timothée Chalamet

Although on many occasions preparation is needed to ensure sessions are effective, a facilitator should find the right balance between structure and flexibility. They should aim to be well prepared while remaining open to the needs and dynamics of the participants. Being adaptable, responsive, and able to change the approach as needed helps a facilitator create a more engaging, inclusive, and effective experience.

OUTCOME AND OBJECTIVES

Taking time to reflect on the purpose of a meeting is a vital first step in preparation. For example, an ideation session may need a different group of participants, space, tools, and techniques than when facilitating a Sprint Planning event for a Scrum Team.

Facilitators often prepare a list of timeboxed agenda items, usually phrasing them with verbs such as *discuss* and *catch up*, leaving it unclear to participants what they are actually trying to achieve. Converting agenda items into objectives instead is a great way to create alignment and focus on the outcome. For example, rather than an agenda point such as, "Discuss team impediments," it is more effective if a facilitator specifies the purpose of the discussion by converting the agenda item to a clear objective such as, "Identify impediments that the team controls and can resolve themselves." This makes the purpose of the meeting clearer and people more aligned on what they are trying to achieve. Therefore, a facilitator should consider:

- Are the objectives clearly framed for participants?
- Have objectives been communicated to all participants?

FACILITATION APPROACH

Different factors can influence how a facilitator approaches facilitation. They may use a different format, content, tools, and techniques when facilitating in different circumstances, such as a large group of multiple teams compared to facilitating a single team event. At a minimum, a facilitator should think about three factors:

- Is the facilitation approach supportive of the purpose and objectives?
- Does the facilitation approach support the Scrum values and facilitation principles?
- Has the timebox been considered?

SCHEDULING AND COMMUNICATING

Scheduling events and meetings can sometimes be a juggling act. The Scrum events are scheduled on a regular cadence, which helps manage expectations of those involved. However, a facilitator can also consider the following:

- Who are the participants? Does the facilitator need a list of the participants?
- Does the scheduled date and time give everyone an opportunity to actively participate? Think of different time zones and working days.
- Has the time and location been communicated to all participants?
- Is the meeting space booked? (physical)
- Is the video conferencing meeting time scheduled and access shared? (virtual)
- Is there some time before and after the start and end time of the meeting to allow for preparing and clearing out the room? (physical)
- Is there some time before the meeting to allow participants to test their technology and to connect with each other? (virtual)

FACILITATION BOX (IN PERSON MEETINGS)

Not every event or meeting needs the same materials or inputs, but it may come in handy to have a ready-made facilitation box available. The content of a facilitator's facilitation box is likely to change over time, with additions and the removal of various items.

A facilitation box includes all the basic necessities to facilitate an event or meeting. Having a facilitation box ready to go saves a facilitator time and stress. The only thing they have to do is ensure that they refill it regularly.

Here are basic necessities for a facilitation box:

- Sticky notes
- Sharpies
- Flipchart markers
- Whiteboard markers
- Whiteboard eraser
- Cable to connect to TV/screen
- Blue tack
- Blue painter's tape
- Sticky dots
- Timer
- Name tags
- A bell or other device to indicate the end of a timebox

FACILITATION SPACE AND EQUIPMENT

Choosing a space in which people can collaborate and be creative is important. This can be in a meeting room or a dedicated team space. But it does not always have to be in an office. We have experienced some effective Sprint Retrospectives with teams outside in the open air or even in cafés, for example.

When it comes to a physical collaboration space, consider these questions:

- Is the space free of distractions and noise?
- Is the location easy to reach in terms of public transport, parking, and so on?
- Does the space have heating or air conditioning if necessary?
- Does the space have a laptop/computer or other device to share from?

- Does the space have a screen or projector?
- Is a screen connector available?
- Will everyone be able to hear the facilitator, or is audio equipment needed?
- Does the space have flipcharts and flipchart markers?
- Does the space have whiteboards and whiteboard markers?
- Is enough wall space available?
- Does the space have natural light?
- Does the space comply with accessibility guidelines?
- Is the layout of the space (for example, cabaret, boardroom, U-shaped) appropriate for the meeting and how will participants be organized?
- Is the space large enough for the number of participants attending?
- Is there enough space for participants to move around?
- Are the safety instructions clear?
- Does the space have wi-fi?
- Does the space have access to fresh air?
- Are snacks or meals required?
- Do any participants have specific dietary requirements?
- Have food and beverages been ordered?
- Is water available during the session?

For virtual sessions, a facilitator can consider the following:

- Is an appropriate video conferencing tool available and installed?
- Does the video conferencing tool have breakout room functionality for smaller group work if needed?
- Does the sound and camera work?
- Do participants have access to an online whiteboard tool in which they can collaborate?
- Does the virtual tooling comply with accessibility guidelines?

Follow-Up

Following up after an event or meeting reinforces the outcomes, decisions, and actions that were discussed and agreed upon during the session. It encourages further engagement and commitment to taking the next steps toward carrying out the intended actions or ideas. Following up also allows a facilitator to learn and improve by gathering feedback from the participants about the session. In addition, following up builds relationships. It can create a supportive environment for ongoing collaboration and foster trust. A facilitator can consider these questions:

- Are there clearly defined actions?
- Is it clear who is taking what action?
- When will the group meet again?
- When and how will progress be reviewed?
- Are follow-up communication and sharing channels accessible to all?
- Have any necessary follow-up communications been made?

Index

Register Your Product at informit.com/register

Access additional benefits and save up to 65%* on your next purchase

- Automatically receive a coupon for 35% off books, eBooks, and web editions and 65% off video courses, valid for 30 days. Look for your code in your InformIT cart or the Manage Codes section of your account page.
- Download available product updates.
- Access bonus material if available.**
- Check the box to hear from us and receive exclusive offers on new editions and related products.

InformIT—The Trusted Technology Learning Source

InformIT is the online home of information technology brands at Pearson, the world's leading learning company. At informit.com, you can

- Shop our books, eBooks, and video training. Most eBooks are DRM-Free and include PDF and EPUB files.
- Take advantage of our special offers and promotions (informit.com/promotions).
- Sign up for special offers and content newsletter (informit.com/newsletters).
- Access thousands of free chapters and video lessons.
- Enjoy free ground shipping on U.S. orders.*

* *Offers subject to change.*
** *Registration benefits vary by product. Benefits will be listed on your account page under Registered Products.*

Connect with InformIT—Visit informit.com/community

Addison-Wesley • Adobe Press • Cisco Press • Microsoft Press • Oracle Press • Peachpit Press • Pearson IT Certification • Que